COMP

Comparative Housing Policy

Government and Housing in Advanced Industrialized Countries

John Doling

First published in Great Britain 1997 by
MACMILLAN PRESS LTD
Houndmills, Basingstoke, Hampshire RG21 6XS and London
Companies and representatives throughout the world

A catalogue record for this book is available from the British Library.

ISBN 0–333–66251–2 hardcover
ISBN 0–333–66252–0 paperback

First published in the United States of America 1997 by
ST. MARTIN'S PRESS, INC.,
Scholarly and Reference Division,
175 Fifth Avenue, New York, N.Y. 10010

ISBN 0–312–17410–1

Library of Congress Cataloging-in-Publication Data
Doling, J. F.
Comparative housing policy : government and housing in advanced
industrialized countries / John Doling.
p. cm.
Includes bibliographical references and index.
ISBN 0–312–17410–1 (cloth)
1. Housing policy. I. Title.
HD7287.D59 1997
363.5—dc21   96–30028
                                                      CIP

This book is printed on paper suitable for recycling and made from fully managed and
sustained forest sources.

10   9   8   7   6   5   4   3   2   1
06   05   04   03   02   01   00   99   98   97

Printed in Hong Kong

For Annie, Sophie, Tom, Sam and Bill

Contents

List of Tables and Figures

Tables

Figures

Acknowledgements

I am indebted to many people – too numerous even to begin to list – who have, over many years, contributed to my understanding of housing policy. I do, however, owe a particular debt of gratitude to Janet Ford who commented in detail on an earlier version of the text. Her efforts, and indeed those of the editor, Catherine Gray, an anonymous referee and others, have undoubtedly resulted in improvements. As usual, I must absolve them all from responsibility for any errors or limitations.

I want to thank a number of people who have been kind enough to give me permission to reproduce tables and diagrams: Lennart Lundquist for Figure 3.4 and Table 5.2; Eva Hedman for Tables 8.1, 8.2, 9.1, 11.1 and 12.2; Dragana Avramov for Table 12.1 and Peter Boelhouwer for Figure 5.1.

Introduction

In those academic fields in Britain which focus on areas of state policy there has, over the last ten or more years, been growing interest in looking at what goes on in other countries. This growing interest can be gauged by the increase in the number of books and journal papers which deal with policy in one or more countries other than Britain, in the proliferation of international networks and conferences, and the growing number of university modules, and even programmes, which seek to explore cross-national comparisons. The present book is part of this wider development. Intended to be of interest to students, practitioners and policy makers, it deals with housing policy in industrialized countries. Its field of interest is concerned with the ways in which the governments of industrialized countries, particularly in the second half of the twentieth century, have taken an interest in their housing sectors. The objective, as frequently elsewhere, is to present information about similarities and differences in what governments have done, and to use that information to provide insights, especially into theory and policy.

My own interest in housing policies in countries other than Britain dates back to at least 1982 when, along with other housing researchers at the Centre for Urban and Regional Studies at the University of Birmingham, I was invited to a seminar held at the Swedish National Building Research Establishment. My understanding of Swedish housing policy had already begun as a result of a reading of Jim Kemeny's *The Myth of Home Ownership* (which for me remains one of the best books on comparative housing), but a few days in Gavle and Stockholm added considerably to that understanding.

An invitation a few years later to take up the position of Visiting Professor in the Department of Social Policy at the University of Tampere in Finland was grasped as an opportunity further to extend my interest in housing in other countries. Specifically, it provided me with opportunities of two types. The first occurred because I took up Briitta

Koskiaho's suggestion to offer a short course for undergraduate students on comparative housing. If nothing else, this forced me into reading and organizing my knowledge and ideas more systematically than I had hitherto done. The second opportunity was to investigate housing in another country in depth. In this I was greatly assisted by many people. One, Jarmo Lehtinen, must be singled out for the immense amount of help he accorded me.

The period of my own personal discovery of comparative study was also a period in which increasing numbers of other people were also doing the same. Bengt Turner and his colleagues at Gavle had been instrumental in setting up the European Network for Housing Researchers. With a large, and growing, membership, a regular newsletter, and an international conference most years it has been a response to interest about, and a catalyst of, international study and collaboration.

From the early 1980s onwards the number of books and papers on comparative housing began to increase. Some of this literature did little more than simply describe, in English, the main dimensions of housing policy in another country. But, some of the new generation of publications were edited collections of papers given at the growing number of international conferences and seminars (for example, Turner, Lundquist and Kemeny, 1987; van Vliet and van Weesep, 1990). Others had chapters about different countries commissioned by an editor (for example, Wynn, 1983; Pooley, 1992), while yet others were single or joint authored monographs. Of the latter group, those involving Michael Harloe (Harloe, 1985, 1995; Ball *et al.*, 1988) stand out as a set of in-depth investigations of six countries. The position now is that there is a considerable comparative literature, although, at the same time, this literature has large gaps.

Aims and approaches

The present book is aimed at university students taking one of the increasing number of courses which cover either comparative housing policy solely or include it as part of a more general investigation of comparative welfare states or comparative public policy. Others, such as those training as professional housing managers, and indeed fellow researchers, may also find it useful.

Something that they will not find here is a set of information that provides an account of the main features of housing policy in any one country. This is not a book that provides systematic country accounts and therefore although it will have a use to those students who, for purposes such as researching for an essay, need to find out some facts about, say, social housing in France in order to compare them with similar facts about Britain, that use will be of a particular kind. For factual information about a specific country, the advice would be to turn to one of the comparative housing books organized by country chapters – for example, Wynn, 1983; van Vliet, 1990 – following up further information through the references they provide.

The aim of this book is to provide different areas of understanding which can complement the 'facts'. It is about the why, how and so what of comparisons. Why should we pursue cross-national comparisons; what do we expect to gain from doing so; and what are the particular difficulties that we might encounter? How do we organize our information so that we can make some sense of it? So, what conclusions can we come to which might make the effort worthwhile, and what theoretical debates or policy conundrums has it enlightened? These questions form the focus particularly of the first part of the book. In the second half the emphasis shifts to exploring the contribution which the existing literature makes to an understanding of a number of housing policy areas, such as tenure and finance.

In the course of providing advice and insights, the book also provides illustrations and examples. I have deliberately tried to find these across all the major, industrialized countries which I have taken to include the countries of western Europe, North America, Australia, New Zealand and Japan. Whereas collectively they provide indications of the range of differences they are nevertheless countries that in most cases have features of their recent histories that are broadly similar. They also constitute those countries about which most is written in English and which students are probably most likely to want to include in any comparative study they attempt. This is not intended to mean that other countries are not interesting or worthy of study – the newly industrialized countries of southeast Asia, or the countries of the old USSR block, for example – but these are other books.

In the present context, one thing, perhaps above all else, that is interesting about the industrialized countries as a collective is that they have all developed welfare policies in general and housing policies in particular. In practice, for governments of industrialized countries, staying out of housing, taking no interest in outcomes, leaving citizens to get on with it as best they are able, has not apparently been an option. One challenge to the housing policy comparativist, therefore, is to seek to explain, not only the differences, but also this and other similarities.

Structure and content

The first four chapters are building blocks providing information and
insights on which the remaining chapters are supported. Chapter One
starts from the observation that all industrialized countries have
housing policies. In other words, in no country has its government been
prepared to leave housing solutions to the free market. It goes on to
provide some initial insights into the nature of the problems which
these policies have sought to solve. Then, through brief case studies of
Britain, Netherlands, USA and Japan it indicates some of the variations
across countries and over time in the nature of the policy interventions.

Following this introduction to the nature of housing problems and
variations in the policies pursued, Chapter Two explores the gains to be
had from their comparative study. It suggests that these derive not from
the comparison of policies as an end in itself – in country 'a' subsidies
are more generous than in country 'b' – but purposeful comparison: for
theoretical and policy learning. Seeking explanations for similarities
and differences provides the opportunity not only to explore and
develop theoretical understanding, but also to identify which policies
might be transferable to where and with what success. But if the desti-
nations are attractive, the path along which we must go to reach them is
a rocky one. Assembling information and achieving understanding
about one country's housing policy is difficult enough; extending it to
many increases the difficulty manyfold. Although considerable progress
has been made by organizations, such as the United Nations, the
Netherlands Ministry of Housing and the Swedish Board of Housing
(Boverket), in collating statistics for a number of countries there remain
enormous problems, for example of missing information, and of definitional differences and changes.

In Chapter Three the spectrum of housing policies is identified. An
intention is to specify the main ways in which national governments
could, at least in theory, take an interest in housing production and
consumption. This involves consideration not only of the content of
policies but also of the groups within societies on whom they might
impact. It is apparent that the range of possibilities is enormous, and
the second part of the chapter attempts to provide some conceptual and
practical frameworks to aid summary.

The starting point of Chapter Four is the observation that housing
policy is a sub-field of social policy, which following common conven-
tion can be described as constituting the welfare state in each country,
and that if we want to understand the former we can draw upon the now

very extensive literature about the latter. The chapter identifies a range of theoretical explanations with some grouped under the heading 'Convergence' and some under 'Divergence'. Whereas writing about the origins and growth of the welfare state has a long history, the chapter also considers another group of theories that focus on the retrenchment of welfare states, which has occurred, or at least has been said to occur, following the economic difficulties, characterized by economic stagnation and high levels of unemployment, facing most industrialized countries over the last 20 years. Considerations of convergence, divergence and retrenchment constitute strong themes running through subsequent chapters.

The remaining chapters each take a particular dimension of housing policy and examine it using the material developed in the opening four chapters. Chapter Five reviews the literature about the nature and content of national housing policy systems taken as a whole. That is, it presents literature which has sought to identify and account for similarities and differences in the overall national approaches to housing. Of these, significant in the extent to which it permeates the work of housing researchers has been David Donnison's social and comprehensive policy regimes with their suggestion of convergence. Whereas the convergence theme is prevalent, too, in writing about the policy consequences of economic development in industrialized countries over the last two decades, increasing attention has also been directed at national trajectories which differ and diverge.

Each of Chapters Six to Eleven takes a specific aspect of housing production or consumption. The selection is not comprehensive. A chapter on government policies with respect to the rehabilitation of the existing stock has not been included for example. Of those aspects included, the treatment is uneven, reflecting the concentration of the literature on some – social housing and home ownership, for example – and relative sparseness on some others. The general approach in each is characterized by three dimensions. The range of possible ways of governments being involved in the stage of housing provision, with which the chapter is concerned, is identified. Evidence is taken from the literature of the actual involvement by governments of industrialized countries. Finally, links are made, based on the theories explored in earlier chapters, to identify and account for the differences and similarities in national policy. This involves the presentation of the existing literature which has sought to classify and explain the pattern of national approaches. Because of both the sparseness and the unevenness of the literature, these dimensions do not all receive uniform attention, and, in particular, the last lacks a comprehensive treatment in most chapters. In addition, some chapters, notably Six, Seven and Eight, in their relative focus on the unsystematic presentation of information about arrangements and policies in different countries, reflect the limited range of the literature.

It is intended that each of these chapters could be of particular assistance to students who wish to undertake cross-national studies of specific aspects of housing policy, perhaps investigating approaches to state involvement with land development and its control and collectivization of the benefits of any increase in land values, or national approaches to social housing provision. The chapters provide an introduction to the literature as well as some data which can be used to locate each country relative to other industrialized countries, as well as some specific country examples. Like the literature, these data, and the range of countries, are also uneven, reflecting their varying availability in secondary sources.

The final chapter (Twelve) picks up on one of the key themes in the second, namely that comparative study can help the learning of policy lessons. It presents some of the literature that has examined questions of which policies work best. This, of course, begs the further question: what do we mean by 'best'? In this regard, a number of different criteria are explored. It also begs the question of what policies would travel: in other words, what would actually work in the same way in another country. Whereas, at one level, these questions are very practical, the answers can also provide theoretical insights about why governments have housing policies, indeed welfare policies in general.

1

Housing Policy: Origins and Variations

Housing is a necessity. It is precisely because it is a necessity that people will always find somewhere to live. This will not always be a well-built, spacious and permanent dwelling with a full range of facilities. In some societies, financial pressures may well force many to live in self-built shanty dwellings sited on illegal sub-divisions and without proper sewerage systems or formal schools; others will illegally squat; some will inhabit dwellings with short-term and insecure contracts; yet others will be forced to live with parents or friends; others to sleep in the metro or in shop doorways. For some, living in a horse-drawn van or squatting may be matters of choice made around lifestyle decisions, but, in general, the solutions people find will reflect the level and stability of their incomes and the cost of various alternative housing solutions. In general, the so-called 'Iron Law' of housing operates: that those groups in societies with the greatest command over material resources will live in the biggest and highest quality homes and those with least command will find the lowest quality solutions; and, for the latter their housing circumstances will be socially unsatisfactory.

Among the advanced industrialized countries, however, there are no examples of governments being prepared to allow the continued existence of a housing system in which all citizens have been left to search only among free market alternatives. In all such countries, governments have intervened to alter the range of solutions available, the balance of advantage and disadvantage of different solutions, and the means of access to them. They have introduced measures to modify the quantity, quality, price, access and control of housing, and in so doing they have also modified the 'Iron Law'. A feature of all governments of all industrialized countries, then, is that they have taken it upon themselves to become involved with this necessity. Whatever the ideological predilections, the level of industrialization, the demographic or social characteristics, the climate or the availability of building materials, governments have intervened widely and deeply with the production and consumption of housing. Moreover, there are grounds for suggesting, following Harsman and Quigley, that, although governments intervene widely in all major areas of welfare – health care, education, pensions and so on – as well as with some other goods and services, the interventions in housing are substantial:

> All developed countries have a housing problem in some form, and all nations regardless of their orientation towards free markets or central planning, have adopted a variety of housing policies. The production, consumption, financing, distribution, and location of dwellings are controlled, regulated, and subsidized in complex ways. In fact, compared to other economic commodities, housing is perhaps the most tightly regulated of all consumer goods. (Harsman and Quigley, 1991, p. 1)

Housing problems

Given the universality of housing problems and of government intervention, the question can be asked: what is the nature of the problems which all this policy is seeking to address? In other words, are there, or have there been, practical difficulties which have stood in the way of individual citizens enjoying an acceptable level of housing? Burns and Grebler (1977) have suggested that the problems can be described in terms of four types of disequilibrium, a term which in this context they use, not in the usual economic sense of a disparity between supply and demand, but as a disparity between the stock of dwellings, on the one hand, and the quantity which is deemed to be 'needed', on the other. There can, under this definition, be an absolute shortage of adequate housing which cannot be closed in the short term by the price mechanism. One consequence is that some people may be without housing of a satisfactory standard or without housing at all.

The distinction, therefore, is between the concept of demand, which is one taken from economics and refers to the ability and willingness of the individual consumer to pay for housing, and the concept of need, which is a socially accepted aspiration describing that standard of adequacy which society as a whole adopts as an expression of the collective interest. Although they have been posed as alternatives they are not in fact independent. What societies adopt as an adequate standard will not be unrelated to the real economy, that is to the 'incomes and prices prevailing in the country concerned' (Needleman, 1965, p. 18). Where there is a real commitment to ensure that needs are met, the concept of social demand can be useful. This describes the ability and willingness of society, as a collective, to pay for housing. Although it is not necessarily the case that all interventions in housing markets will result in a greater consumption of real resources or public finances, nevertheless housing policy itself can be approximately equated with the concept of social demand. On this view, the decisions by governments to intervene in housing systems have the effect of replacing, or modifying, individual demand, as the principle governing housing outcomes, with social demand.

The Burns–Grebler discussion of disequilibria can be presented in the light of the distinction between these concepts, with disequilibria being thought of as statements of need, which governments may choose to translate into statements of social demand. Static disequilibrium refers to the overall disparity between the number of dwellings in a geographical unit such as a country and the number of households. Of course, both sides of the disparity may be inter-related, for example because household formation may be constrained, or facilitated by, the availability of satisfactory housing, but, overall, static disequilibrium provides a crude measure of the current adequacy of the national stock of housing.

Dynamic disequilibrium refers to the trends over time in static disequilibrium and thus to the combined trends in housing stock and households – as to whether the disparity is widening or narrowing. Spatial disequilibrium indicates the mismatch that may occur within the different parts of a country. Over a country as a whole there could be a balance between houses and households, or even a housing surplus, but the houses are not necessarily located in those regions where the households want to live. Spatial disparities can occur where there is rapid migration from rural to urban areas, perhaps associated with processes of industrialization, or with a reduction in employment opportunities in those urban areas whose economies are heavily skewed towards declining industries combined with an increase in employment in growth industry areas. In other words, there can be shortages in some locations and surpluses in others. The final measure is qualitative disequilibrium which denotes that some households may be living in accommodation that falls short of a standard that would be acceptable to society at large. The accommodation may be deemed too small for the number of people living there, it may be missing facilities such as an internal WC, adequate heating arrangements or a fresh water system, or it may have too limited an ability to protect those living there from the elements.

Given that the Burns–Grebler disequilibria represent a way of describing, in general terms, the housing problems with which governments of all advanced industrialized countries are faced, one question is whether they are actually the stimuli for policy making. There has been an assumption among many of those who have studied housing policy over the last 30 years that policy can be interpreted unequivocally as part of a process whereby governments react to the housing problems facing its citizens (perhaps, as here, described in terms of disequilibria) such that the objective is to increase their wellbeing, welfare or quality of life. On this view, therefore, policies start from the difficulties facing individual citizens – homelessness, overcrowding, insecurity of tenure, insanitary conditions – to which governments respond in the form of housing policy in order to improve these housing conditions.

But, as we shall explore in later chapters, the view that the welfare needs of the citizens of industrialized countries are an automatic trigger for the introduction of social policies is contestable. The belief that humanitarian concerns constitute the sole, or even partial, basis or trigger for housing policy, overlooks other possibilities, for example that policy may fulfil a function in stabilizing the economic and political system as a whole. Governments may intervene, in other words, in ways that improve the lot of those who would not otherwise be able to consume housing of a reasonable size and quality, but such an outcome is a consequence of an underlying motivation to preserve the social order. There may be a distinction, therefore, between what policies achieve in improving the housing system and what they are intended to achieve in providing a wider stability.

The argument here, then, is that whereas in all countries there are, or have been, circumstances that can be described in terms of need and disequilibria, and at the same time all industrialized countries have enacted housing policies, the two cannot necessarily be seen as part of a stimulus response system. The possibility of alternative links makes the understanding of the nature and origins of housing policy both a difficult and a fascinating task. It is further complicated because of both spatial and temporal variations. Whereas all industrialized countries have enacted housing policies, there is nevertheless a very wide range of forms taken by those policies. Thus in some countries there is an emphasis on direct provision, in others on regulation, some concentrate more on production, others on consumption, and so on. Equally, there may be changes in policy over time. In other words, there is an historical dimension to policy as from time to time governments repeal old legislation and enact new legislation. The stimulus for such change may be developments in the nature of housing problems, in changing perceptions of need, or perhaps in ideological developments which may lead governments to become more or less inclined to intervene in processes of supply and demand.

The European paradigm

One way of exploring the spatial and temporal variations is by drawing on the presentation of what Bullock (1991) calls 'the European paradigm'. In this he traces what he asserts to be the typical historical development of national experiences of housing and the associated housing policy. Since the paradigm constitutes a number of stages, which can be tied to historical periods or milestones, when the nature of problems, or the perception of them, changed, it usefully emphasizes the historical dimension of national housing policy systems. However, here, it is also used as an ideal type or model against which the developments in individual countries can be compared.

Bullock's starting point is the suggestion that whereas eighteenth century observers of housing had expressed 'objection to inadequate housing or overcrowding' (Bullock, 1991, p. B004), the nineteenth century saw the linking of the phenomenon of urbanization with the sanitary reform movement which was spurred by the widespread occurrences of typhoid and cholera. Under this pressure the mid-century response was typically that governments took responsibility for imposing regulations which would ensure the greater healthiness of those living in the rapidly expanding urban areas. Housing problems were viewed as products of urbanization and industrialization arising from the dysfunctional consequences of free market solutions.

In Bullock's view, a second, typical stage occurred from the 1880s on. Housing came to be seen less as a health issue and more as an economic one, with a recognition that the incomes of the great mass of national populations were too low to enable them to afford the market price for adequate housing. In this growing awareness, the appropriate role of government was again re-assessed. The greater willingness to countenance intervention found expression in the development of non-profit alternatives to the free market. As Bullock recounts it:

In England, for example, enabling legislation is enacted so that cities like London may now build and manage their own municipal housing estates. In Germany, as in France, government is now for the first time prepared to sanction the use of funds at lower than market rates of interest as a source of capital for the housing co-operatives and associations of the fledgling non-profit sector. (1991, p. B004)

Both world wars marked turning points. The First World War was accompanied by a radical, two-pronged approach. Governments adopted regulatory frameworks aimed at rent levels and security of tenure in private rental housing. In addition, they embarked upon large-scale programmes of subsidized housing. The widespread destruction caused by the Second World War, the cessation of new building for half a decade or more and the large-scale movements of population, all contributed to a need to build quickly and in large numbers. The standard response was the mass building of social housing, a response which conformed with wider, welfare state developments. Since the mid 1970s a further turning point has been reached with the typical running down of social housing programmes, as part of a general pressure on welfare states.

So, overall, within the European paradigm the view is one in which housing problems were increasingly recognized from the end of the eighteenth century on, the interventions became more and more comprehensive with a growing emphasis, particularly in the post Second World War period, on social housing solutions, but with a retreat from government responsibility over the last twenty years. To what extent does this accurately describe the historical development of housing policy approaches in European countries? Most observers would undoubtedly recognize elements, particularly in those European countries in the middle latitudes, such as Britain, Germany, France, Belgium and the Netherlands, which experienced mass urbanization and industrialization in the nineteenth century. Actually, the British position fits very closely, as we describe here.

Britain

The basic structure of the British solution to meeting housing needs was established during and shortly after the First World War. Until that time, consistent with what has been referred to above as the European paradigm, housing in Britain was a good produced and allocated according to rules which operated in a largely unregulated market.

Government legislation had, it is true, been having an impact in controlling some of the worst aspects of the market, such as excessive densities and inadequate sanitary arrangements, but market forces remained the dominant ones. However, the market-based approach was resulting in outcomes which were deemed unacceptable. A rent act in 1915 introduced both controls on rents, which tied them to historic rather than current market levels, and security of tenure. With the private rental sector at this time accounting for around 90 per cent of the housing stock, this legislation had the effect of fundamentally changing the balance between the collective and the private interest. In turn, this new balance contributed to the long-term decline of the sector. No longer able to charge rents that reflected market scarcity landlords chose to move out of the business, while tenants increasingly turned their aspirations to other housing opportunities.

The first of these alternatives was developed through further legislation in 1919 setting up arrangements which were to result in the rapid, and eventually extensive, development by local authorities of a public housing solution. Momentum had been growing for two or three years supporting the view 'that some sort of state aid would have to be made available' (Malpass and Murie, 1994, p. 51) and the issue by 1919 was rather more about the appropriate vehicle for doing so. Providing subsidies through private builders would have been a technical possibility, but was rejected. The government in the end built on the established tradition of local authority responsibility for the provision of local services. The remaining part of the housing system, the 10 per cent held in the form of home ownership, was also set at this time for an extended period of growth. Increasing national prosperity extending into higher real wages and greater job security, combined with the growing resources of the building society movement, facilitated the growth of demand.

The period of reconstruction immediately following the Second World War saw a policy shift even further towards a collective responsibility for housing. Indeed, the concept of public housing as a social service was consistent with the wider development of the welfare state in postwar Britain. At first, all new housing was provided by local authorities so that the size of the public housing stock grew rapidly. This period of mass building of council housing continued more or less unabated for two decades, at first making good the postwar shortage and later linked to slum clearance mostly in the major centres of population. With government support for home ownership being gradually re-asserted and then extended, for example through generous tax subsidies, this sector also continued to grow. Through the 1960s and 70s, housing policy could be described as having two main strands: market provision for those who could afford it, and state provision for the rest. Home ownership was seen as the normal tenure, which those with the greatest command over resources would normally seek to attain. Subsidies to home owners facilitated the expansion of the sector so that by 1970 over half the population had achieved this form of tenure. For those who were unable to meet the financial commitments of home ownership the council sector, having grown to around one third of the stock by 1970, was the solution. But, as indicated by its size, it had more than a residualist role, and was a tenure aspired to by a wide range of working people. This two-sided policy could be seen as a reflection of the broadly balanced strengths of the two main political parties.

A major policy shift started to develop in the 1970s (see Forrest and Murie, 1988). As part of the breakdown of the postwar consensus around the welfare state, itself apparently tied to growing economic difficulties, support for the council housing solution was beginning to wane. With the election of a radical conservative government in 1979 pursuing ideals of state withdrawal and the re-assertion of markets in all areas of welfare, housing policy became focused narrowly on the extension of home ownership. The collective solution through state provision was to be dismantled through legislation which would encourage the transfer of council housing into the home ownership and private renting sectors. The 1980s' solution was thus more reliant upon the market as the appropriate institution through which housing needs would be met.

The Netherlands

If we accept that Britain is archetypal, equally most observers would also recognize that the paradigm is not actually common throughout Europe. There are not only the exceptions of those countries whose capitalist trajectories were truncated by their annexation into the communist east, but also those European countries which experienced mass urbanization and industrialization much later than those of the industrial heartland. Thus Portugal, Spain and Greece to the south, while sharing many of the same responses, such as the public health concerns, have seen much of their housing policy developments confined to the second half of the twentieth century. But, even where the time frame was similar to that in Britain, the policies themselves have often been very different in both detail and general philosophy. The case of the Netherlands, summarized in terms of tenure in Table 1.1, provides an example.

Table 1.1 Tenure patterns, selected countries, 1990 (%)

	UK	Netherlands	USA	Japan
Owner occupation	68	44	64	62
Social renting	25	44	3	8
Private renting	7	12	33	24

Source: Hallett (1993); Hägred (1994).

The pre World War Two housing policy in the Netherlands was based on private investment with legislation authorizing the construction of social housing, dating back to 1901, being 'used only as a stopgap' (van Weesep and van Kempen, 1993, p. 185). The postwar era saw a major shift in direction, a direction which was heavily influenced by two factors. First was the shortage of housing, which had resulted from the combination of war damage and the lack of construction during the war years. However, for Dutch governments the housing problems took second place to the wider problem of reconstructing the country's economy, leading them to impose strict controls on prices, wages and investments. In housing terms this meant a continuation of the rent control imposed at the start of the war, and a relatively modest programme of new construction. The second factor was the Dutch political model which is based on wide representation which helps to ensure 'a fair degree of continuity in housing programmes, even when government coalitions change' (van Weesep and van Kempen, 1993, p. 184). The overall outcome of these factors has been that 'Dutch housing policy since 1945 has been one of the most comprehensively interventionist in western Europe' (McCrone and Stephens, 1995, p. 75).

The postwar solution was based on the construction of social housing. As in Britain, the early postwar years saw a dominance of this form of new provision with a gradual shift in favour of subsidized and non-subsidized housing. Unlike Britain, the local authorities were rather minor players in the production of social housing, this role being entrusted to housing associations. This orientation also had its roots in the act of 1901, which according to van Weesep and van Kempen (1993) had lead to a heated debate from which the widespread suspicion of direct state provision was expressed by politicians as being too strongly associated with state socialism. What developed was a sector founded on the philanthropic organizations that had developed in the previous century and that came to be organized largely along ethnic, religious and regional lines. Although the numbers increased in the inter-war period, after the war they first expanded rapidly in size and subsequently grew even larger through mergers.

However, local authorities were also significantly involved in the regulation of the social housing sector. Social housing received 'bricks and mortar' subsidies, with operating subsidies also being made available. The price to be paid was that landlords were faced with restrictions on rent levels, and access to housing was also determined by regulations which set down certain criteria that households needed to meet in order to qualify for a home.

Although production levels increased in the 1950s, the overall shortages remained. It took a large production boom in the 1970s to more or less close the gap. By this time the social and non-social rental sectors had expanded to around 60 per cent of the national housing stock. At this point there was a move to shift the burden away from state subsidized production and consumption of housing to the free market. However, the demand for home ownership weakened considerably with a widespread collapse of prices and confidence, and the government continued to support social housing programmes. Nevertheless, from the middle of the 1970s there have been changes as the Dutch government has sought to reform elements of its housing policy system. The shift away from 'bricks and mortar' subsidy was part of a recognition that the numbers problem had been solved. It was accompanied by a greater reliance on transfer payments to tenants to enable them to afford the higher rent levels, although a reaction to the resulting increase in public spending has been the capping of such payments. Likewise pressure on public spending has led the Dutch government to withdraw state loans for new production in an expectation that housing associations seek finance from the private sector. A White Paper published in 1989 has set out the principles for the 1990s and beyond. They herald an even greater targeting on the needs of the lowest income groups and more reliance on the market and private capital. As McCrone and Stephens conclude:

> the Netherlands seems to have realized that, in the present fiscal climate, a policy on the scale of the past cannot be sustained. If the radical proposals for the social rented sector are implemented, together with the measures already in train, Dutch policy could become one of the least costly, instead of being one of the most expensive. (1995, p. 95)

The USA

The European paradigm, then, disguises inter-country differences, but further it is precisely that: a model or paradigm which is confined to Europe. North America has travelled along a different route, not because its cities did not grow, or that their inhabitants did not experience many of the same sorts of problem as their European counterparts. In the USA, rather, the government was not prepared to develop a social housing sector on anything like the same scale as in many European countries.

In the United States the predominant ideology, throughout the present century, has been, much more than in Europe, centred upon the notion that the individual, and not the state, is responsible for his or her own destiny. Government has seen itself in the role of ensuring some measure of equality of opportunity rather than some measure of welfare. The ideological tradition has also included an emphasis on private ownership. The result, as Wolman suggests, is that social policy is:

> largely designed to play a derivative and residual role. Americans are expected to provide for their needs themselves... social policy is 'selective' – that is, it applies only to the residual not able to provide for themselves and utilizes a means test to identify who those are. (1975, p. 4)

This observation may seem not to fit with the establishment in the Housing Act of 1949 (reaffirmed in 1968) of a national commitment towards the achievement of a decent home for everyone. But in practice the US government has placed little priority on housing, certainly if this is measured by the proportion of the federal budget expended on housing programmes. Wolman (1975) speculates about the causes of the schism between stated intention and outcome, between acceptance of a social services philosophy but not the approach. He suggests that there is both a lack of consensus about the goal as well as competition from other housing goals. In addition, the statement could be seen as an expression of a desirable outcome, but not one that the federal government bears the responsibility for achieving, not least because of the role of local and state governments in fulfilling social programmes.

American housing policy derives its roots, not as in Europe from the shortages and tensions resulting from each of the two world wars, but from the profound shock of the 1930s' Depression. The concern was not primarily about the acceptance of a state responsibility for ensuring that citizens' housing needs were adequately met, but with finding a way out of the economic difficulties through planning at the macro level. Providing an impetus to the construction industry and maintaining confidence in the mortgage market were seen as significant steps in seeking to reinvigorate a depressed economy.

What developed was a housing policy regime strongly oriented towards the private sector in general and home ownership in particular. The promotion of home ownership had dated back at least until 1913 when the federal income tax code provided tax relief to be set against mortgage interest payments and local property taxes, an initiative which was 'conceived as an important incentive for promoting widespread home-ownership' (Howenstine, 1993, p. 25). The continuation of such tax breaks along with support to the mortgage industry in the wider context of a strong cultural predilection towards home ownership saw the achievement of this form of tenure by a large proportion of the population, in excess of 60 per cent, as early as 1960.

In contrast to Britain, the private rental sector was not so disadvantageously treated. On the one hand, rent control in the United States was not traditionally seen as 'an appropriate device, partly for ideological reasons and partly due to the widespread belief that it would not work' (Wolman, 1975, p. 42). On the other hand, tax policy gave sufficient incentives to investors in residential property to encourage the maintenance of a large presence.

Public housing had been part of the New Deal in the 1930s, but it has never been encouraged sufficiently for it to make a major impact on the challenge of meeting housing needs. Even in the 1930s there was powerful opposition to the concept of public housing, but after wider acceptance in the postwar era, its potential was even more limited, according to Howenstine, because housing authorities were 'required by law to evict families, when their income rose above original eligibility limits' (1993, p. 24). However understandable as a means of ensuring that public housing was reserved for the very poorest members of society, it had a consequence of producing a highly stigmatized sector which, in the long run, has lost it widespread support. Table 1.1 shows clearly the resulting insignificance of non-market forms of housing.

The election of President Reagan into his first term of office in 1981 heralded a shift even further towards market solutions and away from social objectives in general. Silver (1990) provides details of the changes with respect to housing. The administration cut spending on new construction with the annual output being reduced from 45 000 to 7 000 units. At the same time rents were raised by 30 per cent, and subsidies increasingly took the form of vouchers which could be redeemed in the private sector. In addition, programmes were introduced that encouraged the sale of public housing units. Overall, then, the 1980s was a decade in which the federal government in North America saw even less need for its own involvement in meeting housing need.

Japan

The case of Japan demonstrates yet further variation. Here, in 1941, the majority of the housing stock, around 75 per cent in the cities, was owned by private landlords (Hayakawa, 1990, p. 676). The great changes that have been brought about over the subsequent half century have been the result of intervention by Japanese governments. There have been a number of factors that have been important in steering these. With the exception of 1947, Japanese governments have been run by the conservative party. Much of the land area of Japan is not easily habitable having twice the population of the UK and West Germany, but only a quarter of their habitable land areas. The large scale urbanization, particularly after 1955, has squeezed the population into the densely packed cities. Numerically, the postwar period has witnessed an increase in the proportion of urban dwellers from under two-fifths in 1945 to almost four-fifths by 1990.

A rent control ordinance of 1946 undermined the economic viability of private renting and had the result that landlords sold their dwellings to tenants and the building of new owner-occupied housing increased. In short, this legislation marked the 'start of the increase in postwar home ownership' (Hayakawa, 1990, p. 676). The large-scale urbanization fuelled the demand for the building of additional housing. Between 1945 and 1985 34 million private dwellings were built, this figure representing about 85 per cent of the total. The Japanese housing solution has therefore been predominantly a private sector one, reflecting the ideological orientation of its ruling conservative party.

But, there has also been some housing built by the public sector. Over the same period about 2.6 million dwellings have been built by local authorities. Treasury subsidies are used to build houses which are let at low rents. Eligibility for the dwellings is limited to those with incomes below specified levels and living in unsuitable accommodation. Whereas in 1951 the income limits encompassed around 80 per cent of the population, by 1987 this had been reduced to 20 per cent

(Hayakawa, 1990). This has clearly acted to suppress the demand for this type of housing. Moreover, the consequence of a tenant's income rising above the prescribed limit may be that they are required to vacate the property. The Housing and Urban Development Corporation also receives public funds which it uses to meet housing objectives, including the provision of both rental and housing for sale.

Not only does the policy system as a whole contrast sharply with that in European countries, but the individual dwellings are very different. They are small in terms of floor area, with adjustable interior space and minimal furnishings, which reflect the traditional lifestyles in which men have worked long hours, entertainment has been carried out outside the home and cooking is minimal (Donnison and Hoshino, 1988). So, whereas residential street scenes in European cities as well as in many cities in the USA often have much in common, those in Japan can be very different.

Conclusions

In all advanced industrialized countries governments have taken the view that they should have considerable presence in their housing systems. Although people will invariably find somewhere to live, no government has been willing to allow all their citizens to make provision for themselves within a framework that has been entirely unstructured by government. Nowhere, in other words, has there been a free market in housing in which outcomes have been solely determined by the unfettered actions of individual suppliers and consumers. In fact, in comparison with many other goods, perhaps reflecting the fact that housing is an essential item of consumption, the level and nature of intervention in housing has generally been considerable.

If intervention in the form of housing policy is common to all advanced industrialized countries, little else seems to be. Whereas Bullock's European paradigm may be useful as a reference point from which to start locating the development of national housing policy systems, few countries fit neatly. Britain with its transition from health to economic concerns, and the policy milestones being established at the times of the two world wars clearly fits very well. But, many countries, now industrialized, have become so according to a quite different time scale. Moreover, even those countries with a similar time scale have developed housing policies that are very different one from the other. Thus, whereas the Netherlands developed a policy system based upon renting and private, non-profit landlords, Britain pursued a twin track of owning and public sector renting. Even these two countries do not represent the full spectrum of policy models, as the case studies of the USA and Japan indicate.

In addition to the variation from country to country, the paradigm also indicates the variation from time to time. Housing policy systems are organic so that they do not develop to some predetermined model. They grow in some ways and contract in others and they change direction. There may be many reasons underlying the developments – demographic, ideological, economic – with each country developing at different stages in time. One of the challenges facing the would-be comparativist, therefore, stems from the fact that there are variations in housing policies over both time and space.

2

Undertaking Comparative Housing Policy Studies

Before approaching the task of examining housing policies across countries in more detail, the present chapter considers a number of prior issues, mainly methodological. It draws upon literature related to comparative policy studies in general in order to explore a number of areas, which can be reduced to three broad questions: what is entailed in the comparative study of policy; what is to be gained by doing so; and, what are the difficulties involved? In practice, these three questions are inter-related and this is reflected in the structure of the chapter.

What benefits?

All social science, indeed all science, is comparative. Researchers compare different units or samples of populations, perhaps across time or space, in order to assist with investigation of how the social and the physical worlds work. In that sense there is nothing unusual or special about comparisons across the boundaries that divide one country from another. But, this does not make redundant the question of whether this has particular uses or value; an opinion which takes on significance against the observation that increasingly international comparative studies have come to be accepted as a good thing. As Willem van Vliet points out:

> Cross-national studies tend to assume the advantages of cross-national comparison as a given, supposedly obvious to the reader, without explicitly stating the reason(s) for adopting this approach. (1990, p. 7)

A case can be made that the comparative study of housing policy in industrialized countries has the potential to inform both the researcher and the policy maker. It has this potential because it introduces empirical information that derives from the historical, geographical, social, political and economic contexts of other countries, which may both share similarities with and differ from that of the country of origin of the researcher. Comparative study broadens the researcher's horizons and brings new experiences against which the existing, own country, experiences can be compared and contrasted. In terms of theory the additional information can aid both hypothesis testing and hypothesis generation. It can assist consideration of whether relationships identified in one country are also apparent in others, as well as provide more data which inform understanding of the world of housing policy. Simply put, it can aid the search for better explanations of the social world.

Additionally, comparative study can help the policy maker. First, by identifying what other policies are possible, or at least which others are in operation elsewhere. This may help the policy maker in one country to come to conclusions about what policy innovations might be worth pursuing. Second, by providing examples of how different policies work in practice – to what extent they are successful or not – the policy maker may be able to come to more informed opinions about appropriate action. If the view is taken that policies are introduced by governments in order to improve aspects of life, learning from the successes and failures of others will often be a worthwhile part of policy formulation.

So, there is a *prima facie* case for arguing that comparative study facilitates lesson learning both in terms of theory and policy. Unfortunately, the gains are neither so straightforward nor so easily realized. As Tim May (1993) puts it: '[c]omparative research is clearly a two-edged sword having both potential and problems' (p. 163). This observation forms the basis of the present chapter.

A method or a field?

It is useful at the outset to establish that comparative study is not a field of study. In itself the term 'comparative' implies nothing about the object of study, with the indication of the object being provided by the term 'housing policy'. Strictly, comparative housing policy describes a methodology or an approach. But, this does not refer simply to the comparison of housing policies. It is the approach which is comparative, using information from different countries in order to come to some general conclusions. This is significant because it can be recognized that much of what is described as comparative study consists, solely, of the study of housing policies in a country other than the researcher's own. But, finding out about what goes on somewhere else is comparative only in the most implicit of ways. Thus, the reader may themselves make connections between what they read and housing policy in a country – their own – with which they are already directly familiar. Any comparison, then, is derived from the reader, using what the researcher has written and bringing to it their own intellectual endeavours to locate differences (and similarities) and explanations, rather than having these explicitly stated by the researcher.

Whereas explicit consideration of more than one country is needed to achieve the status of being comparative, this in itself is also not enough. 'Comparative' means more than taking one set of policies from one country and identifying how they differ from, or are the same as, policies from another country. Achieving the status of being fully comparative requires the use of empirical information to explore understanding. 'The fact', as Pickvance points out, 'that a study is based on data relating to two or more societies is no guarantee that it is a comparative one' (1986, p. 163). So, discovering that person 'x' is taller than person 'y' is comparison (or contrast), but 'such observations are a necessary but not sufficient condition of comparative analysis' (Pickvance, 1986, p. 163). As social scientists we generally want to move further, to discover what processes have resulted in person 'x' being larger, and person 'y' smaller, or why successive Dutch governments have given more support to social landlords than have the Japanese. So, it is explanation rather than observation which lies at the heart of comparative study. Nevertheless, the social scientist can use the observed differences and similarities, and often will start from them, in order to inform the identification of processes. Comparison is not an end in itself, therefore, but a means, perhaps just a first step, of providing insights.

Building explanations

Given that the objective of comparative study is the search for understanding, how does it fit with broader methodological strategies in the social sciences? Put another way, is there anything about using information from more than one country that opens up methodological avenues not available when examining just one country? An argument sometimes put forward in support of comparative study is that it provides the researcher with an approach that resembles the experimental method. The argument is based on the perceived difficulties facing those who study human societies in that, unlike their counterparts in the natural sciences, they are rarely able to set up experiments in which all bar one variable is controlled with the intention that any observed variability can be attributed, often unequivocally, to the uncontrolled variable. The approach is not unknown in the social sciences – the implementation of housing allowances (Friedman and Weinberg, 1985) is an example – but it is rare. There can be ethical issues about putting people into situations which are artificially set up, doing so without their knowledge (or they might change their behaviour in ways not controlled by, or known to, the researcher), and which might result in behaviour that later embarrassed or otherwise disadvantaged them (see Homan, 1991).

But, the problem goes further than the moral, because frequently the necessary 'degree of physical control is not possible' (Dickens *et al.*, 1985, p. 25). Social researchers do not generally have the ability to organize the social world and its actors sufficiently to achieve the required level of control over variables. Indeed, one view is that this is never possible:

> Just as each human being is absolutely unique, both biologically and as a legal person, so each event in the history of mankind and society is singular; neither the one nor the other can be identically reproduced. No experiment can therefore be designed, as in mechanics or chemistry, to analyse a force or measure a reaction and obtain, time and again, the same quantified result. (Lisle, 1985, p. 21)

It is here that comparative study is sometimes seen as offering the social scientist the opportunity to emulate the natural scientist. Since events are historically and culturally specific, the researcher needs to find some way of understanding the significance of these environments. In the case of the cultural environment – customs, institutions, language and lifestyles – these may, in theory, be controlled for by comparative analysis. The view is, then, that investigating the same phenomenon or processes in different countries may allow us to generalize about human behaviour beyond a single country.

While recognizing some potential benefits of comparative study, Dickens *et al.* (1985) argue that there are some difficulties. First, many of the concepts and variables used to describe industrial states are difficult to define operationally. Concepts such as 'a pure capitalist mode of production, a pure ground rent or gender relations' (p. 26) are not easily specified empirically. Second, it is not, in practice, possible to identify pairs or sets of countries which are identical in all significant respects bar one. Even if in general terms they are similar, the details are more likely than not to differ considerably. Moreover, the populations are not controlled as in an experiment, but are already separate and different. Countries may be defined as agglomerations of inter-correlated variables which cannot be separated out and matched with variables in other countries. Part of the problem is, then, that any of the differences may be influential as intervening variables. In addition, as George (1986) has pointed out, there may also be some fundamental difficulties in trying to replicate studies and measuring devices developed in one country in other countries where the cultural differences may give them very different meanings. So, one might agree with Lundquist (1986) that, given the difficulty of finding two, or even more, countries that differed only in aspects central to the study, the pure experimental model might simply not be possible.

Whereas the pure experimental model may not be widely applicable in the social sciences, many researchers do accept and pursue what resembles a looser form in which variables are not fully controlled and it is accepted that extraneous factors may affect outcomes. It can be argued that even under these circumstances, comparison 'adds a dimension to our research which might not otherwise be there, and enables us to form some impression, however imprecise' (Higgins, 1981, p. 6). Likewise, to the question of whether the methodological difficulties mean that it would be impossible to gain any knowledge from comparative research, Lundquist, in writing about his own research into tenure conversion, provides a response:

> No; because the character of cross-national research is to replace proper country names by those aspects of their structure which play a role in the explanation of a particular phenomenon, knowledge can indeed be gained if the relevant aspects are properly identified. This is no easy task, and does not 'solve' the problem of possible intervention from other than these identified variables. However, if the relevant structural and contextual aspects are properly accounted for, and their importance can be assessed, the problem of determining the effects of conversions – as opposed to other features of housing policy and the housing sector – may be somewhat easier to handle. (1986, p. 21)

In such a looser experimental control, then, two or more countries can be selected such that their populations, economies and other significant variables are more or less equivalent. If they have different housing policies these can perhaps be (equivocally) related to any differences in housing output; for example, policy regime 'x' has resulted in higher levels of housing production than regime 'y'. Or, the experiment is used to attempt to understand the origins of social policy. If country 'm' has had an extensive period of right-wing governments in power, and country 'n' an equally long period of left-wing domination, differences in policy developments might be attributed to political choices. In terms of the specific case studies presented in the previous chapter, for example, might the differences in the postwar developments in housing policy in Japan and Britain be attributable to the single-party domination in the former and the two-party interchange in the latter?

So, even if the pure experimental model is not possible, different countries can be chosen so as to reduce, rather than eliminate, variation in key variables. The result is a 'measure of control over complexity and variability' (Dickens *et al.*, 1985, p. 30), which does enable the researcher to gain insights into causal mechanisms and processes. Reducing, even where not fully eliminating, variability may thus facilitate the search for the key processes that aid explanation of different outcomes.

Confronting assumptions

Consistent with this latter view, Dickens *et al.* (1985) suggest that one of the benefits of comparative studies is that it can confront us with our assumptions. In their words, its value lies in the role of 'undercutting the taken for granted' (p. 29). One of the consequences of socialization is that we often come to believe that the ways in which our national worlds are organized – the nature of their institutions or the relationships between different groups – is the 'natural' way to organize. They are as they are because they follow some natural law and are therefore universal. Implicitly, we often expect every other country to organize their affairs in the same way. Probably the most frequently quoted example of this in Britain is home ownership which has been widely considered, without question, as being an innate desire for all groups. Although at some stages in their lives it is accepted that some people may find it preferable to rent, with the exception of some recent doubts raised because of the changes in the market, in general expressing a desire not to own has almost been certifiable behaviour. All of the arguments – equity growth, independence, status, stability – point in the same direction to the extent that buying ones own home is everyone's, or almost everyone's, ambition. In contrast, renting in Britain is often seen as a mark of failure and lack of achievement. These views are encapsulated in government publications which claim of home ownership that it is a 'basic and natural desire' (DoE, 1977, p. 50). However dominant home ownership is in Britain, it is quite clear from even a cursory examination of countries outside Britain that these views are not universal. Home ownership is not everywhere extolled with the same characteristics. More importantly, not everywhere is home ownership considered 'natural'. The study of other countries reveals that in some – the Netherlands, Germany and Switzerland, for example – owning your own home is a minority activity, but not necessarily a rich minority so that renting is not everywhere a concomitant of lower income. Likewise in Sweden and Finland forms of cooperative living in which collective ownership and responsibility and shared facilities are common, and often sought after. In other countries, perhaps because of a stronger sense of individualism, cooperative ownership may be viewed as unusual, suspicious and a second-best pursued by those with few choices. Knowledge of other countries can thus be enlightening about one's own country, forcing a realization that there are alternatives. Existing housing arrangements are not there because of some unwritten law of nature, but are societally contingent.

The corollary of undercutting the taken-for-granted is that of checking generalizations and abstractions made on the basis of knowledge of one country. If a search of other countries does not reveal that in at least one of them housing is organized differently, the perceived uniformity adds support that the generalizations or abstractions do have validity that transcends national boundaries. So, the search for differences can be valuable whether or not they are found. An alternative way of putting this is that comparative study may enable the researcher to identify any general features of housing systems and housing policy, finding what is common to all countries studied and distinguishing it from what is unique to individual countries. The acts of generalizing and particularizing, in turn, facilitate both hypothesis formation and hypothesis testing. On the one hand, new patterns of information may lead us to fresh insights about relationships and processes; on the other, the same patterns help us to support – or not – existing ideas about how systems operate or why policy is successful.

Lesson learning

Up to this point, the main emphasis has been on methodological gains leading to theoretical insights, but comparative studies might also be deemed to have a directly practical value in helping the search for better policies. Here, the term policy is used in a broad sense to include more than content; lessons might be about ideology and rationales, and about instruments and institutions. There may be as much to be learned from policies that failed as those that succeeded. May has outlined the general argument:

> the prediction of programme outcomes is enhanced through comparative work. According to this view, not only can the potential for the success of particular policies, systems or practices in a given society be understood, but also their outcomes can be predicted, once experiences of their effects in other societies and social and cultural contexts is examined. Therefore, organizations or governments may embark upon a [sic] particular courses of action knowing their likely consequences. (1993, p. 159)

A general principle is that no one country, and no one set of politicians, has a monopoly on good sense, wisdom and foresight, so that looking elsewhere for ideas about how to tackle problems seems good common sense. Indeed, this might be taken one step further to the case that politicians who did not take the precaution of arming themselves with whatever knowledge was available concerning the nature of policies and their record of success or failure would be failing their constituents. Learning lessons from others' achievements and failures thus offers an invaluable source of information for the policy maker.

Learning lessons from overseas has in reality been a common activity with some national governments often looking to particular countries. Sweden has frequently been the teacher for its Scandinavian neighbours, whereas in Britain, the appropriate teacher has frequently been viewed as North America. Indeed the Britain–USA link has sometimes been so pronounced that British policy makers have deemed it worthless looking anywhere else (Deakin, 1993). This limited view could be defended on the grounds that the two countries had experienced common developments such as increasing inequality of income and large-scale de-industrialization, which made policy transfer appropriate. There are also persuasive arguments for Britain, as well as much of the rest of the industrialized world, looking east on the grounds that since 'Japanese styles of management have long attracted attention and support' (Jones, 1993, p. 215) there might be a case for considering the extent to which their social policies are also worth emulating. It might, in addition, be recognized that lessons may usefully travel in both directions, as the pupil becomes teacher. Even the USA learnt something from the British example of council house sales (Silver, 1990). In general, as the world has become smaller, the influence of international organizations such as the World Bank, OECD and the EU become greater, so the lessons have perhaps been spread more rapidly and, at times, learnt more quickly.

Common though lesson learning has become, it is not unproblematic and for reasons that bear resemblance to the limits of the experimental model of comparative research. The fact that, in one country, a particular policy appears to work well (or badly), for example because the outputs or consequences exceed certain criteria, is not in itself evidence that the same would happen in another national context. The environment or system within which policies are located will invariably be very complex – different economies, different demographic structures, different aspirations and cultures, different labour markets and so on. The outputs, then, are the result not simply of the policy in isolation but the policy in a specific setting. So, something that works well in one setting, may work badly in another. In essence, this is the holding-everything-else-constant problem of the experimental model.

The classic cases of the non transferability of policy lessons from one country to another perhaps concern the numerous attempts to transplant western technology in developing countries. The history of aid to third world countries is replete with examples of rusting machinery standing idle in fields or in disused factories while around them the local population starves. The exporters of western technology often failed to recognize that though there was nothing wrong with the technology in itself, outside the social context within which it was developed its presence was not necessarily productive. Similarly, the importation into developing countries, often encouraged by the World Bank, of western-inspired social housing developments has sometimes proved an expensive failure (see Pugh, 1990). The situation with respect to industrialized countries and housing policies may well be similar: policies based on Teutonic cooperation and organization may not successfully transfer to Latin countries, for example. As Higgins (1981) puts it: 'lessons may be inadequately learned so that one country is lured into imitating the policies of another without sufficient regard for differences in national contexts' (p. 14).

Hilary Silver provides an example when she notes that American housing policy in the 1980s was strongly influenced by British example, specifically the sale of public housing introduced under prime minister Thatcher:

> Responding to advocates from New Right think tanks and citing the British experience, the President's Commission on Housing proposed public housing sales in its 1982 report. Ronald Reagan himself endorsed the policy in the 1985 State of the Union Address. (1990, p. 123)

In fact, prior to this endorsement, 'many American members of Congress and housing experts warned that the tenantry, scale, and quality of British and American public housing were very different' (Silver, 1990, p. 123). Despite initial acceptance of the inappropriateness of policy transfer, eventually support for sales was achieved, but early evaluation of the policy indicated that the policy transfer sceptics were correct since it seemed 'unlikely to achieve the objectives that conservative Republicans and some liberal Democrats expected of it' (p. 135).

Of course, different national contexts are never going to be identical, so any policy lesson learning needs to address a number of issues. First, what are the processes in the policy exporting country which, with the object policy, result in the desired output, and which of these processes are key? Second, to what extent would the same processes also be found in the policy importing country? A short cut to such comprehensive analysis might be a recognition of which countries have, not identical, but similar policy contexts – that is that the variation in key areas from the importing country is low – so that it would be possible to be reasonably confident that most policies that worked in one would work in the other also. In other words, would the Danish government be more likely to find useful policy lessons in Norway or Sweden as opposed to Greece or Italy? And, would the Canadian government be advised to look to the USA, France or Japan? The point is, then, that some countries might, in practice, be more likely to be used, and useful, as guides.

Time consuming

Having concentrated on the benefits, and nature, of comparative approaches, subsequent sections deal with some of the practical problems involved, beginning with the observation that undertaking comparative study is difficult for a number of reasons, not least because it is time consuming. And the more countries that are included, proportionately, the more time that can be consumed. If anything, then, the size of the task increases exponentially with the number of countries. The basic problem is that most of us, whether comparative scholars or not, have lived all or most of our adult lives in one country only. We have been immersed in the culture, speak its language like a native and studied its housing systems. Knowing more than one country, from the inside, is difficult, and becomes more difficult as the number of countries increases. Visiting a country for a few weeks, even if the researcher has the necessary language skills, will enable little more than a scratching of the surface. Overcoming the knowledge problem is therefore a fundamental challenge facing the would-be comparative policy analyst. In part, these are purely practical and logistical issues, as Michael Harloe points out:

> there is the problem of organizing the research. The sort of flying visit to each country concerned which has often formed the basis for comparative studies is unlikely to result in more than a superficial understanding of specified national housing situations. Yet longer periods of study in each country are usually impractical for financial and other reasons. (1985, p. xvii)

One of the challenges facing the comparativist, then, is to find an appropriate strategy for overcoming the information gathering problem. Harloe (1985) describes the empirical work involved in his own study of private rental housing. For each of the six countries studied he conducted library-based research into their historical development as well as recent political, social, economic and demographic trends. Detailed information about processes was obtained through the device of hiring country consultants. Each was furnished with a brief which, in order to achieve as much comparability as possible, specified data according to precise definitions for specific years. Following submission of the reports, Harloe visited each country in order to carry out interviews with representatives of government and non-government agencies. These enabled the accumulation of more evidence about detailed processes, political attitudes and current problems. Discussions with each consultant also clarified the material in their reports. He was then in a position to write country reports, which were checked out by the consultants.

The Harloe strategy for tackling the information gathering problem, certainly not a cheap one in terms of the human resources it requires, is in fact one of a number apparent in the literature. Oxley (1991) lists these as:

(a) Draw on secondary sources, mainly official statistics, to produce summaries and generalizations. This will frequently involve one researcher who is, alone, attempting to analyse developments in a number of countries.

(b) Experts in each of a number of countries are used as key informants, providing information as well as guidance through relevant literature. This is the Harloe model.

(c) Individuals combining together, perhaps under an organizer (editor), each to provide an account of housing in a single country, according to a loose brief. This may be the outcome, opportunistically seized, of a conference. Someone, acting as an editor, invites researchers who have given papers, perhaps previously unconnected and unsolicited, to agree to their publication in an edited volume.

(d) As (c), but with a strong brief. This is probably not possible without a great deal of prior planning.

Statistical problems

All advanced countries undertake detailed surveys and keep comprehensive records of events and characteristics of their populations. Obtaining information, or at least some information, about a particular country's housing does not generally involve any more difficulty than a visit to one of its specialized reference libraries. There may of course be some translation difficulties, but even that may not be the case since some countries produce versions in other languages, often English. There are in addition statistics produced by international bodies – OECD, the EU and the UN – which should be accessible in the libraries of all advanced countries.

Finding numbers, therefore, is not the problem. But, their meaning, comparability and relevance may well be. Anne Power in her five-nation study summarizes some of the problems:

> Three major constraints on the housing information collected in the five countries were: figures for production, tenure and housing stock were often incomplete, inconsistent and sometimes inaccurate within one country for certain periods (for example, pre-war Germany); some figures were out of date and the latest available figures were from different dates in different countries; different countries collected figures in different ways. Therefore, even national pictures were not completely accurate and comparisons were sometimes based on estimates derived directly from government sources. (1993, p. 16)

The difficulties in part arise because decisions about which things or events to measure, according to which definitions, and which to collate and publish reflect the ways in which national governments see the world, and wish others to see it. So, the statistics that would be desirable from the point of view of a particular comparative study may simply not be available. What may seem absolutely central to thinking about housing policy in one country – whether housing is provided through public or private landlords, for example – may simply not be deemed important enough in another to warrant the collection of relevant information. What are chosen to become official statistics perhaps depends on social and ideological considerations (see Government Statisticians' Collective, 1979). Take the case of housing tenure. In Britain, almost any contemporary discussion of housing policy is couched in terms of tenure. For housing policy one might not unreasonably read tenure policy. The debates mainly centre on issues such as: how many council houses should be built; what should be the role of housing associations; how many more people can be assisted into home ownership? From a perspective close to the change of the millennium it would be inconceivable that statistics about the numbers of dwellings in each tenure were not easily available. Yet, their collection has actually been a relatively recent feature of national statistics. Accurate population statistics have been recorded back to at least 1801 with the first decennial census. But, the earliest widely accepted figure concerning the level of home ownership relates to the turn of the twentieth century. The figure of 10 per cent is, however, only an estimate – in fact little more than a guess (Saunders, 1990). There were some official estimates made in 1938 by the Ministry of Health for the Fitzgerald Committee and in 1953 for the Enquiry into Household Expenditure (Holmans, 1987), but there was 'no completely reliable figure on the number of people in owner occupation in Britain before 1961' (Saunders, 1990, p. 14). So, accurate information about the level of home ownership was only deemed to be important in the last 30 or 40 years. It is not only that tenure has been of significant interest to government only recently, and therefore data has been gathered only recently, but that in other countries there has not necessarily been the same level of concern about tenure at any time.

Another example of an issue that has only recently come to prominence is house price developments in Finland. In the large owner-occupied sector in Finland the investment characteristics of housing have become very important in Finnish society. But, data on prices were first systematically recorded only in 1960 and only for the capital city. In 1970 house price data for ten other towns were recorded, but the sample was only of 232 transactions in Helsinki and a further 254 in the other towns together. It has not been until the 1980s that samples large enough to give precise estimates have been used (Doling, 1990b).

Other examples of some of the statistical problems encountered by the comparative researcher are provided by an examination of the United Nations Annual Bulletin of Housing and Building Statistics in Europe. This series provides information for the whole of the period since 1950. Since its inception the range of tables has increased greatly, so that it provides a useful source of historical data for a large number of countries. However, there are a number of limitations. First, is that of gaps. The UN's sources are the surveys and other data collection promoted by individual countries. Because these are not carried out annually by all countries there are, for some, nil responses in some years. In the cases of some countries there are very few entries with respect to some variables.

Second, where numbers are provided, comparability between countries and between years is sometimes difficult. The problem is not simply that different countries use different definitions of the same concept, but that from time to time some countries have changed their definitions. One example is that a significant proportion of the variables describe characteristics of new housing production such as the proportion of multi-dwelling buildings. In the case of the Netherlands and Switzerland this included two-dwelling houses; elsewhere multi meant a number larger than two. A second example is that the series describing the dwelling stock in each country was interpreted in the case of France until the end of the 1960s as referring to 'all dwellings' but thereafter to 'principal dwellings only'.

A further example of non-equivalent measures is described by van Vliet:

> nations vary greatly in their definition of what constitutes a room. In the Federal Republic of Germany and Norway, rooms with a floor space of less than 6 square meters are not counted as rooms, whereas the Swedes disregard rooms with a floor space of less than 7 square meters and not receiving daylight. In Japan, kitchens with a floor space of less than 5 square meters do not qualify as rooms; in Ireland the cut-off point for kitchens is 10 square meters, and in France it is 12; whereas in Canada only bedrooms are counted and kitchens as well as living rooms are excluded altogether. (1990, p. 10)

These variations in definition are not statistically trivial since the decision to omit kitchens in the count of rooms may make a 20 or 30 per cent underestimate, relative to those countries that do count them, leading to quite different conclusions about comparative space standards.

This problem is compounded where the concepts, and even the operational definitions of those concepts, are complex. Thus one of the key measures of national commitment towards housing – the level of intervention in the housing system – has been taken as government housing expenditure. Wilensky indicates something of the difficulty which this imposes:

> A bewildering array of fiscal, monetary, and other policies that affect housing directly and indirectly – even remotely – have made the task of comparative analysis of public spending in this area nearly impossible. When pensions are increased in a national system, one can trace the sources of financing and the flow of benefits with little pain. But when government monetary policies lower the interest rate in the mortgage market, thereby creating a local boom in construction, and when transportation policies direct road transit to a new area, thereby creating a local boom in rents and land values, the idea of 'government expenditures for housing' becomes slippery. (1975, p. 8)

Language and meanings

We use language in order to give labels to complex concepts such as public, voluntary sector, housing association, home ownership, family and dwelling. These labels can be thought of as a sort of shorthand way of referring to something that we expect others to recognize as we do, but without having to provide each time a full elaboration of what it is to which we are referring. So, we may not feel it necessary each time we refer to the voluntary sector to say that this is something that is not part of the public sector though we might expect that it shares at least some of the same objectives, such as allocation according to need. It may differ from the public sector in important ways, such as in not being democratically accountable, and it will have a different relationship with central government. But, we might add – if we were providing a full elaboration of the concept – that it is not the same as the private, for-profit sector, though it might employ private-sector management methods and seek to be efficient. All of these things we do not usually elaborate. We speak or write down the shorthand and draw upon the shared experience and knowledge of other people who use our mother tongue. From time to time, someone may explore definitions in the literature and this can have a function of both checking and refining our shared meanings. But, on most occasions we find it satisfactory to use the label as shorthand.

In describing a concept in one country and wishing to use a label in the language of another country it is possible that the chosen label is an approximation only. The term housing association might seem adequately to describe the type of non-profit, private-sector housing found. Yet, what is described as a housing association in one country may differ in significant ways from what is described as a housing association in another. One may receive state subsidies, the other may not; one may have voluntary management committees, another a paid board; in one country they may build only apartments for rent, in another houses for sale. It is possible, therefore, that we think that we are comparing like with like, apples with apples: there is a bigger housing association sector in country 'x' than in country 'y', for example. However, we are actually comparing apples and bananas since the two sectors are so different that it makes little sense to set them side by side. One of the problems about language is that it can often give the impression that it can only be an aid to understanding. In fact, it can, unless we recognize a need to check out meanings in different national contexts, be a source of misunderstanding. Particular examples of where this often applies – with the use of tenure labels – will be discussed in Chapters Nine and Ten.

Conclusions

People who advance the case for comparative policy studies have tended to do so on one or both of two arguments. The first is that it offers methodology and empirical information, which are not available to the person who studies a single country, and which may contribute to hypothesis formulation and testing. In short, comparing policies in different countries may help the task of building better theories as well as simply providing better understandings of the researcher's own country. The second argument is that looking at what foreign governments have done in the field of housing can inform policy makers. It may enable policy makers in country 'p' to come to the view that a policy, or some part of it, in country 'q' could be usefully imported.

When summarized in this way the advantages of comparative policy study seem clear and quite straightforward. However, there are, as the chapter has also indicated, implementation difficulties. There is a set of methodological issues around the extent to which a quasi-experimental approach, modelled on the natural sciences, is appropriate. The balance of opinion seems to be that it is not. Some weaker form of experimentation that does not rely on the rigid holding constant of variables does seem to attract wider support. Likewise, there are issues about the extent to which policies will travel. Put simply, to what extent is the context or environment within which policies operate as important, if not more so, than the policy content itself?

In addition to these difficulties there is another set of practical considerations facing the would-be comparativist. There is no doubt that the size of the task involved is greater, often considerably so, than the task of looking at one country alone. Gathering the facts, understanding sufficient about the cultural context, tackling the language all add to the size of the task. There are well-used strategies to overcome these, but sometimes there are problems that have no easily practicable solution. When data have been collected, maybe three decades or even three years ago, according to one definition in one country and another definition in another, the differences may be irresolvable, except by crude approximation. Comparative analysis is not, therefore, necessarily an easy option.

3

Policy Options and Frameworks

The case studies included in Chapter One reveal variation in housing policy but the range of possible policies is actually much wider. The aim of the present chapter is to identify the range of policy options that, theoretically at least, policy makers are able to adopt as a means of achieving their policy objectives. It is thus concerned with the content or substance of possible policy as well as the institutional arrangements through which policy can be implemented. Drawing up a comprehensive list of options, this chapter produces policy terrains that map out where national policy makers could locate themselves and provide aids to the task of making cross-national comparisons.

How, then, can we begin to construct the terrains? An initial approach can be taken by drawing upon the similarities in the principles underlying housing policies and policies in other areas of welfare states. So, for housing and non-housing policy makers alike issues of public versus private production, of universal versus means-tested subsidies, of provision versus subsidies and so on are equally important. This chapter begins, then, with the identification of the policy options that can be introduced across areas of welfare in general, though for purposes of exposition and example, the case of government interest in the double glazing of windows will be used. In practice, this policy issue is of more relevance in some countries, depending upon climatic conditions and the desirability of insulating the interior of the dwelling from the outside environment.

The chapter goes on to explore the nature and significance of two limitations to the identification of the options in the way indicated. The first limitation is that in identifying options which fit the general case of social policies, an assumption is that these are also relevant to the specific case of housing. In fact, there are grounds for suggesting that in some respects housing is different and it is therefore important to investigate the particular characteristics of housing and of housing policy through which the general can be translated into the specific. One outcome of this is a recognition that the production and consumption of housing involves many stages and that governments may intervene at any combination of them. This recognition follows on to the second limitation: once the full picture has been drawn of where the housing policy of a specific country is located, it is generally extremely complicated. If understanding the significance of one complicated picture is difficult enough, the problem multiplies as the task moves to comparing a number of national pictures. In the last part of the chapter, a number of frameworks are identified which provide ways of summarizing and simplifying national pictures so as to make the task of comparison easier.

The range of policy options

The identification of policy options includes consideration not only of their content, but also of the institutional arrangements for implementing them, as well as the target population. Each is considered in turn.

Content

One way of looking at policies is to regard them as attempts by governments to bring about changes in the behaviour of all or some actors, be they private individuals or organizations such as firms. The identification of policy content can then be presented according to the strength of the mechanism whereby behaviour is to be modified, that is whether their provisions are mandatory and thus force change, or whether they are voluntary and intended only to influence or coerce. A second scale along which policies can be located is with respect to the extent to which they may have any direct impact on either price or the ability to pay. Together, these scales suggest six strategies: non-action; exhortation; regulation; taxation; subsidy; and provision. Each constitutes a different approach though they are not mutually exclusive and in practice are often implemented in various combinations.

(1) *Non-action.* Logically a decision to do nothing, and thereby to leave some area of life to be played out through whatever social

and economic processes are otherwise operating, is nevertheless a policy. The decision may of course be taken by default or positively. A policy by default would occur where a government had not considered whether or not a policy, perhaps with respect to double glazing, was appropriate; in other words, it did not constitute, for the government, a problem. A positive decision could occur where a government had adopted a policy objective but believed that the objective would be met anyway without further government action. The motivation for this non-action could be varied: that it was genuinely thought that the target would or should be reached, perhaps because of the perceived effectiveness of marketing by the private sector; that the target was being set/advised by a superior body (the EU perhaps) and it was considered that the target was undesirable; or that it did not want to accept the implications – perhaps financial and fiscal – which it actually thought were necessary to achieve the target.

(2) *Exhortation.* Governments may in various ways seek to exhort individuals as well as organizations to behave in ways consistent with their policy aims. Thus governments may mount a publicity campaign, through ministerial speeches, media advertising, or mail shots, which is intended to make people aware of the advantages of double glazing. The message may be that double glazing will lead to lower heating costs or will bring householders the admiration and envy of their neighbours. But governments may also exhort through threats – the future introduction of a surcharge on fuel costs for dwellings without double glazing – and through moral disapproval – non-fitters of double glazing are damaging the national economy by forcing higher than necessary imports, or harming the environment by increasing the use of fossil fuels. A further type of threat is that unless actors 'voluntarily' modify their behaviour, in other words they self-regulate, the government may introduce legislation which will be even more onerous.

(3) *Regulation.* Governments may decide that certain specified behaviour ought to be prohibited with transgression being punishable generally through the legal system. Regulation can take the form of specifying minimum or maximum standards of materials or behaviour. Thus the achievement of at least a minimum value for the potential heat loss from a building, the utilization of specified materials for glazed units, or the achievement of double glazing in at least, say, 80 per cent of the

window area of a house are all examples of regulatory specifications. There are a number of ways of punishing failure to conform to the regulations, for example by fine, confiscation or imprisonment.

(4) *Taxation.* Governments may increase taxes on those goods and services of which they wish to reduce consumption. Thus single-glazed window units may attract a higher rate of taxation than double-glazed units. The rationale, as with taxation on tobacco and alcohol, would be that people would consume less of the disapproved commodity than they would otherwise, and so spend more on approved commodities. Taxation can be imposed in various ways: for example through a tax on sales, on property, or on income.

(5) *Subsidy.* This can be thought of as the reverse of taxation. Governments may introduce subsidy either because the market price of double glazing is too high for some people to afford (if they are also going to buy food, clothes and other 'essentials' and so would be literally beyond their means), or because double glazing is within their means but they are deemed to require a financial inducement to encourage greater consumption. Such inducements can be partial – representing some proportion of the cost – or full. In the latter case the government is in effect supplying the good or service for free, that is at zero cost to the user. The subsidy may be given in a number of ways: as the good itself; as a voucher or coupon which can be redeemed only against expenditure on specified items; as a tax break; or as a money transfer. The subsidy can be given to producers so that they can, and may be made to, provide the good at a price lower than the market price. Alternatively, consumers can receive the subsidy so that they are able more easily to meet the market price. Whatever the form of the subsidy there may be some upper limit to the amount supplied to any one user, or to the total amount of subsidy. Thus government may place a cap on the cost to the public purse of the subsidy, which may involve the drawing up of some bureaucratic rules that facilitate rationing.

(6) *Provision.* It is open to governments to consider the direct provision of goods or services. This can sometimes be considered as the special case of a 100 per cent subsidy, and may involve provision by the state itself or by a private or voluntary organization. In the latter cases, the cost of provision can be met by the government. In such a scenario, double-glazed windows

might either be made available to house owners who wanted to fit them, or supplied because their fitting was mandatory.

Institutional arrangements

From the discussion of the list of possible ways in which policy can appear, it is also clear that policy may be delivered through different types of institution. Housing policy, and indeed policy in other welfare fields, does not correspond only to public provision. It may be the case that central government organizes its civil servants so that they are responsible for delivering a subsidy, drawing up a regulation, practising exhortation and so on. Alternatively, some other level of government such as regional assemblies or local authorities may perform them, as may QUANGOs and nationalized industries. But, government may also harness the voluntary – private, non-profit – sector, or for-profit companies. For example, governments may decide to promote the production of social housing by offering subsidies, along with any appropriate legislative and regulatory framework, to encourage non-profit organizations to undertake the desired action. It is entirely possible that these organizations would not exist in the absence of government inducement so that they may be considered in a sense creatures of statute. But, they do constitute an alternative to direct public provision.

Housing policy cannot be simply equated with the public sector, then. Indeed, welfare in general may, as Titmuss (1963) argued in his analysis of the mixed economy of welfare, have multiple sources: as well as provision by the state, there may be the fiscal system (tax incentives) and the workplace (tied cottages, company pensions and private medical insurance). One of his arguments was that, in addition to the action of governments, the private sector may deem it in its own interests to provide welfare goods for its own employees so that welfare becomes part of the contract between worker and firm. In fact, this idea of the mixed economy of welfare has been widened, for example by Rose, with the development of arguments that it is important to consider 'the contribution that each of three social institutions – the household, the market, and the state – makes to total welfare in society' (1986, p. 14). Norman Johnson (1987) has extended this yet further by adding the voluntary sector to the sources of welfare provision. These views are important because they make it clear that individuals receive their welfare by virtue of a number of different institutions and mechanisms. The state may be a prime influence on some – through state provision and taxation – but not on others. But the action taken by governments will influence the non-state sectors' actions and vice versa. In a national setting where firms or the voluntary sector take on large-scale responsibility for, say, the provision of housing, the pressures on government to legislate may be low. An understanding of the totality as well as the parts is thus important.

However, it is also important to recognize that whereas there are several different sources of welfare, they may not be functional equivalents. Thus Mishra (1990) has argued that the source may have consequences for the nature of welfare since the different sources reflect or follow from different values and principles. Thus housing provided by a firm may have very different connotations to housing provided by the state: the former may be sought, or aspired to, as representing high status; the latter may be stigmatized and avoided. Consequently, it is important for the comparative researcher to recognize that what individuals receive in welfare should be measured not only in terms of the total amount, but also the balance between different sources.

Recipients

In taking an interest, then, in the lives of their citizens governments have a great many choices concerning the ways in which they can influence their behaviour. Moreover, within each of the six, broad approaches and the different institutions presented above, it is clear that there is a variety of strategies and levels, so that a complete list of the possible means of achieving social goals is very long. As long as this list might appear there are, in fact, still other choices. One set of choices concerns the extent to which the policy is to apply to all the citizens of a country or to some subset. A universal subsidy would be one for which all citizens are eligible, but, frequently, only sections of the population can receive help. The selection might be on the basis of income so that the subsidy is means tested, or of some other characteristic such as location (inner city or conservation areas), ethnic group (positive discrimination in favour of an ethnic minority group) or families with children (dwellings with gardens) or age (older persons' housing).

The fact that a particular subset is selected as the recipient of policy does not necessarily exclude other subsets from consideration. Indeed, it is not uncommon that people in different income brackets are subsidized according to different criteria. Thus, the poor might be subsidized through state provision and the rich through the tax system. To take a particular example, a government could decide that it wanted to achieve the renovation of the houses in a particular area, perhaps because of their architectural or historic interest, and in order to achieve this introduces legislation requiring house owners to undertake the necessary work, providing all with an income tax allowance, but providing some, whose incomes are below a threshold at which they pay tax, with financial assistance in the form of a grant.

It is also important to note that although different households may receive the same amount of subsidy, the form in which subsidy is given may have a significance. It can be the case, for example, that middle- and higher-income groups receiving subsidy through the system of income tax benefit are not stigmatized by their position. Indeed, their obtaining of the benefit may be thought sensible (everyone should take advantage of the concession) or even envied (it would be nice for others if they could get the same). In contrast, welfare through direct provision, particularly if means tested, may be thought of as inferior (lower status) or even arising from moral deficiency (dependency and scrounging). The way in which different groups in society receive their welfare may be an important indicator of their power in society. In addition, in circumstances where there are external pressures on governments to take austerity measures (as so frequently in the period after the oil crisis in 1973), the welfare enjoyed by more powerful groups may be less susceptible to cuts.

Finally, it is also important to distinguish between policy inputs and policy outcomes. Policy may have stated aims to assist specified groups in the population in specified ways, but the groups in the population that actually do benefit may be different than those apparently intended. For example, a policy to assist the low-income tenants of a slum area by providing grants to renovate their dwellings may make the area so attractive that other, higher-income groups exercise their market power to displace the former residents. A policy, which on the surface looks like a progressive one, therefore, may actually have regressive effects.

The distinctiveness of housing

Up to this point the chapter has considered content, institutions and recipients of welfare using examples for illustration from both housing and non-housing areas. However, the overlap between what might be called general policy options and housing related options is not exact. Indeed, it seems reasonable to suggest that as the product or service provided in different areas of welfare states differs – health care from education from pensions from housing, and so on – the range of possible options may include some that are unique to any particular area. There may thus be possible policies in relation to the regulation of medicines that have no parallel in some other policy areas, and vice versa. A further stepping stone for the survey of options with respect to housing can usefully be established with a consideration of what is distinctive, if anything, about housing as an area of welfare.

The first distinction is that houses are physical artefacts, which in most forms – the mobile home being an exception – are located, immovably, on a defined area of land. Unlike, say pensions or unemployment benefit, houses are not portable across space. On any large scale, the import of housing into a country, or even from one part of that country to another, may be technically difficult. As a consequence, if a government wishes to ensure that its citizens are housed to a satisfactory standard, there may be an onus on the government to ensure the conditions under which the necessary level of house production will take place. Unlike television sets, clothes, medicines and food, adequate levels of consumption cannot be ensured simply by providing enough money to purchase, if necessary from abroad. Any housing policy ends directed at providing houses across the population of a country have therefore to address issues of how to ensure not only that households are able, for financial and other reasons, to consume them but also that there are sufficient numbers of appropriate dwellings and that they are in appropriate locations in the first place. In short, housing policy commonly addresses both production and consumption issues, and rarely more so than when there are large shortages.

Another important characteristic of houses is that they are durable commodities. They are not produced, and then consumed, at one point in time, but rather provide a flow of services over time. They are not, like food and drink, consumed instantaneously. The period of time can be considerable. The materials and the methods used are important determinants of the durability, but houses, in countries where brick, stone and concrete constitute the normal building material, which had lifespans of less than, say, half a century would often be unusual. Equally, the way in which the house is consumed – how it is tended and how maintained – will have important consequences for durability. Moreover, in some cultures as houses get older they may, like vintage cars, attract a premium, not simply because they are scarce, but because of what is deemed to be their intrinsic attractiveness.

Durability also means that 'housing systems are not designed from scratch' (Ambrose, 1992, p. 172). The high capital costs involved, together with the other resource constraints, such as the availability of building skills, mean that European countries have only rarely managed to add more than a few per cent to their housing stocks in any one year. Even in those countries that experienced large-scale damage to their housing stocks in the Second World War, very large parts of their current housing stock predate 1939. Social security systems, pension eligibilities, educational provisions may in many ways be fundamentally altered in quite short periods of time. But, much about housing endures. Even the 'revolution' in council housing in Britain with the Right to Buy provisions had, after fifteen years, left around 80 per cent of them still owned by local authorities.

Finally, many areas of welfare state spending – child benefits, income support and pensions for example – take the form of transfer payments. For whatever reason, individuals are considered appropriate recipients of the nation's money which they can spend on specified goods (perhaps via vouchers) or unspecified ones. Spending in many other areas – health care and education, for example – is heavily weighted towards the payment of salaries of the service providers – teachers, nurses, doctors and so on. Housing production, however, is very capital intensive. The development of new housing demands access to large sources of capital. Since in practice, loans which finance the capital expenditure may be repaid over many years, the payments households make in the form of mortgages or rent frequently constitute not only the repayment of the capital, but also a payment to cover interest. A further feature of this capital is that it needs to be periodically renewed if the quality of the service provided by a dwelling is to be maintained. Housing is not a single, durable commodity which is paid for at the outset, but a set of capitals which have different lifespans. The basic structure – the bricks and mortar, or concrete – may be very durable, but the internal decorations and the external paint work may, from time to time, need renewing. The capital intensive nature of housing production, re-production and some forms of consumption, notably home ownership, ensure that the arrangements whereby capital is accumulated and lent are crucial and distinctive parts of the housing policy equation. More so than in any other major area of social policy, therefore, governments cannot easily ignore the characteristics and requirements of finance capital.

Housing as a process

John Turner was perhaps the first to observe of the word 'housing' that in English it:

> can be used as a noun or as a verb. When used as a noun, it describes a commodity or product. The verb 'to house' describes the process or activity of housing. (1972, p. 151)

In addition to the collective noun, therefore, housing can be viewed as a process. For Turner, the important aspect of this process was the role the occupant could play in bringing the noun into being. But the recognition of a process can also be useful in identifying elements or points in the process at which government may become involved in order to effect policy ends. The benefits as well as the procedure have been described by Peter Ambrose:

> One analytical approach that may clarify the policy issues is to 'unpack' the process of provision into its constituent stages. ...This subdivides the provision process into the relatively discrete stages through which all housing units pass. (1992, p. 173)

Figure 3.1, based on Ambrose (1991, 1992), identifies what most observers would probably agree are the main stages. These begin with the act of development whereby an individual or agency initiates the conditions that can support the construction stage. This will probably involve them in ensuring that a specific plot of land is available, which in turn entails both that the promoter has legal title to that land and that any appropriate planning permission has been obtained. Promoters will also need to ensure the availability of sufficient capital, either from their own resources or from an external source, to finance the next stage. The availability of land, labour and materials is, then, a prerequisite for the construction stage which may also be carried out by an individual or an agency. As at the development stage, the actor may also be a member of the private, public or voluntary sector. This stage involves the bringing together of the factors of production in the building process in order that physical structures are produced.

Following construction is an allocation stage at which decisions are made about the persons who are to occupy the dwelling. At this, and indeed at any other, stage in the process, the legal title to the land and the dwelling may change hands. The allocation stage may involve an owner deciding whether or not themselves to be the occupier, to allow a friend, relative or employee to occupy, or to let it to a member of the wider population. This stage thus involves a shift from the production phase to the consumption phase. It is also at this stage that the user price of the dwelling – in the form of the amount of capital required to purchase, of loan repayments or of rent – will be determined. Sometimes the allocation stage will occur only once in the lifetime of the dwelling but, more frequently, there will be periodic re-allocations, for example a tenant leaves or the owner decides to sell the property. Similarly, the final stage, when the dwelling is repaired or maintained, may occur several times over the lifetime of the dwelling. This stage represents the periodic injection of capital in order to renew broken or worn-out parts of the dwelling: a phase of periodic re-production. But it may also constitute additional capital in order to bring about improvements through, for example, the building of an extension or the installation of better insulation.

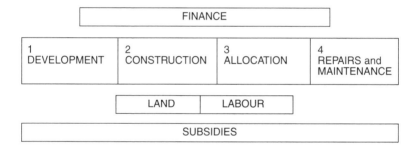

Figure 3.1 Stages in the housing provision process

Running in parallel with all four stages is a requirement for finance and the existence of subsidy. It has been noted earlier that the former need is particularly acute in the case of housing because it is generally very expensive relative to average incomes. Finance may take the form of lumps of capital or small payments, but frequently is facilitated by large financial institutions which provide credit. Subsidies provided by governments to the actors at each stage of the provision process are a common feature of national policy systems. Periodic access to sources of labour and materials is also necessary.

Whereas Figure 3.1 describes stages in the housing provision process, they are of course located within a wider framework or context. The behaviour of actors and the range of possibilities with which they are faced are influenced by events in the wider economy such as developments in wages, in national income, and in interest rates. Thus it may be expected that where prosperity increases households are able to exercise a higher level of demand, being willing to pay for larger dwellings with higher standards of facilities such as heating and kitchen equipment. Or, rates of return in other sectors of the economy may be significantly higher and attract developers and builders away from housing, perhaps to build offices or shops. In addition to those in the economic environment there are other important processes. Demographic developments can result in temporally uneven demands for housing from newly created households, from families with large numbers of children, or from elderly persons. New technologies or new fashions in architecture or in living styles may bring about new sets of preferences. What all this amounts to is that the boundaries set on Figure 3.1 are quite artificial and that, while they are useful for allowing us to explore the terrain on which the main parts of housing policy are located, they largely remove from our vision many non-housing policies that may have significant impacts upon the housing system.

It should also be recognized that each of the boxes in Figure 3.1 may summarize a great deal of detail. Later chapters in this book will show, for example, that the box representing finance may constitute a wide range of actors who relate to one another in a variety of ways. In each country the particular configuration of actors and relationships will vary.

Frameworks

One point about the schema in Figure 3.1 is that it maps out the locations of interest to governments seeking to involve themselves in the housing of their citizens. The locations are not exhaustive, although beyond the boundaries any involvement would probably be considered not to be motivated with respect to housing, but to be thought of as health, labour market or education policy, for example. Governments may choose to act, or not, but their decisions will not necessarily be the same for each stage. At one stage government may regulate, at another do nothing, and at a third subsidize and regulate. Thus, housing for a specific population group such as older people might be left to the private sector to develop and build but with the standard of provision, in terms of the physical fabric and the standard of care, being regulated by government and linked to rent subsidy. One way of using the schema therefore is to develop a matrix, as in Figure 3.2, which combines the stages in housing provision with the types of policy content described earlier. For each country being compared, a separate table could be completed by noting for each stage in the provision process the nature, including absence, of government intervention. This would aid systematic presentation but, unfortunately, for purposes of locating the complete policy regime of any one country, there are, as we have seen, more than two dimensions: the institutions of policy as well as the recipients are important. Technically, therefore, we have a multi-dimensional space – institutions, recipients, content and stages – and along any of the dimensions there may be more than one entry.

POLICY INSTRUMENT	POLICY STAGE			
	Development	Construction	Allocation	Renovation
Non-action				
Exhortation				
Regulation				
Taxation				
Subsidy				
Provision				

Figure 3.2 Policy instruments used at each stage in the housing provision process

Adding a further level of complexity, many of the interventions listed here may be implemented to various degrees and at various levels. Take the case of rent control, which has been common throughout industrialized countries in the postwar period. In addition to which properties and which people might be affected, there are issues concerning the rigour with which the policies are implemented – do some groups or regions avoid the legislation – and the severity of the control? Are rents so low that housing is consumed at near zero user cost? Or are they sufficiently high that they provide developers a return on their capital that compares favourably with what they could get in other sectors? There can be no doubt, therefore, that not only can policy regimes vary considerably from one country to another or even from one time to another but that they can be complex or multi-dimensional.

Putting ownership and subsidies together

In response to the recognition of the complexity of national housing policy systems, an alternative approach is to map them on other two-dimensional matrices, where each dimension records some aspect of policy. An example is provided by Figure 3.3 where the ownership of dwellings – whether by a private individual or company, a private, non-profit organization, and the public sector – is set alongside the extent to which the user cost is subsidized. There could be many other pairs of dimensions, but Figure 3.3 is sufficient to illustrate how such matrices can be used.

WHO PAYS?	WHO OWNS?		
	Private company or individual	Voluntary organization	The state
User	1	2	3
Part subsidy	4	5	6
Full subsidy	7	8	9

Figure 3.3   Housing ownership and payment

Cell 9 represents a pure public model in which housing is provided by some branch of the state at zero cost to the user. The pure private model is represented by cell 1 where housing is owned privately and the user pays the full cost. The remaining seven cells represent various hybrids. All are technically feasible, and although in practice some are unusual combinations, there are examples of all of them. So, governments can be landlords providing homes at full cost or market rents (cell 3); equally, tenants of private landlords may have all their housing costs met by the state (cell 7). Identifying where the housing in a country was located in this matrix would facilitate cross-country comparison. Thus most housing in the USA is located in cells 1 and 4, whereas much housing in many western European countries is located in cells 4, 5 and 6, and in eastern Europe there had until the start of the 1990s been considerable parts of their stock in cell 9.

Such matrices could be based upon alternative dimensions, such as the type of developer or financing, as well as of institutions or recipients. The choice of dimension would depend on the particular aspect of housing policy being studied.

The cost–income gap

Given that national policy systems are frequently extremely complex there is a danger that, even with the devices suggested, the national pictures are still so complex that they present considerable problems in seeking to understand any one of them, yet alone to make comparisons: a danger of not being able to see the wood for the policy trees. In addition to the frameworks described through Figures 3.2 and 3.3 another approach can be pursued through a re-formulation of the policy terrain as a challenge to reconcile the, so-called, cost–income gap.

This re-formulation is based on a view that the problem facing national governments is that of finding ways in which their citizens can afford to meet the cost of housing. The problem of affordability arises because the real cost (that is the full economic cost of the resources consumed) of producing housing of a standard below which it would not be socially acceptable, generally greatly exceeds the incomes of households at the bottom of the income distribution. This situation arises in the first place because all governments in western countries have specified levels of housing, in terms of size, quality, materials, infrastructure, which they consider to be the minimum acceptable. Generally this has taken the form of regulating – often through land use planning and building legislation – the nature of residential development. Insofar as such legislation has increased the quantity and quality of housing that households would otherwise consume, it creates a problem in that social objectives outstrip private means, the distinction introduced in Chapter One between need and demand. This outcome can be described in terms of two columns, which are proportional in height to the real cost and to incomes respectively, with the housing problem occurring because the former is higher than the latter. The difference between the two then describes the cost–income gap. Even for those sectors of the population with higher incomes who may be able to afford housing of the minimal standard, it is frequently the case that there is still a gap between their individual income and their individual housing aspirations.

There are four broad strategies governments can pursue in attempting to resolve the existence of the difference in the heights of the two columns. They can do all four together or in different permutations. They can, and sometimes are, permed differently for different tenures or population groups.

(1) *Doing nothing.* This strategy will ensure that while some households – generally those with higher incomes – live in houses

of socially acceptable minimum standards, many are unable to do so. They will be forced either to live outside mainstream society in shanty settlements, or double up with other household members, perhaps parents. In the latter case, the policy is in effect reflecting a view that standards in the shape of overcrowding are not important. Moreover, while recognizing that minimum standards may be desirable, this approach fails to acknowledge either that their imposition creates a cost–income gap, or that some sectors of the population do not merit the socially defined minimum.

(2) *Reducing real costs.* This policy approach attacks the very heart of the contradiction by attempting to reduce the real resources consumed in the production of housing. In effect, this reduces the height of the cost column to a level closer to the height of the income column. This approach will involve influencing aspects of the production process including the factors of production – land, labour and capital – in order to ensure that production uses fewer resources. On Figure 3.1 it will be implemented within stages 1 or 2, and perhaps 4, and could involve, for example, the implementation of methods of house construction based on pre-fabrication.

(3) *Reducing user cost.* This approach is based upon the reduction of the cost facing the final owner or user of the dwelling. It is achieved by providing a subsidy so that, while the real cost may be unaffected, the price the supplier charges is lower than the real cost. The actual height of the cost column is not reduced, therefore, but the height facing the consumer is. Such supply-side subsidies may be in the form of, for example, land provided by a local authority at zero cost, reduced interest rates on construction loans, tax breaks on specified expenditures or rent control. Whereas such subsidies are generally provided by governments they may, as in the case of rent control, be imposed by government but be paid for by the supplier. In cases where profit-maximizing companies are suppliers of housing there may be a tendency to try to convert the subsidy into profit, so that subsidies are generally accompanied by regulations governing the prices that can be charged.

(4) *Increasing ability to pay.* Demand-side subsidies are a form of income redistribution whereby users of housing are enabled to increase the amount of money they can pay. In effect, they increase the height of the income column. The redistribution may take the form of a money transfer, which the recipient is able to

spend in any way that he or she chooses, even if this is on non-housing expenditure. It may also take the form of a money transfer, sometimes a voucher, which can only be redeemed against housing expenditures. Demand-side subsidies, therefore, may be part of general income distribution policy or be thought of as housing specific policies. In both cases the policies can be progressive, that is providing in relation to income proportionately more help to lower-income groups, or regressive, that is less help.

Lundquist has proposed a different representation of the range of policy contents that governments may adopt, but one which implicitly also relates to the cost–income gap:

> To get to the logically possible *content* of policy regardless of national context, we may begin with the proposition that the housing sector is a system characterized by a perpetual *process* of adjusting households and dwellings to each other, i.e., by the incessant interplay between producer supply and consumer demand. ...The system involves two major analytical categories, i.e., *subjects* (producers and consumers) and *objects* (dwellings). (original emphases, 1992a, p. 4)

For Lundquist, then, policy is the process whereby the system elements are brought together and in some way resolved. This may be according to principles, at one extreme, of the market and, at the other, of human need. The options can be represented by two dimensions: household purchasing power and dwelling prices (see Figure 3.4). The former will be determined by personal income and wealth, as well as state transfers to the individual household. The latter will follow from the factors of production used, which will depend on both technology and the size and quality of the dwelling. The number of dwellings will affect prices. The state may also influence prices through regulation, provision, taxation and subsidy. Figure 3.4 thus outlines the courses of action, or inaction, that are open to states and that have consequences for the resolution of the two sides of the market.

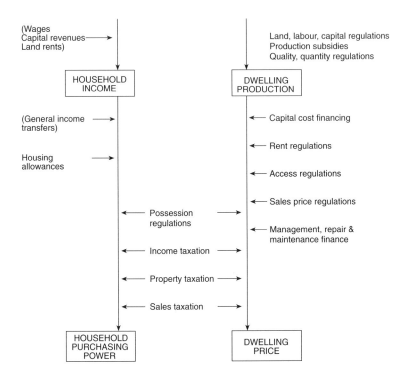

Source: Lundquist (1992a).

Figure 3.4   State interventions in the housing sector

Conclusions

Forming one of the book's building blocks, this chapter has done two things. First, it has identified the options that face national policy makers in their deliberations about the housing of their citizens. These options have been identified in terms of the possible content of policies, with governments facing different opportunities including regulation, subsidy and provision. Although the list of options is in fact general across all areas of social policy it is useful to relate them to the particular characteristics of housing. In this, the recognition that the gestation period as well as the lifespan of houses may cover many years is relevant to the view of housing as being characterized by a number of stages stretching over time and including both production and consumption. A significant feature of these stages is that governments may choose to intervene in any combination of them, and for each may choose from a range of policy options. To make reference to housing policy, then, is to deal with a multifaceted involvement by the state so that a full description of housing policy in any industrialized state involves the construction of a highly complex picture.

It is this recognition that forms the basis of the second part of the chapter. If describing one nation's housing policy is difficult, describing and comparing more than one is even more difficult. One of the challenges facing the comparativist is therefore that of finding ways in which complexity can be reduced. The chapter introduces a number of approaches, based on matrices, which force a systematic appraisal on the researcher. A further approach is based around the inequality between the cost or supply side of housing systems and the income or demand sides. The so-called cost–income gap then provides a conceptualization of the housing problem facing national governments as well as a basis for classifying policy effects or intentions.

4

Policy For What Ends?

If the previous chapter sought to explore what, theoretically at least, were the options facing policy makers, the present one seeks to explore not what policy makers can do, but why they do what they do: why do they intervene at all, and why do they intervene in the ways they do? It attempts this by presenting a range of theoretical perspectives, each of which throws light upon the macro-processes within which policy makers operate, and which help to explain national patterns in housing policy. Taking the case studies in Chapter One as illustrations: why have Japanese governments encouraged home ownership and private sector solutions to an extent that has not been apparent in the Netherlands, and why have both North American and British housing policies in the last two decades been characterized by a greater insertion of market principles? In other words, we seek some assistance in the understanding, rather than the description, of differences and similarities over both time and space.

Organizing theoretical perspectives

There are numerous theoretical perspectives from which a selection is drawn of those that, implicitly or explicitly, have been the main ones informing housing policy researchers. The starting point for including and then organizing perspectives is a recognition that neither housing problems nor housing solutions, nor indeed the links between them, are necessarily what they seem. As indicated in Chapter One, they do not necessarily constitute a stimulus–response system in which housing problems somehow get translated into housing policies. How can we, therefore, start to understand why housing policies exist? One way of finding insights to help understand both why industrialized countries have developed sets of housing policies, as well as the form of those policies, is to review those theoretical perspectives that purport to explain the growth and nature of welfare states. The rationale for this is that the theories might not be specific to particular areas of welfare but apply equally to health care, social security, housing and so on. So, we can draw upon the larger focus of study in order to inform us about the smaller one. In addition, there is now a considerable amount of literature on these issues in the social policy field as well as in the main social science disciplines of sociology, political science and economics. This literature can provide perspectives from which national housing policies can be understood, contrasted and compared. These perspectives also shed light on the origins and objectives of social policy which take us beyond simplistic notions of mechanistic relationships between problem and policy.

Although there are actually a large number of theoretical perspectives it would be possible to review, here only those deemed most relevant to the task in hand are presented. They are grouped under half a dozen or so headings. Under each heading, however, there is in fact a range of views so that in the context of a single chapter it is not possible to do justice to the full variety. These reviews are not detailed ones, therefore, but merely intended to provide, in each case, an indication of the main thrust of the argument, only sometimes drawing attention to the variations in interpretation. They draw on a number of sources (for instance, Mishra, 1981; Pierson, 1991) to which the reader is directed for fuller discussion.

For the purposes of exposition, the theoretical perspectives are located within two competing schools or tendencies. Of these, the first views welfare states as a common feature of industrialized countries. They have been developed as a consequence of industrialization and its correlates, with the distinguishing feature being cross-national similarity. Welfare states are seen as developing over time along similar trajectories and converging on common solutions and responses to common circumstances and problems. The second, and competing, tendency emphasizes cross-national differences. Broadly, the argument is that even if there are some common circumstances in different countries not only are these not precisely the same but societies have responded to them in their own ways. It is quite possible, and indeed is deemed to happen, that policy regimes can remain different and even become less similar over time. One of the organizing frameworks of this chapter, therefore, is a distinction between theories based on increasing similarity or convergence and those based on increasing dissimilarity or divergence.

Whatever the usefulness of this as a device for presenting theories of welfare state development, it would be a mistake, however, to consider the two theoretical schools as mutually exclusive. Contestable and competing they may be, but restricting the field of interest to one of these tendencies to the exclusion of the other would be to pursue an over-simplistic model. As Harloe (1995, p. 528) has put it: 'any comparatively based theory that aspires to explain the overall development of a field of social policy, not just selected aspects, has to account adequately for similarities and differences'. This may mean that studies are needed which explore processes which during specific historical periods are presenting nations with similar influences and which are leading them to similar actions and responses, as well as processes which identify nationally specific circumstances and responses. It may be most helpful, in short, to pursue understandings of both similarities and differences, convergence and divergence.

A second organizing framework is based on a recognition that there are some common dimensions to the histories of industrialized countries. Broadly, in all now industrialized countries at some point over the last two centuries or so, the pace of industrialization quickened. The shift from agricultural and feudal societies to industrial and urban ones led to the growth of large cities. The concentration of masses of people who sought to make a living from working in the growing manufacturing industries, and the development of markets as the mechanism by which goods and services were allocated became central parts of the way of life. There were fundamental shifts in social and economic relations with the previous systems for the acquisition of welfare often being replaced by markets so that the amount of housing, education and health care people obtained was a reflection largely of their own financial resources. Those with well-paid and regular jobs could purchase a lot; those with neither purchased little. The timing of these developments varied from country to country: in some, such as those bordering the Mediterranean in southern Europe, they have been features mainly of the present century; in others, such as Britain, Germany and the USA, of the previous century. But, in general, the developments of commodified forms of labour and welfare have been part of the process of industrialization. It was against this background that national governments began to put in place sets of social policy – collectively constituting welfare states – which modified the relationship between the ability of people to sell their labour power and the levels of welfare that they could consume. In other words, some goods and services became decommodified so that they could be consumed independently of the consumer's job position.

The transition from industrializing states to welfare states has not in any country been a smooth or even one. Ginsburg argues that it has 'been crucially shaped by the crises, slumps and booms in capitalist economies' (1992, p. 13). Occurring in some countries in the 1870s, 1930s and 70s, these economic crises and their consequent social crises have been crucial in the development of social policies. His argument is that industrialization may form a common back-cloth, but the periodic crises have constituted the trigger of re-evaluation of the social policy status quo. For example, the USA case study in Chapter One pointed to the importance of the Depression in setting the direction for later housing policy, and of the Second World War in the case of the Netherlands. In the period up to 1970 these re-evaluations were typically resolved in the direction of social policy expansion by which governments increased their commitment to, and expenditure on, welfare. In many countries this meant the introduction of housing subsidies and social housing provision, followed by even greater commitment in this direction. It is this expansionary phase that forms the explanatory focus of much theorizing about the development of welfare states. Accordingly, the first part of this chapter presents the various perspectives against the context of explaining welfare state growth.

This emphasis recognizes, however, that for many now industrial-ized countries, industrialization occurred after 1870, and for some after 1930. Crises of the type described, therefore, may have prompted the development of welfare policies, but they are not necessary precursors of welfare state developments. However, all advanced industrialized countries have experienced (even if not so markedly) the third of the crises identified by Ginsburg, namely that occurring in the post 1970 period. Where this has been quite different from earlier periods is that it has lead to a period of re-assessment with a downward pressure on welfare spending and commitment that has, across a wide spread of countries, thrown welfare states into reverse. This retrenchment has been accompanied by different or modified versions of the old theories about welfare states. Thus the second part of the chapter specifically examines theoretical perspectives on welfare state shrinkage or retrenchment.

In summary, then, the rest of this chapter is organized in three sections. In the first a number of theoretical perspectives which propound increasing convergence in policies are presented, in the second they propound increasing divergence, while the emphasis in the third, on retrenchment, presents both convergence and divergence.

Theories of increasing similarity: convergence

Many of those writers who have studied the growth of welfare states in industrialized countries have implicitly or explicitly developed theories that view welfare states as becoming more alike. With the advancement of time and the transition from one phase of industrialization to another, they have viewed countries as having adopted welfare policies that have had more and more in common. On this view, welfare states are not unique, therefore, precisely because they are being driven by a common logic often related to economic development. On this view, housing policy is primarily the product of the economic position of individual countries. Four theoretical schools are included in this section: theories of moral necessity, of citizenship, of the logic of industrialization and of the logic of capitalism.

The welfare state as moral necessity

This perspective states that in all economically advanced countries the processes of industrialization and urbanization have brought with them new divisions within societies, one expression of which has sometimes been an ignorance on the part of ruling elites of how the mass of the population lived. In many countries it was a feature of the transition to industrialization that those engaged in social research about the conditions in which the poor lived firmly held the belief that their findings would be inexorably translated into political action. The elites would see, for the first time, how impoverished many groups were and their sense of conscience and fair play would lead them to act. Amelioration would follow since when the 'facts were discovered [they] would speak with a single unequivocal voice to indicate practical solutions' (Abrams, cited by Bulmer, 1982).

Along with knowledge of the problems, then, there has often been a moral dimension: some policies, intended to improve the position of disadvantaged groups, are deemed appropriate on grounds of fairness. Implicitly or explicitly this theme has run through much of the social sciences with the development of central concerns about equality. This 'moralistic' approach sometimes forms the discourse of popular discussion, so that welfare state reforms are couched in terms of normative statements about everyone being enabled to share certain minimum levels of welfare and society taking responsibility for the disadvantaged. Under this model, welfare policy is driven by social conscience.

So, on this view decent housing is a moral imperative which reasonable people would expect all members of society to be able to enjoy, and government interventions in the housing system reflect that moral position. According to Joan Higgins (1981) this is a view that had general credence, during the 1940s and 50s in particular, within both the population at large and the academic community in Britain. Moreover, there was often an implicit assumption that 'the humanitarian impulse would – in time – lead to a recognition that all civilized societies had an obligation to provide for their dependent members' (Higgins, 1981, p. 28). What is common to all societies, therefore, is deemed to be a shared human disposition towards a sense of fairness with this sense of fairness eventually surfacing so that governments everywhere would seek to improve the lot of those inadequately housed.

Marshall and citizenship

The influential work by T H Marshall on rights of citizenship and modern democratic states was written as an interpretation of developments in Britain. Although the setting is geographically limited and has been criticized for being Anglocentric (see Kemeny, 1992), the case can be made that it can 'be seen as valid for at least western industrial countries, whose political and economic structure is broadly similar to that of Britain' (Mishra, 1981, p. 27). The essence of the Marshallian thesis is that alongside the industrial and economic changes which have characterized the developments of some countries to their present stage of advanced capitalism, there have been political developments. These developments have taken the form of the achievement, over the long run, of three sets of rights: civil, political and social. These rights are seen as cumulative, with civil rights – the freedom of speech and faith, and the freedom to enter into legal contracts – being gained in the eighteenth century, and these, in turn, making possible the acquisition in the nineteenth century of political rights – to vote, and the rise of mass political parties. Both these sets of rights, in turn, paved the way for, and in some senses made necessary, the third set, social rights, which have been manifested in the social policy provisions of access to education, health care, social security and housing. Both the welfare state in general as well as interventions to ensure minimum standards of housing can in the Marshallian scheme be seen as dimensions of a macro-process of modernization.

The developments of rights can also be viewed as the outcome of tensions between the development of citizenship which are based on notions of equality and the development of capitalism which is based on inequality. The gaining of political rights, including the growing strength of political parties which drew their strength from the mass of the population, against a context of economic and social developments which meant continual or periodic deprivation for many, resulted in the granting of social rights. These can be seen both as ameliorating the adverse effects of the developing capitalist system and as acting to defuse moves towards more radical, even revolutionary, political action, hence decisions by governments to remove insanitary and unhealthy housing and to set down at least minimum standards for new housing. In expressing these developments in terms of citizenship, Marshall sets out a justification for access to decent housing and other social goods as matters of rights rather than of social conscience, stigma or residualization.

The logic of industrialism

The essence of the logic of industrialism as an explanation for the rise and the form of welfare states is that they are a necessary concomitant of industrialization. The 'logic of industrialism' (also known as 'convergence', 'end of ideology' and 'politics doesn't matter' theories) is taken to be that long-term social, economic and demographic developments associated with the course of industrialization in advanced capitalist countries, have led, just as surely as night follows day, to a response in the form of welfare states. It is thus the correlates of industrial progress that ultimately explain the way in which countries have developed social policies. The theory also posits that the further that industrialization develops – the more advanced it becomes – the closer or more similar welfare states become. Convergence theory is thus used to explain both the fact of the development of modern welfare states, and their increasing similarity.

Much of the development of, and support for, this explanation of developments occurred in the late 1950s and 60s, with some of the influential work of Wilensky being published in the 1970s. In an early study with Lebeaux, Wilensky concluded that 'all industrial societies face similar problems', and, most emphatically significant, that the solutions to those problems 'are prescribed more by industry than by other cultural elements' (Wilensky and Lebeaux, 1965, p. 47). Likewise he concluded, on the basis of a national comparison of social security spending in relation to GNP, that over the long term, it is the latter – GNP per capita – which 'overwhelms' other predictors (Wilensky, 1975). Although within the disciplines of politics and sociology the influence of the logic of industrialism thesis has subsequently waned, among housing researchers it has remained pervasive and influential (Schmidt, 1989; Oxley, 1991).

Mishra (1981) provides a generalized summary of the processes by which industrialism might be seen to effect social policy developments. Industrialization itself transforms the labour process and with it the relationship between people and work. To a large extent pre-industrial arrangements of self-employment are replaced by waged employment. With this change, wages become the dominant source of livelihood, but only for those in work. For others – the unemployed, the sick, the elderly – the problem of acquiring even the means to exist may become acute. Insofar as industrialization is also associated with urbanization, as production sites congregated together, so it led to new problems of housing – overcrowding and insanitary and unhealthy conditions. Increasingly, industrialization also comes to need employees who have achieved an adequate level of education or skill and an adequate level of physical fitness, so that provisions for mass education and minimum levels of food consumption and living become important. The geographical movement of labour may mean that extended family networks are fractured. There are two types of development, therefore, one whereby industrialization leads to the undermining of traditional forms of welfare provision – such as the family, or voluntary groups – and the other where there are new social problems such as unemployment and insanitary living conditions. The result of these (universal) developments is that 'industrialization creates the preconditions for a substantial growth of specialized or "structurally differentiated" agencies of welfare' (Mishra, 1981, p. 40).

Posited in this 'pure' form, convergence theory is an explanation founded on technological determinism in which values and choices – the politics – are not simply marginalized but discounted as having no impact upon outcomes. Hence the common observation that the theory amounts to one based on the premise that 'politics doesn't matter'. Indeed, as Mishra (1981, p. 45) notes, 'the claim that everything is already decided in advance by the nature of modern technology and economy denies the very possibility of a "policy" about anything, social or otherwise, since policy presupposes the act of deliberation and choice'. The evidence supporting this position is by no means water-tight as Higgins points out:

> It was rapidly becoming clear, even from a superficial examination of different societies, that a wide range of policy responses to social need had evolved since the nineteenth century. (1981, p. 40)

In addition, Kemeny (1992) has taken issue with what he sees as a misreading of the literature: a state of affairs which has followed from 'a search for theoretical simplicity in explanations of social change' (1992, p. 54). Kemeny's reading indicates (to him) that in the literature there is not an argument suggesting a rigid inevitability about social policy arising from industrialism, but rather a recognition of a 'contest between the forces for uniformity and for diversity' (Kerr *et al.*, 1960, cited in Kemeny, 1992, p. 54). But, even if this is a simplification, others – Taylor-Gooby and Dale, for example – point to what is arguably a considerable strength of convergence theory, namely 'an immense capacity to handle the considerable evidence of world-wide structural uniformity in social welfare' (1981, p. 114).

The logic of capitalism

In common with some of the other explanations of the processes driving the development of welfare states which are discussed here, the Marxist approach is characterized by a range of explanations. Marx himself was formulating his thesis at an historical point before the development of mature welfare states so that what Marxism has to say about them has come rather more from the later disciples than the master. Nevertheless, consistent with, that is following and developing from, his basic tenets it is possible to identify positions that appear firmly of the Marxist school.

At the heart of the Marxist position is an understanding of the capitalist system as having a number of distinct characteristics which set it apart from other systems. Under capitalism the means of production, through which wealth is generated, are privately owned. This applies to land and raw materials as well as to labour. Workers sell their labour power through the market in labour and in return receive wages. Capitalists who employ these workers produce goods whose value is greater than the wages paid so that in effect some unpaid labour is extracted and, through that profit, capitalists in general increase their wealth. The system of exploitation of workers is thus one in which the welfare of capitalists as a class is met, while the welfare of the workers themselves is squeezed. Workers can use their wages to purchase through other markets what levels of housing, health care, insurance and education they are able, but their ability will be squeezed always by the extraction of surplus. Capitalism is thus an antagonistic system, driven by competition, which has a tendency toward the dis-welfare of workers.

Marx's position concerning the role of the state was that it was an expression of the exploitation of workers. In this there was a contradiction: on the one hand, the state represents the members of the community over which it holds sway responding as appropriate to political pressures applied on it; on the other, it is also the protector of the class-based exploitation and so, in the long run, cannot act against the interests of either the capitalist class or the viability of the system as a whole. For Marx, it followed that the state could not act to effect a permanent enhancement of the welfare of workers since this would necessarily undermine the very foundation of the exploitation of workers and reduce the profit of capitalists. In addition, the dominant value of capitalism was one in which state intervention in general was seen as undesirable, and anything that was done in order to enhance the welfare of workers, particularly if this was guaranteed irrespective of their ability and willingness to sell their labour, would undermine the will to work, produce a nation of idlers and thereby undermine the basis of the system itself. Under this system human needs might be recognized politically but they could not be translated in the long run into social demand – the willingness of the state to meet those individual needs. For Marx, therefore, the development of meaningful and permanent social policy was inconsistent with the long-term functioning of capitalism as an economic and political system.

While holding on to much of the core of this argument, later Marxists have modified and refined it in the light of the development of welfare provisions across all the countries of the western world. O'Connor (1973) argues that whereas the state is of course involved in ensuring the circumstances whereby accumulation can thrive and will thus promote investment and stability, it also has to ensure legitimacy. The latter involves it in creating social harmony and ideological support for the continuation of the economic and social status quo. This has been expressed also in terms of a role of the state as that of maintaining social control (Ginsburg, 1979; Gough, 1979). On this view the benefits that social policies bring to workers is not disputed. However, the motivation for introducing social policy stems from the needs of capitalists, rather than from workers, to ensure the reproduction of capitalist social relations. Thus, the introduction of social security systems which modify the financial consequences of unemployment may well be welcomed by workers, but their introduction will follow from the requirements, clearly of interest to capitalists, that a pool of reserve labour is established and that widespread opposition to the system as a whole could be dissipated. According to Offe (1984) social policies can be viewed as mechanisms whereby the periodic crises of capitalism can be managed. Under capitalism there are constant tendencies towards dysfunctional outcomes. These are the results of unfettered capitalism, such as pollution, epidemics and starvation of the unemployed, which would threaten the very existence of the system. Given these threats the state acts through provision and legislation to obviate their consequences. Everywhere, according to Offe, it became an:

> obligation of the state apparatus to provide assistance and support to those citizens who suffer specific needs and risks which are characteristic of the market society… the welfare state has been celebrated throughout the post-war period as the political solution to societal contradictions. (1984, p. 147)

Intervention in the form of the welfare state, therefore, may vary in its form but not in its fact: the welfare state is a compromise forced on capital to protect its own existence and in that way can be seen as functional to capitalism.

In support of these views, in general and as a rebuttal of the position that the welfare state owes its existence to political projects reflecting the aspirations of the poorer elements within societies, Pierson (1991) offers eight observations:

(1) Social policy is established to meet the needs of capital rather than labour.
(2) Many social policy innovations were initiated by elites rather than as the result of bottom-up pressure, and they were initiated to reduce hardship or personal disaster.
(3) Social policy has been recognized by the elite as a mechanism to counter socialism and the overthrow of the established order, for example the use of home ownership as a means of giving workers a stake in the country.

(4) The changes in the nature of the welfare state reflect changes in the needs of capital in historically specific periods, for example the need for a fit and educated labour force as the labour process advanced compelled governments to introduce appropriate policies.
(5) At best the welfare state has been redistributive across the working class or across the lifecycle. At worst it has been regressive.
(6) The form of the welfare state has frequently been through large bureaucracies rather than community or self-organization.
(7) Legislation has often promoted the rights of state officials to interfere directly into people's lives and thereby to control their behaviour.
(8) The benefits provided by social provisions have bought off opposition to the system.

Theories of increasing dissimilarity: divergence

In contrast to those theoretical perspectives which have seen the outcomes of the processes of industrialism as inexorably leading countries to adopt welfare policies, is another set of perspectives which places greater emphasis on the role of individuals and groups within societies in their capacity to make free choices. On this view, social policy is the outcome of human beings exercising choice within the political arena, and, with choice leading to diversity, welfare states diverge.

Individualism

Individualism is one of the bases of neo-classical economics. Society is seen as being composed of individual people who pursue their own interests in the sense of seeking to maximize their own welfare. This leads them to have views about what, from their point of view, is the most appropriate or desirable package of social policies. As individual consumers they will 'calculate' the gains and losses to them of different goods and services being provided collectively and, of these, whether the local or central state is the more desirable provider. The political market place is characterized on the demand side by the votes with which individuals can elect or threaten to elect and, also, by the political pressure of lobbying groups which can help to influence the nature and impact of voting intentions. On the supply side of this market, political parties bring different packages of policy. Parties and their policies thus buy votes, so that the policies which get enacted in any country reflect the sum of individual calculations about their desirability. In other words, countries have housing policies that their electors want and have voted for through the ballot box.

Pluralism

Pluralism shares some of the features of individualism. It has two central tenets. The first is that modern democratic states pursue the satisfaction of the interests of the members of that state. States behave in this way because of the second tenet: societies are not made up of uniform masses of people all sharing common beliefs and pursuing common ends, rather, societies are seen as being characterized by a wide range of interests and with power widely dispersed. The combination of opposing political parties, elections, pressure groups, the division between legislature, judiciary and executive, which are all characteristic of modern democracies, contribute to a system in which power can never be monopolized by one group or interest.

Within this framework the role of the state is generally perceived as a benign sieve through which the interests of groups in society are channelled. Appropriate legislative action is then taken. The state, in other words, enacts policy in response to the demands made on it by a multitude of formal and informal interest groups within society. Crucial to pluralism is the formation of pressure groups and the development of policy as the outcome of their lobbying activities. Thus the level of public expenditure on housing, the growth and decline of different tenures, and the nature of housing subsidies would, for a pluralist, all be the outcome of a bargaining process in which interest groups brought political pressure to bear.

Both individualism and pluralism place the locus of decisions about policy formulation and adoption firmly in the political arena. Individuals and groups come to views about how their interests are to be met, and they pursue those interests through democratic processes.

Corporatism

As a perspective on advanced capitalist societies, corporatism was developed in the 1970s. It can be seen to have origins in dissatisfaction with existing pluralist analysis on two fronts: with the underlying assumptions of pluralist analysis itself, and with what were perceived to be the failure of pluralist analysis to account for certain developments in advanced societies, such as the extent of the political power and influence achieved by both industry and labour unions. Phillipe Schmitter (1974) and others put forward a perspective on policy formulation and implementation which focused on the incorporation of interest groups.

As with the other perspectives discussed in this chapter, corporatism constitutes a school of thought within which there is often quite wide disagreement, even down to what might be considered as the key propositions (see Williamson, 1989). Even so, it is agreed by most observers that the central proposition concerns the role of interest groups acting as negotiators and, to an extent, consensus seekers between the state and their members. As such, the proposition is not unlike pluralism. However, there are some fundamental differences. For pluralists, the role of interest groups is set within a competitive framework such that they vie for political concessions on behalf of their members. Corporatism, in contrast, posits that the objective, and outcome, is a monopolistic arrangement whereby the state and the interest group collude in a manner that excludes other interests. There may initially be competition among interest groups but, once the winners have been established, others are excluded. Being thus favoured, the elites of certain interest groups are enabled to represent the interests of their members. In this respect corporatist states make and implement policy in ways that are often beyond the immediate scrutiny of the normal democratic processes, with arrangements and negotiations going on behind closed doors.

Such arrangements can be beneficial to both the state and the licensed interest group. It may be that the interest group has to accept some constraints on its, and its members, behaviour, but in return it receives some stability and assurance over the continued activity that furthers their interests. This can take the form of restricting entry into a market so that the licensed group can pursue the accumulation of profit in a protected environment. From the state's point of view, corporatism provides partners in policy making and implementation thus helping to ensure that the state's policy objectives are achieved. Corporatism as consensus building thus helps to establish outcomes that are concurrent with the direction the state seeks to pursue. But, this also creates a mutual dependency. The licensed group becomes reliant on the state in order to ensure its own continuation or at least its continuing to carry out activities under the protective umbrella of the state (though this is of course a minimum condition for continuity since, among other things, the group also has to be profitable). The state may, in turn, become increasingly reliant on the licensed groups for knowledge of what is happening, and what is possible, in the real world.

Much of the literature on corporatism concentrates on industrial policy and the incorporation of elite groups in the form of labour unions and business organizations. In the case of housing, the elite groups are likely to be drawn from the professions involved in the provision of social housing, labour unions and businesses concerned with housing production and exchange. They might include, therefore, organizations representing the interests of housing managers, building workers unions, building companies and mortgage lenders. As David Clapham and his colleagues point out (Clapham *et al.*, 1990), the nature of these groups has certain consequences. In particular, and consistent with corporatist arrangements sitting outside the otherwise normal democratic procedures, the decisions reached will not directly reflect the interests of consumers. Corporatism involves bargaining with and among suppliers. The result may be that the nature of what is provided may reflect the interests of those whose livelihood is tied up with the supply of housing services. And, if the numbers of houses provided is greater than would have been the case in the absence of corporatist bargaining this may of course benefit consumers, but that may be a by-product of other interests being successfully pursued. Therefore, as is frequently the case under monopoly arrangements, the interests of the consumer may not be the central dynamic.

Social democracy

A particular perspective on the role of political processes in achieving the development of welfare states, is one which attributes them to the success of the social democratic project. According to Pierson (1991) this perspective has three distinguishing features. First, the Marxist view that capitalism will inexorably result in an increasingly impoverished working class is rejected, because it is not supported by the evidence. The working classes themselves, particularly through the gains achieved by social democratic parties on their behalf, have succeeded in intervening in, and thereby counteracting, the inequitable outcomes of capitalism: in short, prosperity can be shared. Second, the class structure of capitalism can be modified. The growing middle class, the rise of professionalism and a managerial class all can be seen to have contributed to a weakening of the position of capital. Third, capitalism offers the best prospect for increased prosperity. In practice these views were established on the basis of real achievements, which followed in turn the creation of parliamentary democracies and the election of social democratic parties:

> Of decisive importance is the winning of democracy which brings a new social and political order under which it is *political* authority which exercises effective control over the *economic* seats of power. (original emphases, Pierson, 1991, p. 25)

The social democratic project received yet further weight with the acceptance of the Keynesian view of economic management, according to which economies could be managed so as not only to create increasing prosperity but to do so in ways in which the interests of non-capital groups could be protected and developed. Growth and equality were not mutually exclusive, if anything the reverse. The development of welfare states, therefore, was not something which was seen as inimical to capitalism. It did constitute the acquisition for the mass of the population of benefits through redistribution, but it did not achieve this at the expense of capital accumulation. The economy could be managed in ways that ensured both growth and full employment, while social policies ensured the redistribution of the benefits of growth. On this view, therefore, better, that is more, larger and higher quality housing at lower user cost, could be considered as one of the gains achieved on behalf of the working class.

Welfare state regimes

There is a long tradition of writers attempting to identify patterns of dissimilarity. Gosta Esping-Andersen is perhaps the most influential of those who have recently attempted to identify distinct welfare state types. These can be seen not only as being different but as maintaining, if not increasing, those distinctions over time. His analysis begins with the view that welfare states are responses to situations where the development of capitalism had resulted in the commodification of many aspects of welfare. The creation of a market in labour meant that the life chances of individual workers depended on their ability to sell their labour power. The result, at the level of the individual, could mean, quite simply, that unemployment could threaten their very survival. The development of welfare states can thus be viewed as attempts to decommodify some goods and services such that they could be enjoyed, to varying degrees, independently of the ability to earn. The particular form of this decommodification provides a key to international variation to the extent that distinct types of welfare state or regimes can be identified. These forms developed from the nature of the struggle, negotiation and accommodation between class interests. Particularly significant was the 'pattern of working class political formation', or in general the 'political coalition building' (Esping-Andersen, 1990, p. 32) which developed differently in different countries. He develops these ideas through the drawing up of decommodification measures which indicate the extent to which people in different countries can gain access to welfare benefits such as pensions, social security payments and health care, independently of their offering their labour power as a commodity. On this basis he is able to identify three distinct regimes.

The liberal welfare states, of which Britain, Ireland and the USA are examples, are characterized by an approach to welfare in which the market and the resources of the individual are viewed as forming the primary solution. The state is considered an appropriate avenue for the provision of welfare only when the 'normal' channels do not work. These welfare states, therefore, are directed at those with no or lower incomes. Assistance will generally be means tested rather than universal, and frequently stigmatized.

The conservative–corporatist states – for example Germany and France – are characterized by welfare provision through or related to occupation. The thrust of this is that existing status differentials are maintained. Social policy was seen as a means by which authoritarian regimes could defuse working-class mobilization, but without actually conceding any great redistribution. The Church and the family are key participants in the provision and structuring of welfare.

The social democratic welfare states – for example Sweden and Denmark – are based on a broad working- and middle-class consensus. Principles of universality and widespread decommodification are pursued in order to achieve equality of a high standard. The state is not seen as a safety net in the event that the market fails, but as the first resort. Also, unlike the other two regimes, the social democratic states have seen full employment as a key element which helps to ensure some types of equality (as between genders for example) and to reduce social transfers.

Welfare state retrenchment

Whatever the perspective taken on the long-run development of welfare states, there has clearly been a situation in the last two decades or so where the earlier advances have come under scrutiny. The 1973 oil crisis, which with the benefit of hindsight can be seen to have been at least one mark of the ending of the long period of postwar expansion of western, industrialized economies, also marked changes in the growth of many welfare states. Their development up to that time had been generally expanding, particularly since 1945, as they took larger amounts of resources, both in absolute terms and in proportion to national GDPs. In the 1980s and 90s, however, growth has sometimes slowed down – though not necessarily in all policy areas and all countries – sometimes stagnated or even gone into decline. With the slowdown in economic growth, the welfare state has been reconsidered with it becoming, in Claus Offe's words, 'the object of doubts, fundamental critique, and political conflict... the most widely accepted device of political problem-solving has itself become problematic' (1984, p. 148). These doubts led to, and incorporated, many well-known developments in the dismantling of welfare states, for example, those associated with Thatcherism and Reaganism. Housing policy has, of course, been part of these same patterns of reassessment.

Initial attempts to theorize about these developments were dominated by two schools: the Marxist and the neo-liberalist, both of which argued, in much reduced form, that economic developments have resulted in circumstances where welfare states, as they had developed up to that point, were no longer sustainable. The message, therefore, was that across industrialized countries there were forces that, beginning from the economic sphere, would force countries to reduce social expenditures.

Klein (1993) usefully conflates the arguments of what are probably the three leading exponents of the Marxist critique: O'Connor, Gough and Offe. Basic to their argument (O'Goffe's Tale) is the premise that the capitalist state contains a mass of contradictions. It has elements within it which are favourable to capital (but unfavourable to labour) and some unfavourable to capital (but favourable to labour). Consequently, in the long term the compromises that constitute the welfare state are unstable, and as the external world itself changes, are from time to time subject to strain and re-negotiation. The distinctive aspect of the O'Goffe position was that the crisis facing the welfare state has been a crisis that is internal to capitalism and is thus part of the nature of the capitalist state, and has the features of a contradiction. This occurs because of, in Klein's words:

> [the] in-built, inescapable conflict between the needs of legitimating, consumption and the demands of capital accumulation. To maintain political legitimacy, the capitalist state had to spend on welfare services and programmes: to maintain the machinery of capitalism, however, it had to promote capital accumulation and ensure profits. And all this was in addition to freeing enough resources for consumption. (1993, pp. 7–8)

While the western nations were growing ever more prosperous in the long, postwar expansionary phase, the illusion was created that these contradictory objectives could be reconciled. But when growth slowed down, tax revenues decreased and unemployment increased putting upward pressure on social security transfers, the national systems faced crisis.

The view from the neo-liberalist perch was similarly sceptical about the future of welfare policies. There are many facets to the neo-liberal position which can be summarized by the statement that the welfare state, indeed the state in general, is seen as part of the problem. Building on the earlier writings by Friedrich Hayek and Milton Friedman, the critique developed, and gained considerable support in some countries, that the appropriate role for the state was a minimalist one in which, beyond defence and law and order, most exchanges in society should be transacted through markets. Whereas the welfare state might have been established in order to reduce the inequalities resulting from commodification, it was widely seen as having failed. Moreover, any state intervention was seen as denying or eroding the freedom of the individual, making their legitimate self-interest subservient to the interests of the state. One of the consequences was that rather than strive to further their own interests citizens became dependent on welfare and sought to achieve their own interests only by bringing political pressures on the state to concede yet more benefits. The state sector itself was inefficient, its practices and procedures being producer or bureaucrat led, and this was adding to the costs of funding the welfare state. Increasingly welfare was seen as a burden on the wealth-producing parts of national economies. As an OECD report was to put it in the mid 1980s:

> rather than being widely regarded as a major contributor to economic growth and macroeconomic stability, the view that the growth and financing of the public sector has, on balance, stifled growth now attracts widespread support. (1985, p. 14)

On this view, then, reducing the welfare state, both in size and in cost, was a necessity if economic growth was to be sustained further. Reducing public expenditure was a necessary, not a retrograde step (King, 1987). Those countries that would be most successful would be those that pared social policies back to the bone. So, on the issue of welfare state retrenchment elements of the political left and right foresaw a similar picture. In terms of housing, this picture was a convergence characterized by a withdrawal of states from responsibility for meeting or supporting the housing needs of its citizens.

By the end of the 1980s it was widely recognized that the crisis of the welfare state had been over-predicted by both Left and Right, and that divergence persisted. Capitalism had apparently shown an ability to adapt pragmatically to the changing context. Welfare states may have been questioned, but their responses had proved remarkably robust. With respect to Britain, it was clear that welfare spending's share of GDP had remained more or less constant over the decade (Hills, 1992), showing a 'surprising degree of resilience' (Le Grand, 1992, p. 3). So, even in a Britain led by a prime minister, Mrs Thatcher, whose name became an international by-word for privatization and pushing back the frontiers of the state, the general trend was not a cut at all. The welfare state was certainly changed, and some areas were certainly cut, but overall the level of state involvement in the welfare of its citizens remained.

Klein demonstrates, on the basis of data from 14 countries, that elsewhere 'there were varieties of adaptive strategies and degrees of success' (1993, p. 14). In some countries such as the USA and Norway there was an over-reaction in the sense that welfare spending declined at a rate faster than the fall in economic growth. In others – Sweden, for example – there was an under-reaction, so that welfare spending continued its existing rate of increase. For Klein, the reason for this variation is that any crises or conflicts 'are mediated by specific national factors: the nature of the political culture and the political system' (1993, p. 15). For Esping-Andersen (1990) the nature of the welfare consensus in each country was crucial in influencing the extent to which the forces of retrenchment or further growth would prevail. As with the logic of industrialism theses which had flowered in the 1960s, however, the lesson of the 1980s and 90s is that economic determinism is not a good predictor (Mishra, 1993).

Conclusions

Notwithstanding the general tendency, often implicit, to see policy makers as responding to the needs and aspirations of citizens, in other words with the state as a benign institution willing and able to introduce ameliorative policies, it should be clear to the reader that there is a range of contestable theories about the origins of housing policy. Some of these theories posit that the state has very little room for manoeuvre. It intervenes not from a position of free will or even from a position of honest broker, but in response to the imperatives of economic development and capitalism. On such views, not only is the fact of intervention determined by economic processes, but so, increasingly, is the nature of that intervention. In short, national housing policies are on a trajectory of convergence. Other theoretical perspectives place more emphasis on the role of politics and divergence, but this does not always imply that the political decisions are the outcome of collective voting powers of equally influential citizens.

In addition to these theoretical perspectives which have been influential in the study of comparative social policy in general and which illuminate the search for explanations of differences and similarities across countries, this chapter has also identified theoretical perspectives on the retrenchment of welfare states since the 1970s. This discussion has helped to emphasize the importance of time and the particular historical circumstances within which states make decisions about intervention.

It seems appropriate to draw this chapter to a close with a brief note about the extent to which the forces shaping all sectors of social policy can be usefully considered equivalent. It has been part of the argument here that in exploring theories about the development of social policy in general these would apply equally to housing. Thus the chapter has to a great extent concentrated on inter-national differences and similarities, but this begs the question of how typical or uniform are housing, health, education, social security and so on? There are some grounds for arguing that the intra-national variation will be less than the international since 'many of the key actors, from parliamentarians, to finance ministry officials, to government auditors, serve to extend homogeneity among the policy sectors' (Heidenheimer *et al.*, 1990, p. 353). This has been the basis of much of the discussion in the present chapter. However, any initial thoughts about sectoral differences need to be established empirically. The challenge and the difficulties have also been recognized by Heidenheimer and his colleagues:

> Up to now there have been very few systematic attempts to compare functionally different policy areas cross-nationally. One could seek to determine, for instance, whether policy processes in housing conform more to general national policy styles than do those in economic management. One difficulty here would be agreeing how to select and measure the relevant indicators. Another would involve the fact that national policy styles change over time. (1990, p. 353)

Aspects of this issue will be explored in later chapters.

5

Exploring Whole Housing Systems

Up to this point in the book much of the focus has been on what policy makers could do and why they might do it. To a large extent, it has drawn on literature related to social policy in general, being as much about health and social security as about housing policy. The remaining chapters of the book deal with what policy makers have actually done and is thus housing policy specific. Whereas later chapters each focus on individual stages in the production and consumption of housing, the aim of the present chapter is to present the literature that has attempted to compare whole housing policy systems in different countries. In order to achieve this, it presents the work of a number of authors whose writing is either seminal or typical. It thus provides the reader with a broad, not necessarily comprehensive, view of the studies that have attempted to provide comparative statements about housing policy. These examples are organized under a number of headings which mirror those in Chapter Four; as there, the first order headings of convergence, divergence and retrenchment are used. Under each of these at least one example from the literature is presented so that most of the theoretical approaches – Marxism, corporatism and so on – are illustrated.

Before starting the task of presenting the selected studies, some comments are made on the task of summarizing the key dimensions of housing policy in two or more countries so that a manageable under-standing of the nature of that policy can be achieved. The challenge here arises, because, as we have seen in Chapter Three, the list of possible policy means, and the range of institutions and of beneficiaries is enor-mous. Unless somehow the detail can be broken through, there is a danger of being overwhelmed by complexity. So, one area of note is the nature of the summaries that researchers have proposed. Of course, the processes of measuring, fact finding and summarizing cannot be disassociated from the theoretical perspectives from, and to, which researchers work so that identifying similarities and differences, and seeking to provide theoretical explanations and insights are not separate activities.

Many of the comparative studies have achieved their summarizing by adopting one of two devices:

(1) *Models or types.* This approach attempts to find simplicity through taking the multitude of dimensions on which national housing policies can be described and, in effect, identifying agglomerations of points in this multidimensional space. The agglomerations can be regarded as ideal types to which no one country will fully conform, but which seem adequately to describe the main features of their housing systems. This approach allows the researcher to identify each country as conforming, more or less, to one of the ideal types.

(2) *Stages and trends.* These differ from models in that there is some notion that over time countries may be moving from one policy state to another. Moving may be from one model to another, that is the models represent a progression and countries move along this progression. Alternatively, countries stay within the same model but the model itself changes over time. Sometimes the progression between stages is blurred so that it is more appropriate to think in terms of trends or directions of change.

Therefore, many of the existing studies of comparative housing policy can be located under one of these headings. However, there is another important dimension, that of the period of study. Some attempt to examine developments over the entire postwar period during which housing policy systems were built up; some have covered even longer periods; and others concern themselves with at most the last decade or two, frequently when the old systems seem to be subject to processes of retrenchment. The distinction between the long term and the short term provides different perspectives on the way in which different countries have responded to the environment within which policy is formed.

Convergence approaches

Comparative housing policy research has been dominated by perspectives which propound convergence. In other words, most comparative analyses of housing policy are based around explanations that economics or industrialization constitute the major explanation for difference and similarity, with politics taking a minor role. Thus Barnett and his colleagues comment that from the viewpoint of the mid 1980s: 'an analyst would find that on the question "Does politics matter?" the mainstream of literature on international housing adopts a broadly negative view' (Barnett *et al.*, 1985, p. 130).

Table 5.1 Classifications of national housing policy systems

HARVEY	*DONNISON*	*KEMENY*	*BARLOW–DUNCAN*
NO RIGHTS	**EMBRYONIC**		**RUDIMENTARY**
Greece	Greece		Greece
Ireland	Portugal		Portugal
Italy	Turkey		Spain
Spain			Italy (South)
DIRECT OR INDIRECT RIGHTS	**SOCIAL**	**HOME OWNING**	**LIBERAL**
Belgium	Belgium	Australia	Ireland
Denmark	Ireland	Canada	UK
France	Switzerland	New Zealand	USA
Luxembourg	UK	UK	
Netherlands	USA	USA	
Portugal			
UK			**CORPORATIST**
West Germany			Austria
	COMPREHENSIVE	**COST RENTING**	France
	Denmark	Austria	Italy (North)
	France	Netherlands	West Germany
	Netherlands	Sweden	
	Norway	Switzerland	
	Sweden	West Germany	**SOCIAL DEMOCRAT**
	West Germany		Denmark
			Netherlands
			Norway
			Sweden

Source: Harvey (1994); Donnison (1967); Kemeny (1981); Barlow and Duncan (1994).

Citizenship and rights

Notwithstanding the general propensity for adopting convergence perspectives, studies of housing policy based on the development of rights of their citizens, which in Marshall's terms are social rights, are rare. One example is provided through a consideration of policies in

EU countries with respect to homelessness. Table 5.1 indicates that in a number of countries – Spain, Italy, Greece, and Ireland – there was no right to housing enshrined in their constitution or contained in law, though there were, particularly in the case of Italy, some local practices that provided 'coherent municipal or region housing responses' (Harvey, 1994, p. 8). In the remaining countries rights with respect to housing were established in principle, but the outcomes in practice were often muted. Taken over European countries in general, 'a right to housing exists only to a very limited degree', with the most common approach being 'to treat homelessness as a condition to be avoided for the public good rather than in terms of individual rights' (Harvey, 1994, p. 8). Whereas Avramov (1996) indicates some amendments to the Harvey classification, she previously suggested that in these approaches to homelessness in the EU countries there are 'no signs of convergence' (Avramov, 1995, p. 158). It can, nevertheless, be noted that the countries with the weakest statement of rights are, with the exception of Italy, the least developed economically so that a principle of the relationship of the development of different types of rights to the development of national economies might be supported.

Logic of industrialism

Donnison

One view is that the preponderance of convergence explanations can be directly attributed to the seminal work of David Donnison. At a time before housing studies, yet alone comparative housing studies, had been widely established in any of the industrialized countries he published a book (Donnison, 1967) that has had an enduring influence on thinking about national policy systems. Followed up fifteen years later with a revised edition (Donnison and Ungerson, 1982), these books have set a framework which continues to be a point of departure.

Notwithstanding a certain obfuscation resulting from a shift in the 1982 publication, the Donnison–Ungerson thesis has been referred to as explicit convergence theory (Schmidt, 1989), the point being that a theoretical model in which the role of industrialism is dominant underlies their work. The 'enormous influence that explicit convergence theory has had over housing research' (Schmidt, 1989, p. 84) is evident from the identification in the comparative housing literature as a whole of two variations. An implicit convergence model is characterized by the use of socioeconomic variables as explainers of housing developments but with no clear suggestion that the developments will conclude in convergence (for example Burns and Grebler, 1977). The exponents, Schmidt claims, of what appear as covert convergence models not only deride the explicit and implicit models but themselves go on to present something that closely resembles them (for example Harloe, 1985). The logic of industrialism is rejected, in Schmidt's words, 'in support for some kind of "logic of capitalism"' (1989, p. 84).

What did Donnison propose which has had this enduring and wide-spread influence? Appearing to draw on earlier analyses of welfare states by Wilensky and Lebeaux (1965), Donnison applied the concepts of institutional or comprehensive, and residual or social policies to housing. National housing policy systems could be described, in his view, as being located in one or the other. In addition, he proposed what appeared to be an antecedent of both so that countries could, in housing policy terms, be located in one of three stages: 'three roles, or patterns of responsibility, [are] to be seen amongst the governments of the market economies of Europe' (Donnison and Ungerson, 1982, p. 67).

The first pattern is to be seen in the countries of southern Europe, such as Turkey, Portugal and Greece (see Table 5.1), which had only recently experienced the transition into industrialized states. Income per head was still relatively low by European standards and unemployment rates were high. With the economic developments, people were flocking from the countryside into the larger cities. The governments of those countries had only just begun to intervene in their housing systems. Housing was seen as an area of consumption, rather than production, and therefore constituting investment which would be at the expense of economic growth. With priority given to industrial expansion, only limited attempts were made to control the flow of jobs and labour into the towns. For many people their housing needs were met through illegal squatting and the self-building of shacks. The pattern of government responsibility for housing in these countries, then, has been generally passive with housing taking a subordinate position to the needs of economic development.

The second pattern of responsibilities is found in those countries such as Switzerland, the United Kingdom, Canada, Australia and the USA which have social housing policies. Their salient feature is that 'the government's principal role is to come to the aid of selected groups in the population and help those who cannot secure housing for themselves in the "open market"' (Donnison and Ungerson, 1982, p. 75). The intention is to respond to particular sets of needs and problems only when they occur. For most purposes, and people, the market is considered to be the best mechanism for meeting housing needs. Government may intervene in the market but intervention is often seen as exceptional and to be discontinued once the normal, market mechanisms are able to continue the task. Policies are 'designed to meet particular needs and solve particular problems, and, whether they consist of building, lending, subsidy, rent controls or other measures, these measures are seen as exceptional "interventions" – often temporary interventions – within an otherwise "normal" system' (Donnison and Ungerson, 1982, p. 75). So, this response is not based on a view that the government bears responsibility for the housing of the whole population and that it has to develop a long-term housing programme. Rather, governments take responsibility only for selected groups such as 'residents of inner city areas, lone parents, migrant workers and others who are distinguished by the difficulties they have in the labour market and hence in the "normal" housing market' (p. 75).

The comprehensive pattern – the third model – occurs where governments accept the responsibility for ensuring that the housing needs of all their population are met. In such countries as Sweden and West Germany, housing will not be viewed as a burden on national prosperity, but as itself making a contribution to economic development. Government intervention will thus be thought of as a permanent rather than a temporary feature. Although the specific policy means may vary, the general commitment will be towards long-term projection of needs and resources, and long-term programmes of housing provision – though not necessarily through direct public provision. Indeed, the governments of these countries may rely heavily upon 'quasi-public bodies' which 'encompasses a wide variety of investor types, from semi public utility companies (whose directorship is part public and part private) to non-governmental cooperatives, housing corporations and housing associations' (Heidenheimer *et al.*, 1975, p. 72). Governments may also control access to existing housing.

Although these models are in places presented as being quite clear cut, actually 'the categorization of policies... is a generalization' (McGuire, 1981, p. 11) so that they might more accurately be said to be tendencies. No one country can be expected to pursue policies which ensure that it fits unambiguously into one of these models, not least because of the 'often crucial differences in national contexts of housing policy' (Lundquist, 1986, p. 13). Heidenheimer *et al.* (1975) argue that the models have become less useful over time: the models 'are helpful in distinguishing the different evolutionary patterns which housing policies have taken, [but they] appear to have diminishing utility in describing current government housing programmes' (p. 73).

Criticisms of the Donnison models extend from concerns as to how accurate a picture of policy intention they provide, to how useful they are in portraying outcomes; whatever governments have meant to achieve, the actual results of comprehensive and social regimes can appear remarkably similar. According to Pinker (1971), this blurring of the differences occurs because where governments pursue comprehensive or institutional policies these will be frequently 'supplemented where necessary by selectivist services' (p. 107), and the residual or social model will be 'supplemented where necessary by universalist services' (p. 107). Both trends arise because intention becomes modified by reality:

> so long as conditions of scarcity prevail and demand potentially exceeds the supply of social services, forms of rationing prevail. The institutionalist begins with a generosity and is driven reluctantly towards stringency in allocation. The residualist starts with stringency and is driven towards generosity. (Pinker, 1971, p. 107)

Donnison and Ungerson admit to wide variations between the countries grouped together:

> the countries we have described as pursuing 'social' housing policies differ in all sorts of ways. In Switzerland the role of government is severely limited, being based on short-term legislation, typically authorizing no more than a four year programme, with the intention – so far unrealized – that these powers be eventually terminated altogether. But in the United Kingdom the government financed the bulk of the house building programme for several years after the war, and in 1949 it removed the restrictive phrases about 'housing for the working classes' which had hitherto confined the powers of the Housing Acts. (1982, p. 77)

Rather than rigid blueprints, therefore, the models might be more appropriately thought of as ideal types or caricatures, with some countries fitting the caricatures better than others.

One view of the Donnison–Ungerson models is that they describe not just models but stages through which all countries can be expected to progress. In terms of the categorization presented at the outset of the present chapter, therefore, the concepts of time and convergence have been introduced. Because the putative dynamic is the needs of economic development, with time, countries progress from one stage – embryonic – to another – social – and another – comprehensive. This view was expressed strongly in Donnison's first book on the subject, but in a weakened form in the second (see Schmidt, 1989). In the latter the authors indicate that economic development is not a sufficient explanation of policy type since that would 'ignore advanced economies, such as the United States, which have retained "social" housing policies' (Donnison and Ungerson, 1982, p. 79). Nevertheless, even the more equivocal interpretation of the second book presents the first housing interventions as occurring in those countries in an embryonic stage of economic and urban development, with countries with social housing policies having 'a longer industrial history' (p. 74), and those with comprehensive policies having attained even higher 'levels of industrial and urban development' (p. 78). The authors give further support to convergence theory in a number of other claims: 'a comprehensive housing policy may appear to be the ultimate stage which sufficiently advanced economies attain' (p. 79), and, 'the size and quality of Europe's houses are becoming steadily more similar' (p. 91).

From the perspective of 1965, or even conceivably 1982, there may have been contextual grounds for considering that nations were moving forwards to some common end state. The long period of postwar expansion throughout the industrialized nations may have prompted the observation that economic progress, which had everywhere been accompanied by the growth of public expenditure, meant that all countries would increase their involvement in housing. In all of them, small, social interventions would develop into large, comprehensive ones. From the perspective of the mid 1990s when the 'golden age' looks to have passed, it is possible that the governments of many countries are withdrawing rather than progressing their interventions in housing systems. Quickly, the direction has changed and former comprehensive models are apparently being transformed into social ones. Of this, more later; for now we might note that the fact that the stages may have changed does not of itself invalidate convergence theory. If the course of industrialization worldwide were to change, as it has over the last twenty years, it might be expected that the path along which their social policies moved – the successive stages – also changed.

Burns and Grebler

The Burns and Grebler study also follows an examination of stages or trends. It differs from Donnison, however, in a number of ways, particularly in its use of multivariate analysis. It involves a search for the differences between nations with respect to the amount of resources invested in the construction of residential dwellings, and concludes that

they can be described in terms of positions along a trajectory.
Following the findings of existing studies – including Donnison – they
posit that there should be a relationship between housing investment
and stage of economic development. They also consider how important
economic determinants might be in comparison to 'the need criteria of
the housing advocate – the growth of national and urban population and
their derived needs for shelter' (Burns and Grebler, 1977, p. 29).

Their empirical investigation drew on data for the period 1963 to
1970 over 39 countries covering the spectrum from the underdeveloped
like Kenya, Honduras, Bolivia and the Philippines to the highly developed, including most of the countries of western Europe together with
Japan, Australia and the USA. They fit a multiple regression equation
with H – the share of housing in total output – the dependent variable
and the independent variables being gross domestic product per capita,
population growth and urbanization. They conclude that all the independent variables contribute to an explanation of the level of housing
investment, but particularly significant is the non-linear relationship
between investment and economic development. Indeed, they conclude
that economic development is probably far more significant as an
explainer than either of the population variables:

> The inverted U-shaped function which best approximates H with respect to devel-
> opment level may be described as follows. At the earliest stages of economic
> development, H is low. A relatively small share of total resources is allocated to
> housing because other investments presumably yield higher expected returns.
> With development, H rises as housing outbids many of the types of investment
> seen as critical during the earliest development stage. Past some point on the
> development continuum, H falls as alternative investments once again outbid
> housing. (1977, p. 30)

The approach adopted by Burns and Grebler sits firmly within a
convergence framework. Rules governing human behaviour, which
transcend time and national boundaries, can be established, and these
rules relate welfare to economic development and its social and demographic correlates. Their work implies that as countries have advanced
economically their housing sectors have moved, inexorably, along a
common route. If we want to know the future of housing in South
Korea or Puerto Rica, for example, we need only predict where their
economies are moving. Nevertheless, their analysis stops short of the
convergence theory discussed in Chapter Four since it is about
outcomes rather than policy formation or policy regime. It is not part of

their argument therefore that it is possible to read off policy type from national economic characteristics.

Boelhouwer

On the basis of an examination of housing policy in seven European countries over the period 1945 to 1990, Boelhouwer and van der Heijden (1992) identify four policy stages. An assumption seems to be that the stages are consecutive – so, as with Donnison, countries move from the first to the second and so on. At the same time, they recognize that the stages may overlap so that a country may, in any period, be conforming to more than one stage. In addition, countries have entered and left each stage at different times, with some countries not yet having progressed through all four. A further contrast with Donnison is that the stages are at a lower level representing the foci of policy rather than their regime or principles.

The common starting point for all seven countries was the special features characterizing the immediate post Second World War period. Housing shortages resulting from war damage to the existing stock, a dearth of new construction during the war, as well as large-scale migratory movements together – though in different combinations – contributed major challenges to national governments. The characteristic response was the mobilization of national institutions and resources to promote high levels of new construction. This was a stage in which the numbers of units built and the closing of the gap between supply and demand quickly was of paramount concern.

At the second stage, which Figure 5.1 indicates began in some countries – Belgium and England – within a decade of the start of the postwar period, the emphasis shifted from quantity to quality. Governments began to adapt policies so that new construction conformed to higher standards with respect to both size and facilities. There were also moves to increase the quality of the existing stock through both slum clearance and redevelopment and the renovation of lower quality dwellings. Boelhouwer identifies a further feature of this stage, namely that governments shift from need, as the principle on which provision and allocation should be based, to demand. In effect, this constitutes a shift from considerations of equity which countered income inequalities to considerations which accepted that inequality was the appropriate determinant of housing consumption.

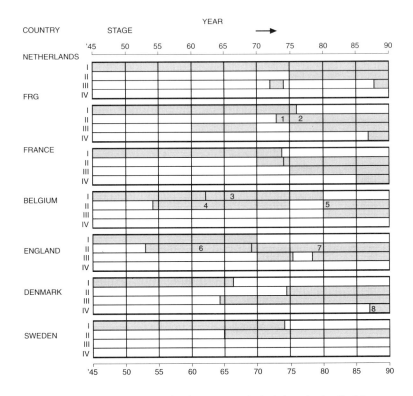

I   High degree of government involvement, particularly in order to alleviate
       housing shortages.
II   Greater emphasis on housing quality.
III   Greater emphasis on problems of housing distribution and targeting specific
       groups, and the withdrawal of the state in favour of the private sector.
IV   Reappearance of quantitative and/or qualitative housing shortages; state
       involvement increases in some countries (FRG and France).

1.   Improvement in the quality of new housing construction.
2.   Improvement in the quality of housing stock.
3.   Housing construction used as an element of economic policy.
4, 6. Improvement in the quality of the stock by slum clearance programmes and
       substitute new construction.
5.   Emphasis on housing improvements in addition to slum clearance.
7.   Emphasis on maintenance and improvement instead of slum clearance.
8.   Housing shortages, mainly caused by the collapse of the owner-occupied
       sector, and consequently a significant increase in demand for (cheap) rented
       housing.

Source: Boelhouwer and van der Heijden (1992).

Figure 5.1   Boelhouwer's schematic outline of housing policy stages

The third stage is seen as a direct consequence of public expenditure pressures on national governments, themselves a result of economic developments of the last quarter of a century. The total amount of subsidies to the housing sector is reduced and restructured with a switch from production to consumption. The consequences include both an overall reduction in the levels of new construction and an increase in attempts to target subsidies toward low-income groups. The final stage is associated with the re-emergence of housing shortages which take the form of both an absolute shortage and a shortage of houses at rents (and capital prices) that are affordable by those with lower incomes. In some countries there have been policy initiatives directed at these 'new' problems.

Figure 5.1 indicates during which periods, if at all, each of these four stages is characteristic of the countries examined. While there is a general tendency for the stages to be sequential – shown most clearly in the cases of France and England – there are also exceptions. In general, however, the existence of patterns in the data is not immediately apparent. With the exception of the first stage, the others have been adopted in different years – even different decades – and endured for different lengths of time. In no two countries in the sample is the pattern identical. An additional level of variation is evident when we consider that each stage can be pursued with varying degrees of intensity. Boelhouwer's stages do not, then, appear to be the basis for a classification of countries.

Finally, it is important to note that despite the emphasis on stages and general similarities in the housing policy systems across the range of countries examined, and with that emphasis an apparent foundation in convergence, Boelhouwer and van der Heijden themselves have rejected notions of convergence:

> there is no convincing evidence to suggest that the characteristics and the problems associated with housing systems in the countries under review are tending to converge. Housing market structures, which are the product of a series of historical developments unique to each country, the institutions that have been established in the course of time, and the activities of government, which are influenced partly by tradition and by ideology, are far too diverse for this to be a credible supposition. (Boelhouwer and van der Heijden, 1992, p. 295)

Other stage models

Boelhouwer's observation of policy stages is consistent with a large body of literature which has also interpreted developments in national housing policies in terms of the changing policy environment. For some, significant changes have occurred within the housing system. Thus, the great progress made with attempts to meet the large shortages after the war brought about situations where the success of policies meant that the need and/or political pressure on which they were based had been dissipated. If policies are likened to medicines prescribed for someone with an illness, the success of the medicine creates a situation where it is no longer needed. Thus McGuire (1981) proposes that it is a general feature of advanced nations that as they industrialized and urbanized they entered the first of four stages of housing development. The first stage consisted of the struggle to provide the rapidly expanding numbers of town dwellers with a minimum of housing. Once achieved, this aim was followed by a second stage of attempting to provide more than the minimum level of space. The emphasis on numbers gradually petered out as a balance between numbers of households and numbers of dwellings was achieved. Typically, countries moved to the third stage which involved an emphasis on quality. Finally, once the larger part of the population is housed in good quality dwellings states increasingly target their assistance on low-income groups leaving most people to find their own housing solutions through the private market, and increasingly in home ownership.

Logic of capitalism

Probably the best known, certainly the best developed, of the studies within the Marxist tradition are those carried out by Michael Harloe and his colleagues. In his book on the development of private rented housing in Britain, France, West Germany, Denmark, the Netherlands and the USA, Harloe (1985) begins with a critique of existing, comparative study that was based on models of the world in which benign, if not benevolent, governments do their best to solve housing problems but can never quite get the solutions right. He posits, as his alternative, a Marxist framework. But, despite analysis of the political and ideological in the formation of policy, a major theme is the apparent universality of the long-run decline of private rented housing brought about by broad, structural processes. In a later book with Michael Ball and Maartje Martens (Ball *et al.*, 1988) covering the same six countries, the similarity or convergence of trends is frequently stressed. Thus, the increasingly worldwide concurrence of economic cycles is seen as a major influence on home ownership markets:

> The housing market booms of the late 1970s were in all countries followed by a major market down-turn, during the early 1980s... A major crisis in the world economy contributed to cause the housing market slump, as it was associated with sharply rising unemployment, stagnating real incomes and extremely high levels of nominal and real interest rates. (Ball *et al.*, 1988, p. 123)

Elsewhere in the same book, there is presentation of common trends in the financial institutions providing housing loans, particularly general moves toward deregulation and increased competition. Even if the authors themselves would reject the suggestion, it is, therefore, not difficult to understand Schmidt's reference to covert convergence theory.

Testing for convergence

Many of the attempts to locate national housing policies in the same or different categories are based on description, argumentation and theoretical assertion. Much of it is hypothesis forming. In some studies empirical data are presented – often in the form of tables and graphs – from which conclusions are drawn. In some, data are largely absent. Attempts, as Oxley (1991) points out, to develop quantitative approaches whereby hypotheses may be tested are rare. The multivariate analysis by Burns and Grebler (1977) is an example, as is a more recent study by Schmidt (1989) which uses data for 18 industrialized countries, over the period from the early 1970s to the mid 1980s, in order to derive operational definitions that enable him to test for convergence. For each of his variables, which include the number of dwellings constructed in different time periods, the rate of owner occupation and government housing expenditure, he computed a coefficient of variation. His test for convergence was whether or not the values of the coefficients decreased over time. The results showed no indication that over all the countries the spread had become any less, so that the basic tenet of convergence – that housing markets and housing policies become more similar over time – could not be supported. Indeed, the statistical evidence if anything suggested that there had actually been evidence over this period of some widening of the spread, that is divergence. A more extensive examination of similar data suggested that over the immediate postwar period through to the 1960s there was evidence of some convergence taking place, but that during the subsequent period the picture is a confused one showing a mixture of convergence and divergence (Doling, 1990a).

Divergence approaches

Although divergence perspectives have been in a minority they have
not been insignificant or uninfluential with, in recent years, the balance
of the literature perhaps shifting in their direction.

Corporatism

The notion of the corporatist state has not featured strongly in studies
of comparative housing policy, but has been utilized as the basis for
understanding developments in individual countries. Thus, Lundquist
(1988) has considered corporatist arrangements in the Swedish public
rental sector and Boddy (1989) the role of the building societies in the
drafting of the British Building Societies Act of 1986. Notwithstanding
the fact that corporatism as a perspective has made only a limited
contribution to our understanding of why countries have different (or
similar) housing policies, two studies are reported on.

Lennart Lundquist's examination of privatization in Swedish
housing provides an example of how corporatist developments have
contributed to policy formation and implementation. For the Swedish
government in the immediate postwar period, there was an intention
both to base provision around public rental housing and to enlist specified organizations in order to help to achieve targets. The Municipal
Housing Companies through its national association (SABO) became
the favoured recipient of housing subsidies, accepting, as part of the
'deal', rent control. The National Federation of Tenants (HGR) was
granted a monopoly in representing tenants in negotiations over
increases in rents. Both had strong ideological and personal affiliations
with the Social Democratic Party which has been in power for much
of the postwar period. Later the Association of Real Estate Owners
was added, while the HGR gained a right to financial resources.
Together they became the normal mechanism – the recognized interests – through which decisions about rent levels throughout the stock
were decided.

Schmidt (1989) has attempted to test a corporatist model for a
number of countries using operational definitions that are both limited
in range and of contestable validity. He argues that in corporatist policy
regimes a small number of large building companies dominate house
construction, and that, in contrast, countries with non-corporatist
housing policies tend to have a greater concentration of small firms. On

the basis of variables measuring construction industry size, he concludes that countries with corporatist policy systems tend to have a higher level of public expenditure on housing. They do so because the corporatist system is 'simultaneously a system for voicing and channelling demands, and implementing policy' (Schmidt, 1989, p. 92). It does not necessarily follow from this conclusion that both state and private actors share common goals around the increase in state promotion of housing provision, but that it is the compromise between the sets of actors that leads to policy expansion.

Kemeny

A major development in the understanding of housing policy systems occurred in 1981 with the publication of a book by Jim Kemeny in which he argued that there were two, generically distinct models (see Table 5.1). Utilizing data from a range of industrialized countries as well as case studies of Sweden, Britain and Australia, he has, in a number of publications (principally 1981, 1992 and 1995), presented a distinction between home-owning and cost-rental societies. The former consisted of those countries, particularly countries of the English speaking world, such as Australia, New Zealand, Canada and the USA, in which home ownership numerically dominated and with access to public forms of renting being limited to those with lower incomes. The latter were mainly located on the European mainland and had much more evenly balanced tenure structures. A large part of their housing stock was available at rents related to the cost of provision rather than being determined by the forces of supply and demand.

Kemeny explained the development of these two models with reference to social structures. His thesis was that there has been a divergence between those industrialized countries with collectivist and those with private forms of social structure. This was not a matter of countries being at different stages of industrialism, through which all advanced countries had progressed, nor of the extent to which their welfare states were developed. Rather they represented distinctly different models not only with respect to housing policy but also to wider social arrangements:

> Sweden is an example of a society in which a high degree of collectivism has been established in terms of a well developed welfare state, highly developed collective transport based on high density urban form derived from a dominance of rental and co-operative flats, and public child care facilitating predominantly wage-labour female roles. By contrast, in Australia there has evolved a high

degree of privatism, as reflected in a poorly developed welfare state, low residential densities deriving from privatized dwelling type and housing tenure, private transport, and predominantly 'domestic' female roles. Britain represents an intermediate form of social organization, with a welfare state more developed than Australia but less so than Sweden, more social housing than Australia but less than Sweden, predominantly semi-detached and terraced housing rather than free standing villas as in Australia or apartments as in Sweden, female roles neither as domestic as in Australia nor as wage-labour based as in Sweden, and so on. (Kemeny, 1992, p. 121)

He argued that in all countries there has been in effect what he called a political tenure strategy. This should not be thought of as a strategy in the sense of a thought-out and planned course of action, but rather as a collection of *ad hoc* government actions, resulting in statutes, regulations and institutional arrangements which had the effect of altering the balance of advantage and disadvantage facing households making tenure decisions. In home-owning societies they made the acquisition of home ownership both more desirable and more feasible. In cost-rental societies forms of cost renting – that is where rents reflect the cost of provision rather than current market values – were likewise favoured. Both models were deemed to be the outcome of actions by governments which were guided by the extent to which underlying social frameworks were characterized by privatism and collectivism.

Thus in the case of home-owning societies the political tenure strategy typically had a number of dimensions. First, there were established some arrangements whereby middle-income groups had access to loan finance to facilitate purchase. Often this meant the formation of financial institutions, such as building societies, which served the housing sector and which operated within an environment protected from other financial markets. Second, governments set up tenure-specific subsidies which gave more assistance to owners than renters, or in a form which was less stigmatizing. Thus in many countries owners receive subsidies through the tax system, whereas tenants receive them through highly visible benefit payments. Third, the legal rights enjoyed by owners are more favourable than those enjoyed by tenants. Fourth, governments may prevent the development of a large, cost-rental alternative. Prevention may take the form of dampening demand by the stigmatization of the tenants of cost-rental landlords. It may also be by making allocation criteria highly restrictive – being means tested or requiring a minimum number of children – or by selling off the stock to private owners. More simply, prevention may take the form of not providing initial subsidies to enable a cost-rental sector to grow.

A cost-rental system is one where the rents charged relate to the initial costs of construction rather than to current market values. Inflation in building costs and market rents in industrialized societies mean that cost rents of older dwellings are generally lower than both cost rents of new dwellings and current market values. A cost-rental system, therefore, results in lower user costs (although there is not of course any lowering of the actual real resources consumed by the occupant). Where government regulation also facilitates rent pooling, the cost rents of new properties can be cross-subsidized by the cost rents of older properties. This helps to improve the viability of new construction. In such systems the costs set in the public sector will often dominate the market and tend to drive private rents down. In addition to cost-rental dwellings there may be a large cooperative housing sector which combines elements of both owning and renting. In those countries which have pursued cost-rental tenures to the point that they compete with private forms of provision, access to the former is not restricted to low-income groups. As a result it is not stigmatizing, and households will have a realistic (socially and economically) choice about the form of tenure they want to consume at different points in their lifecycle.

Kemeny's work is further discussed in Chapters Nine and Eleven, but it is appropriate here to note that the strength of his thesis is not simply that he has identified different models which apparently demonstrate no tendency to converge over time, nor simply that he is able to identify detailed lists of how the models differ, but that he offers an explanation, based on social frameworks, for the development of the models.

Barlow–Duncan

In a study by Barlow and Duncan (1994) of the relative effectiveness of markets and governments in the provision of housing, there are elements of the discussions which have connections with the work of both Donnison and Kemeny. However, they follow more closely the Esping-Andersen framework as the basis for case study selection. Since Esping-Andersen himself does not include housing as a main feature of his welfare state regimes, they extend the original by deducing what the housing implications are. In the liberal regime countries there will be limited government support for social housing; what there is will be highly stigmatizing and intended for lower-income groups. There may well be considerable, though less overt, government subsidy supporting mainstream, market provision. The countries in this group – Ireland, UK and USA – all have large owner-occupied sectors. It is to be expected that in corporatist regimes subsidy will be quite overt and not ideologically tainted but, there will be no intention that housing opportunities will weaken existing social differentiation. In social democratic regimes there will be an intention to manage the market so that housing standards are increased and housing costs lowered for all. Barlow and Duncan add a fourth regime – rudimentary welfare states (see Table 5.1). Although not included by Esping-Andersen, a group of countries can be identified – Greece, Portugal, Spain and Southern Italy – in which there is no strong right to welfare. Traditions of self-help, family support and a welfare role for the Church remain important even with the rapid moves towards industrialization. This regime type reads much like Donnison's first stage. In housing terms, they both translate into minimal involvement by the state in direct provision with a large onus on self-help.

Retrenchment

As explored in Chapter Four, the 1973 oil shock and the subsequent ending of the long, postwar period of economic growth for many countries faced governments with challenges to their ability to sustain previous levels of expenditure on social policies. Some writers have used this shift in the macroeconomic environment as the peg on which to hang a perceived redirectioning of national housing policies.

One such example is to be found in the publications of Ivan Tosics. Working within what appears to be a convergence framework, he combines examples of internal and external housing system change in a discussion of privatization. In his view privatization in western countries can be characterized by two phases. The first phase 'took place in the context of booming capitalist economies with increasing housing production, mainly due to changes within the housing sector' (Tosics, 1987, p. 65). Production subsidies which had previously proved effective in reducing shortage came under review. Characteristically governments withdrew from their position as the primary source of credit, more emphasis was placed on private financial institutions and subsidies were switched to the demand side in terms of rent allowances and tax reliefs. The result was less that the financing by states shrank, but rather that it was restructured into more indirect forms.

In contrast, the second phase was seen as 'a consequence of economic followed by political-ideological changes, which were independent of the housing sector' (Tosics, 1987, p. 65). Notwithstanding the indication of political developments, his next sentence suggests an economic determinism interpretation:

> Decreasing production, stagnant wages, and rapidly growing unemployment are the spectacular signs of the economic recession, as a result of which the capitalist states are forced to limit their expenditures. (1987, p. 65)

The changes at this second phase are presented as being those of reducing eligibility for social housing, selling social housing, reducing state-subsidized construction, and encouraging private finance.

The Tosics formulation is consistent with both a logic of industrialism approach, since it presents policy changes following from the economic context, and with an end of the welfare state thesis. It is thus a parallel of the views discussed in Chapter Four that economic developments of the last 20 years were leading governments in industrial countries to re-evaluate their commitment to the securing of welfare for their citizens. In a similar vein, Lundquist (1992b) has argued that as a result of both economic and political changes impacting upon western countries there has been a fundamental shift away from Donnison's convergence on comprehensive models to a convergence towards the market end of the state–market continuum. Consistent with both these formulations has been the use of the term 'privatization' to describe the perceived withdrawal by states from involvement in housing provision towards a greater reliance on the private sector. While, as is commonly recognized, the sale of council housing in Britain is the best known and the clearest example of this withdrawal, the label has been applied almost indiscriminately.

Retrenchment has also been considered by researchers in the divergence tradition. Notions of divergence provide an understanding not only of differences in the development of national housing policies throughout the postwar period generally, but also of responses to the economic malaise of the last twenty years. In contrast to convergencists, divergencists argue that the differences inherent in national welfare states (and within them housing policy) have also meant that they have been more or less resistant to forces of retrenchment. The Esping-Andersen argument, for example, is that welfare states that have been built around a middle-class consensus and beneficiary, in general those with universalist benefits, have proved more resilient than welfare states that operate on residualist principles:

> The risks of welfare-state backlash depend not on spending, but on the class char-
> acter of welfare states. Middle-class welfare states, be they social democratic (as
> in Scandinavia) or corporatist (as in Germany) forge middle class loyalties.
> (1990, p. 33)

Kemeny, likewise, argues that welfare states in countries where there has been a deep and enduring social structure based on collectivist notions will be relatively immune to retrenchment:

> welfare states characterized by shallow collectivism have not had their welfare
> systems buttressed with collectivized social relationships in the wider society...
> Such welfare states are likely to be unstable, with low degrees of congruence
> between the wider society and welfare formed, as a house that is built on sand.
> Welfare states characterized by deep collectivism are, by contrast, buttressed by
> forms of social organization that complement and reinforce collective welfare
> provision. (1992, p. 112)

Utilizing this general perspective, a study by Lundquist starts from an analysis of the meaning of the term 'privatization', emphasizing that it represents a shift in the location of responsibility for housing matters: being 'actions taken by actors legitimately representing the public sector to transfer the hitherto public responsibility for a certain activity away from the public and into the private sector.' (Lundquist, 1992a, p. 3). The content of housing policy, for which responsibility could be shifted, he classifies according to a typology similar to that presented in Chapter Three, namely that housing policy can, in his view, take the form of regulation, financing and production. So, privatization can be said to take place whenever responsibility for one of these dimensions shifts into the private sector.

But, why should privatization take place at all? Lundquist responds with another question: if theories are proposed to explain the growth of the welfare state, should not the mirror image of these same theories provide an understanding of why they may go into reverse? On this test few perspectives appear satisfactory. Why has some privatization of welfare taken place in countries even when their economies have again begun to grow and what does this say about logic of industrialism theories? How can social democratic theories be squared with the existence of privatization occurring even in those countries with left-wing governments?

Lundquist suggests that a power resources model better passes his test. Here, welfare state growth can be thought of as the result of groups, representing those with little command over market resources, gaining in political power and pursuing rational strategies to switch the balance of welfare provision away from the market and towards the state. The corollary is that welfare state contraction would be a consequence of market-strong groups gaining political ascendancy. Such an argument rests, as Lundquist points out, on an 'assumption that actors on each side of the labour-capital divide seek political power, not just for power's sake, but to use it to adjust the boundary between state and market to satisfy the perceived interests of their constituencies' (1992a, p. 7). However, he is also at pains to emphasize that there is more in this than political reductionism. Also influencing outcomes will be the institutional context and earlier policy decisions which provide the framework within which the outcome of political power is manifested. Thus in countries where there had been the development of a strong state bureaucracy which delivered housing services, a strong professional body and interest groups able to mobilize political influence, or where housing policy had developed to the point of taking on responsibility across all groups in the population, the potential to frustrate market-strong groups would be relatively great. Where countries had got to, in terms both of policy content and institutions, was, therefore, significant in influencing the nature and extent of privatization. In that sense the scale on which privatization should be measured is a relative one, and privatization will, if it can be said to have occurred, take a different form in different countries.

Table 5.2 indicates the diversity of response to the relative shift. In Britain, privatization is evident in the rental sectors, with action in all three policy avenues: freeing up the private sector through deregulation; reducing subsidies to social housing and encouraging the greater utilization of private finance; and enabling stock transfer away from the social to the private sector. In Sweden, by contrast, the measures used are restricted to definancing, but they apply equally to all tenures and to both production and consumption. The Netherlands has also concentrated on definancing, although the concentration has been on production; whereas the Norwegian government has additionally pursued deregulation.

Table 5.2 Privatization in four European countries

	HOUSING SUB-SECTORS							
	Owner Occupiers		*Renting*				*Cooperatives*	
Privatization			*Private*		*Public*			
Alternatives	Prod.	Cons.	Prod.	Cons.	Prod.	Cons.	Prod.	Cons.
Deregulation			GB					
			N			N		
Definancing	S	S	S	S	S	S	S	S
					GB			
	N					N		
	NL		NL		NL			
Dispossession					GB			

S = Sweden   GB = Great Britain   N = Norway   NL = Netherlands
Prod. = Production   Cons. = Consumption

Source: Lundquist (1992a).

Notwithstanding the differences in detail, with the exception of Sweden, the broad thrust of privatization has been biased with production subsidies being cut and consumption subsidies being restructured so that they are more narrowly targeted, sometimes with the lowest income groups getting more assistance than hitherto. Overall, Lundquist, concludes:

> European welfare states have moved a long way from the large-scale public programs of the postwar period. But the contraction of the welfare state has not meant a total dislodgment; while withdrawing from support to new production, governments increasingly subsidize the demand for 'marketable' tenures. (1992a, p. 129)

Conclusions

In the housing policy literature there are a number of examples of studies which have set out to explain why housing policy systems vary across countries. The balance of this literature lies with explanations that stress convergence, a balance which appears to indicate the continuing influence, over three decades, of David Donnison. Throughout this period, during which the literature has expanded, logic of industrialism and logic of capitalism models have continued to dominate, so that the general tendency is to see industrialized countries, at least in their housing policies, becoming more similar. In recent years, however, there has been a growing counter tendency to argue that politics is influential, more so than industrialism, in moulding national models. Here, both Kemeny and Barlow–Duncan have been important in providing empirical and theoretical evidence to support the view that housing policy systems have become less similar.

At the same time it is instructive to examine the groupings of countries proposed by different researchers (Table 5.1) which show clear similarities. With the exception of Kemeny, they group together those countries which are least economically advanced and in which urbanization and industrialization has been largely a late twentieth-century phenomenon. Likewise, liberal regimes (Barlow–Duncan) which have social policies (Donnison) and concentrate on home ownership (Kemeny) include many of the same countries. It might be said, therefore, that there is more agreement about groupings (ideal types or models) than there is about the processes guiding their developments and thus whether they are getting closer together or further apart.

6

Housing Development and Construction

The aim of this chapter, as with the following five, is to explore in greater detail individual stages of the housing provision and consumption process described in Figure 3.1. In part this involves providing additional information about the significance of the stage and how it fits with the other stages. In the present chapter, where two stages are considered, the ways in which they mesh together at the same time as they can be seen to stand individually are explored. Following this, as with each of the remaining chapters, a number of broad issues are pursued. These include issues of: how governments could intervene in this stage of the housing provision process; how they actually do intervene, that is the inter-national variations; and what can be said by way of explanation for those variations. In other words, the intention is to reflect the approach of Chapters Three and Four, applying them not to whole housing policy systems as in Chapter Five, but to individual elements of the policy system.

In common with at least some of the remaining chapters, the relevant literature is fairly sparse. In part this follows from the general lack of truly comparative writing. Many housing policy publications deal with just one country perhaps telling an audience in one country what happens in another, while some other publications tell parallel, but largely unconnected, stories about a number of countries. In fact, literature which looks across the industrialized countries, presenting statistical and other information which provides systematic understanding of differences and similarities, is not plentiful. Actually, the sparseness of the literature with respect to development and construction (as well as finance) is a general feature of both comparative and non-comparative housing studies. As Michael Ball (1983) has argued, there has been a strong leaning amongst housing researchers to concentrate on issues, particularly tenure-related issues, which are located in the consumption phase. Although there have been a number of notable exceptions over the last 15 years (for example Dickens *et al.*, 1985; Barlow and Duncan, 1994) the overall consumer orientation of the literature has endured. One consequence of this sparseness is that, drawing only on the existing literature, a comprehensive treatment of the issues outlined above with respect to all the stages in the provision–consumption process, is not possible. Whereas this leads to a certain unevenness of treatment, that very unevenness indicates where there are gaps in existing knowledge.

The development–construction stages

Reference back to Figure 3.1 indicates a separation of the development and construction phases in the provision of new dwellings. The basis of this separation is founded in the distinctive nature of housing provision. It is argued elsewhere in Chapter Three that housing has characteristics which may set it apart from those other goods and services that are central to welfare policies in industrialized countries. But there are also important differences that set housing production apart from the general case of commodity production. In a pure capitalist form of production, as may occur commonly with, say, consumer durables, a manufacturing capitalist will generally obtain money from a finance capitalist. This enables both the setting up of a production process, which is located on an area of land, as well as the purchase of other factors of production in the form of labour and materials. Goods are produced and sold on to an end user at a price that provides the capitalist with sufficient to repay loans and leave a profit. In this model there is a separation of the manufacturing and finance agents.

In what ways, then, does the provision of housing differ from the provision of other goods? Short, Fleming and Witt (1986) identify four specific characteristics.

(1) Each dwelling to be built requires land. This brings the developer's field of interest into the fields of interest of landowners and of society at large. In part these interests are represented by the land use planning system.
(2) The gestation period for housing, from its initiation to completion and sale, is a long one. Money is expended throughout the process, but the relatively high cost of land and materials may be

expended towards the beginning. The construction phase itself may last many weeks, if not months, while the finding of a customer may also be time consuming. There is often a long gap, therefore, between investment and realization. This can make the speculative builder particularly dependent on loan finance and vulnerable to changes in market conditions.

(3) Completed dwellings are expensive in relation to household incomes. The speculative housebuilding industry requires a well-developed financial system through which households can obtain long-term loans.

(4) The consumption phase of housing requires investment in infrastructure. This includes basic services such as electricity, water, sewerage and roads. In addition, the use value of the dwelling will be enhanced by the presence of other land uses such as shops, schools, parks and cultural facilities. The provision of these infrastructures by the developer will increase costs. At the same time their presence will increase the market value. In these circumstances it is in the interests of developers to divert the costs of infrastructural development to public authorities.

In summary, unusual features of the provision of housing relate to the difficulties of realizing returns given the high cost of the finished product and the length of the production process, the problems of assembling land and infrastructural developments and the site-specific nature of production. These features can be usefully expressed also in terms of sources of profit, since, potentially, developer/builders can make profit in their relationship with the other agents involved; for example, if they are able, through marketing devices, to convince potential buyers (and the organizations from whom they obtain loan finance) that the houses they have brought to the market are superior to those brought by other developers – perhaps because their design is particularly attractive – they may be able to charge more. As with commodity production in general, market share and profitability are greatly influenced by the costs of the factors of production – land, labour and capital. In general, however, there are two broad areas where individual developers may be able to widen the gap between costs and price. The first of these is through land development profit.

Peter Dickens and his colleagues (Dickens *et al.*, 1985) identify two ways in which this can be realized. The input of infrastructural invest-ments into land, made by a body other than the developer, may not be fully realized until the land is developed. So, if a developer purchases a plot of land and subsequently (and unknown at the point of purchase so that the price was unaffected) a public authority builds a rail link or a private institution a shopping centre, the value of the land for residential development is enhanced in the sense that the developer would be able to command a higher price for the same physical structure built on it. Another potential source of land development profit occurs in countries where there are planning controls over the use of land. In circumstances where land is zoned for agriculture or forestry, say, its value, which will be related to the economic return that the owner can extract from it, will generally be lower than land zoned for commercial or residential uses. If a developer can purchase land at its agricultural value and subsequently its zoning is changed to residential use, there will be an increase in land value, or 'planning gain'. Land development profits, then, occur where land is purchased at a price that reflects one set of circumstances and sold, along with a dwelling, at a price that reflects a second set of circumstances.

The second general way in which profitability can be increased is in the building process itself. This consists, in turn, of the processes of preparing the site – by levelling, landscaping, providing drainage and so on – and of assembling the materials – bricks, wood, wires and tiles – to form a physical shelter to an appropriate specification. Sometimes builders can find cheaper ways of achieving these outcomes: mechanical diggers can replace men with shovels, or a new way of fixing bricks together, or even a cheaper material for building external walls may be developed. Different materials and different technologies have the potential to lower production costs. Where a builder is able to do this in ways which meet building regulations at the same time as not losing appeal to consumers, and where this is in advance of the practices of other builders, they are in a position to make larger profits and to exploit the market. If land availability is a constraint on operations the larger profit per unit may enable them to outbid other developer/builders. In a case where the builder is contracted by a developer, the cheaper production costs enable a lower tender and the opportunity for an increased volume of work.

Together, these characteristics of housing result in there being an exception to the pure model of capitalist production. While there is in the builder a direct equivalent to the manufacturer who seeks to achieve a profit from a production process, there may be an additional agent in the form of a developer who seeks to make profit from the land-specific characteristic of that production process. Placed at the juncture of the cycle of production and the cycle of consumption, the developer initiates the production process and owns the product of labour during production. The source of the developer's profit is, however, quite different from that of the builder.

The developer types

If such an institution as a market in housing which was totally unfettered by state intervention could exist, the characteristics of the provision of housing discussed here might result in private companies and individuals undertaking the functions of developer and builder. It might also be anticipated that developers and builders would relate one to another in a variety of ways, ranging from being totally separate to being the same entity. In practice, as elsewhere in the housing system, governments have not taken a non-interventionist position. Willem van Vliet has indicated the range of such interventions:

> Although the private profit motive propels housing provision in all capitalist systems, there are considerable differences among capitalist countries in, for example, the places where investments enter the system, the ways in which public funds are channeled once they are in the system, and the arrangements under which profits exit… These differences have multiple, complex antecedents and reflect the different roles played by the state. (1990, p. 21)

One of the consequences of the interplay of profit-oriented businesses and government intervention is that there is a range of developer and builder types, as well as relationships between them, crossing the spectrum of public and private sectors. So, whereas attention has been drawn to a land development process which is profit driven, in all industrialized countries there are also developers who pursue non-profit objectives. Folin (1985) provides a typology of developers which specifically recognizes their different objectives:

(1) *Private individuals.* These are individuals or households who initiate the production of a single family house, which to begin with, at least, is intended for personal use. It may subsequently be traded in the market but the first aim is the provision of a home. Having taken a decision to proceed in this way, the individual will be faced with the tasks of acquiring an appropriate plot of land, an appropriate design, planning permission, and assembling sufficient funds, materials and labour to effect the construction. In some cases these sub-stages may involve the engagement of

external actors; in others they may be internalized. Thus the individual may have sufficient of their own financial resources, may have held a plot of land in the family for some years, or may apply their own labour to the building process. There can be many different combinations of own and external actor involvement. There are also examples of private individuals combining together, with a view to joint provision for individual consumption.

(2) *Private companies.* Here the developer/builder is a company which is in the business of housing provision in order to pursue profit. Such companies produce houses and flats for the general market. There is no single model. In some cases the company will assemble large tracts of land well in advance of building, undertake the construction process themselves using their own financial resources, and will bring the finished house to the market for speculative sales. In other cases the developer and the constructor may be different companies, and both may utilize finance capital. Indeed, sometimes finance capital initiates development. In yet other cases, the company may retain ownership of the completed dwellings making a profit from their role as landlords. A particularly important variation is the profit-maximizing company which provides housing for its workers. This has a long tradition in many countries, being distinctive because the housing provision itself is not viewed as a source of profit, but the profitability of the wider company requires a labour force which in turn requires housing. So housing may be viewed not as a potential source of profit in itself, but as an element in the cost of labour.

(3) *Non-profit companies.* These can also take a variety of forms and undertake all or only parts of the complete development–construction process. Variously referred to as being part of the voluntary or third sector, non-profit companies are also given a variety of labels: housing companies, trusts and associations. In some countries they have descended from philanthropic organizations, in others from cooperative and labour union movements. The distinguishing feature of their activities is that they are not engaged in housing provision with a view to making profit. They may provide and subsequently sell to an owner occupier, but the more usual model is either joint ownership or renting.

(4) *Semi-public bodies.* The distinction between this and the previous
    category is blurred, but their main distinguishing feature is the
    level of public initiative. In Folin's words:

> Such bodies are semi-public because they arise from public initiatives. They
> exhibit many similarities to the previous category… Their activities are
> strictly state-controlled, especially as regards selling prices or rents, generally
> fixed in relation to a dwelling's 'production costs'. They enjoy special condi-
> tions for obtaining credit and receive subsidies from the state or local govern-
> ment. (1985, p. 57)

(5) *Local authorities.* As with the previous two categories, most
    housing provided by local authorities is intended for their own
    retention, to be let to appropriate tenants. Frequently they have
    statutory powers in relation to access to building land – including
    compulsory acquisition – and to planning permission. They may
    also have preferential access to credit and be eligible for state
    subsidies. Finally, they can act as developers only, or have their
    own construction – direct labour – departments.
(6) *Government departments.* In common with local authorities, central
    government departments may develop housing in their capacity as
    employers. The individual dwellings will generally be expected to
    be retained by the department concerned and provided at a
    subsidized, even free, rent. The particular elements of the
    development–construction process for which they take direct
    responsibility and for which they engage external actors varies
    considerably.

The development amalgam

The agents involved in development may in practice come together, in
different combinations so that the division between the development
and building functions/agents is not always clear cut. Thus, Cardoso
and Short (1983) have drawn up a typology of the relations between
agents. The case of self-promoted and produced housing constitutes a
situation in which there is an absence of a market in that the object is to
create for the individual use of the promoter/developer. Alternatively,
the individual promoter may employ a builder to organize the construction process, whereas a separation of developer from consumer occurs
where an institution contracts a builder to construct houses. Yet another
case is that of speculative housing production which actually most

closely matches the pure capitalist form of production. The develop-ment process is initiated by an individual, or a private company, who obtains finance, buys land and other production inputs, and who may take on a builder to carry out the construction process. Although, as Barlow and Duncan (1994) point out, speculative developers will 'attempt to tailor their output to demand as closely as possible to avoid carrying unsold stocks of completed dwellings, production is not for a specific client on a bespoke basis' (p. 33). Because the final product is sold to those able and willing to pay the price, getting the market right will influence the profitability of the enterprise.

The interplay of these models with the public sector provides another dimension to the cross-national variation in the development–construction nexus. A few country examples illustrate this variation. Thus the activities of limited dividend housing companies in their provision of social housing in West Germany was nested within a general framework and specific initiating tasks both of which are attributable to government. Central government provided the legal and financial framework within which housing provision was located. It gave grants to the Lander (regional governments) who had responsi-bility for developing housing strategies including the identification of land and other resources. They could provide further finance. In Power's term (Power, 1993), they 'fostered' the construction of company-owned, new towns. At the next level in the government hier-archy, local authorities had responsibility for registering those house-holds who were eligible for social housing and through this activity obtained a measure of need. Their involvement in housing provision went much further, however:

> They had planning powers and power to acquire land – they could liaise directly with the social housing companies over needed developments. Many large cities had a major share in companies. In this way they were able to influence develop-ments directly. The location, size of building sites, distribution of dwelling sizes, rent levels – all were heavily influenced by the local authority's role. (Power, 1993, p. 116)

In Denmark, local authorities 'acted as planning authorities and part-ners in development with the social housing bodies' as well having a 'major role in organizing land deals'; they had 'jurisdiction over non-profit housing companies' making sure that 'access was arranged fairly'; and the local authorities 'were represented on the boards of housing companies' so that, overall, they had 'a significant influence over the activities of social housing organizations' (Power, 1993, p. 265).

In some countries, therefore, social housing developers do not act alone in initiating the provision of housing. Government authorities at local, and other levels, are involved at both a strategic and detailed level so that the function of developer in those countries describes the partnership of government and non-government agencies. One of the implications is that Folin's typology, while being useful in identifying the different developer type, underemphasizes the extent to which in some countries the different categories of developer collaborate.

It is also important to recognize that the importance of the land speculation element in the development process varies across countries depending on the ways in which the state and markets intertwine. Though not focused directly on residential development the work by Molotch and Vicari (1988) provides insights into the nature of the variation. Their study indicates that for the real estate entrepreneur in the USA a major source of profit exists in their ability to influence those state decisions – with respect to infrastructural investment, taxation and zoning – which structure the real estate market:

> A commercial property owner lobbies the transit authority to put the new subway stop in front of her own building rather than in front of some other owner's investment. Or a property syndicate fights for high-rise zoning at the site where it has purchased an option to buy. Such investors are betting not on their skills at choosing or developing products that have intrinsic merit but, rather, on their capacity as politically skilled actors to alter the spatial structure of the city. (Molotch and Vicari, 1988, p. 190)

In the USA this dynamic is supported by an ideological context in which the buyers and sellers of real estate 'should have maximum entrepreneurial freedom, with resulting spatial patterns best left to the market', since intervention not only undermines 'efficiency but threaten[s] democracy itself' (p. 197).

Development in Japan is founded on a different ideology: one which supports the commodification of property and land, but which at the same time places emphasis less on market freedom and more on the achievement of national goals. The latter may take precedence over other considerations. The centralized power of the state in practice generally means that '[l]ocal governments and individual citizens... defer to central bureaucrats whose technical skills can best manage [the] complex set of tasks' (p. 197) involved in land (and other) development. Rather than competition between entrepreneurs (and cities) as the motor of development, in Japan a government–corporate nexus shapes the location and nature of development.

Land development in Italy is different again. Ownership of land is dispersed, though much of it is held by public agencies, and subject to strict controls. This is founded in the power of state bureaucracy which is itself founded firmly in the political party machinery. The influence of the party system is pervasive through its control of government jobs, public and semi-public control of organizations, such as banks, involved in development and the co-option of business interests. All of this gives local party officials and technocrats considerable autonomy over the development process which undermines 'opportunities for speculation in spatial relations' (Molotch and Vicari, 1988, p. 203). Profit is still made but this derives from the development of specific parcels of land made available through the political machinery.

The way in which local entrepreneurs, large-scale capital, local and central governments as well as local inhabitants interact in the development process has significant consequences for the nature of land development in general and housing development in particular:

> The Japanese economic juggernaut combined with corporate domination of a single ruling party produces high gross national products and the poorest environment in the industrial world (tiny apartments, congested streets). Out of the seeming chaos of the Italian system comes stability for both the urban physical and social environments. The U.S. spatial entrepreneurialism yields dramatic unevenness within and across urban areas and local governments that are often mere adjuncts of the real estate business. (Molotch and Vicari, 1988, p. 307)

Development types and welfare regimes

Up to this point information has been presented that provides an understanding of the different ways in which the agents involved in development and construction relate to one another, their different objectives and the different ways in which national frameworks, including the role of the state, can influence the national patterns. The information provided about the arrangements that exist in different countries has not been systematic, but relied rather on a limited number of country examples. A somewhat more comprehensive picture is afforded by the work of Barlow and Duncan in which they relate the development–construction nexus to welfare state regimes. Their starting point is that, as with other aspects of the ways in which housing is produced and consumed in industrialized countries, the patterns are not random:

To some extent these promotion forms can be related to the different welfare capitalist regimes. Speculative promotion is the hallmark of the liberal regime type, as in Britain. It is also a feature of the rudimentary welfare state but here self-promotion is important. The social-democratic regime emphasizes social housing and restricted profit private promotion, while the corporatist cluster typically mixes various forms of self-promotion and restricted profit private promotion. (1994, p. 34)

Barlow and Duncan show how the construction process itself can be related to welfare regime type. Their starting point is the range of possible state interventions in housing provision. First, states can, in a number of ways, influence the production regime in which firms operate. They can, as they have indeed done in many countries, attempt to bring down production costs by encouraging system building, or subsidies can be used to bring about a reduction in user costs. States can influence the balance between short-run speculative gains and longer-run productivity gains. In general they can, and do, influence the market in terms of quality, quantity, and location of the product as well as its price and end user. These influences on the production regime will in turn influence the balance between small and large firms.

Second, through the planning system states can influence the location and amount of land made available for housebuilding. Planning systems can be classified into three types, each of which has different consequences for developers and builders. 'Negative' or 'reactive' planning occurs where states operate through development control to sanction or reject proposals made by developers to develop land. Under such systems the initiative rests with the developer and the state simply responds. This is the characteristic system operating in liberal regimes. In corporatist regimes, states are likely to pursue a more proactive role where they set out in advance an agreed land use plan. Developers may still be expected to take the initiative but will be doing so in a context of reasonable expectations of the state's responses. In addition, states can take ownership of land they wish to see developed and in this way collectivize development gain. Builders can then be invited to tender for contracts to build on the next tranche of land to be released for housebuilding. This is characteristic of social democratic regimes.

Third, states can intervene in provision by influencing consumption. Demand-side subsidies will impact on the prices different types of household are able to pay. Nomination rights or access criteria can affect the market or the section of the population for which provision is being aimed. Legislation can make providers charge prices that reflect production costs rather than current market values.

Omitting the influences on consumption, Barlow and Duncan have drawn up a schematic allocation of western European countries, which relates the characteristics of their housebuilding and promotion activities with their welfare regime type, based on the Esping-Andersen typology.

(1) *Rudimentary regimes* (Greece, Portugal and Spain). Land can be speculatively purchased with profit to be made from development gain. Promotion is balanced between non-profit and private institutions but firms tend to be small.
(2) *Liberal regimes* (Ireland, Switzerland, UK). Characterized by private-sector companies, with the balance towards large firms, pursuing speculative profit from land development gains.
(3) *Corporatist regimes* (Austria, Belgium, France, Italy and West Germany). Here the balance between private and non-profit promotion, between development gain and building profits, and between large and small firms is much more evenly balanced. Land supply, however, tends towards the speculative rather than public ownership.
(4) *Social democratic regimes* (Denmark, Finland, Netherlands, Norway and Sweden). Land supply is controlled by the state with large, private-sector firms forced to compete over profits from the building process.

Whereas this provides a view of the broad similarities and differences among the countries of western Europe, Barlow and Duncan have analysed the situation in more detail in one country representative of each of the last three regime types.

Britain

With the exception of the 1945–60 period, housing provision in Britain has been dominated by the private developer/builder (Dickens *et al.*, 1985). This has been particularly the case during the 1980s when around three-quarters of construction was carried out by the private, speculative builder (Barlow and Duncan, 1994). The firm buys land, often to keep in reserve for some years, hoping to obtain planning permission and to begin construction when demand for housing is deemed to be ready and the building process will be compatible with the firm's other activities. From beginning to end this is a speculative undertaking with the firm gambling on its ability to read and influence the market. In practice, the potential development gains are very much larger than the often incremental gains that result from increases in efficiency in the construction process. As Michael Ball has argued, this has resulted in business strategies in which getting the land deals right has obviated the need greatly to pursue efficiency in construction (Ball, 1983). During the 1980s most of the remaining provision – around 20 per cent of the total – was initiated by social housing agencies in the form of local authorities and housing associations, with the construction process itself being carried out mainly by private-sector firms. In addition, about 5 per cent of housing was developed by the self-promotion sector, with a further 2 per cent by the private sector operating under a restricted profit regime, many building 'under license on local authority land' (Barlow and Duncan, 1994, p. 41).

France

The private-sector, speculative developer/builder accounted for only about a quarter of housing provision in France in the 1980s, with social rented housing (mainly through the HLMs) accounting for a further 15 per cent. Over half of total output was in the form of self-promoted housing (Barlow and Duncan 1994). In France, taxes and other restrictions on land speculation are limited, and even in the case of self-promoted housing there are large profits accruing from development gain. In the main, these are taken by companies which speculatively acquire land, sometimes organize services to be provided, and sub-divide it into plots for individual homes. Although, self-promotion is the single largest form of housing provision in France, accounting 'for over 40 per cent of all new completions and over 80 per cent of new single dwelling completions' (Barlow, 1992, p. 256), it is nevertheless an industry dominated by capitalist firms extracting profit 'from both land speculation and the construction process' (p. 256). The construction process itself is frequently carried out by specialist builders, many of which could be described as 'industrialised catalogue builders' (p. 257). Houses are often finished to weatherproof standard, with the internal fittings uncompleted. But, pure self-build is relatively rare.

Sweden

Before the Second World War the great majority of housing provision was by speculative builders. As an intended result of government policy, this form of provision had, by the 1980s, declined to just a few per cent of the total. Although self-promoted housing is a significant sector accounting for around a quarter of total production, the greatest share – about half – was attributable to non-profit developers. The remainder – about 20 per cent – took the form of restricted profit, private housing. The majority of housing provision in Sweden thus takes the form of building to contract. There are three elements to this. First, the promoter – whether private or public – receives the State Housing Loan (SHL) which covers between 22 and 30 per cent of costs and has some special features:

> [It] is not just financial, in terms of lower interest rates than would otherwise be available on the open market. It is also a matter of availability, stability and the reduction of business uncertainty. Access to development land is also much easier. (Dickens *et al.*, 1985, p. 85)

Second, construction firms build 'bespoke', literally so for state developers, being invited to bid for contracts to erect housing of speci-fied design on land provided by local authorities. Even where the developer is private, the receipt of an SHL subjects the housing to spec-ifications laid down by the local authority in whose area the housing is to be built: '[d]evelopers must enter into development contracts with communes which regulate the allocation of SHLs and the building they are used for' (Dickens *et al.*, 1985, p. 85).

Third, and following on from the second, the contract form restricts access to land. Local authorities control both the use of land and its release for construction. The development gain accrues to the state and firms are forced to compete around their ability to build better and cheaper than their competitors. The Swedish system has therefore been one based upon a strong commitment by the state to intervene in the housing market. By removing development gain from the private sphere and by placing firms in a structure where the most efficient constructors can undercut their competitors, the real resources consumed in the building of houses has fallen. The Swedish strategy has reduced the real cost of housing, so that the gap between cost and income is smaller than in countries where the market has been less socially regulated.

The extent and nature of state intervention has consequences for the size distribution of building firms. In Sweden, the contract form of building has encouraged the growth of large firms to the point where it 'has one of the highest levels of ownership and production concentration of any capitalist country' (Barlow and Duncan, 1994, p. 44). Concentration has been encouraged by the need for firms to pursue strategies for achieving efficiency in construction. The result is that in the 1980s about 60 per cent of total production was undertaken by the ten largest firms. Moreover, most of their activity was carried out by their own employees with limited use of sub-contracting except for specialist tasks. The small firm sector is limited and mainly engaged in the production of single family homes.

Conclusions

Normally houses have extremely long lives so that at any one time the housing stock in each country is the product of decisions about development made over many years. Thus the decisions in the 1960s and 70s in many European countries to utilize new technologies in the form of the prefabricated, high rise apartment blocks has left an enduring legacy in their urban landscapes. Being the accumulation of many years of development, this store of housing is many times larger than the amount of new development which could take place this year, or the year after. Indeed, it has been only rarely that annual production has exceeded 2 or 3 per cent of a country's existing stock. But, over the long run, the nature of development and construction as processes and the nature of state intervention as part of those processes has considerable importance for the nature of the physical product and the nature of the household experience of housing. One consequence is that any understanding of the nature of the housing stock presently existing in any country must be founded in an understanding of its historical development.

Although, in theory, it would be possible for the profit-seeking sector of economies to be given an entirely free rein to provide housing, in practice this is never done. The relationships between developers and builders, and between both of them and the state are extremely complex and variable. Policy, more generally the role of the state in capitalist countries, relating to the production of housing has not been a major focus of housing research either of the single country, or of the cross-national, type. A notable attempt systematically to consider housing production across a large sample of countries and to relate the empirical patterns to the literature discussed in Chapter Four is that by

Barlow and Duncan. Their analysis points to the significance of distinctive and diverging welfare state regimes having expression in the ways in which they have organized housing production. Thus in Britain the liberal regime of social policy is translated into a production process which both provides a regulatory framework and also facilitates the pursuit of private profit. In Sweden, by contrast, the social democratic regime has fostered a system of production in which the interests of the private sector have been harnessed such that the long-term benefits are more widely shared with consumers in the form of lower prices.

Actually, probably more so than with other stages in the housing provision process, the literature has tended to concentrate on countries as unique case studies which has the effect that differences rather than similarities are stressed. As it happens, the Molotch–Vicari and Barlow–Duncan comparative studies, in setting their analyses in wider social frameworks, also stress divergence.

7

Housing Finance

The role of finance extends throughout the whole of the housing provision process. Even dwellings achieving only the minimum standard acceptable in advanced societies consume considerable amounts of real resources and consequently their production entails large sums of money. Insofar as developers expect their investment to generate a profit, subsequent purchase by landlords or owner occupiers will, in the absence of a collapsed market, also require large sums. Moreover, the long gestation period for new housing may mean a lengthy delay separating investment and return. Companies and individuals may raise the initial costs directly from their own resource but, generally, the circumstances contribute to a situation where production and consumption is facilitated by well-developed arrangements for making finance available.

In some cases, general financial institutions operating across several areas of national economies may make funds available, but in many countries special institutions have been developed which only serve the housing sector. Often these operate within regulatory frameworks which both restrict the range of their operations and provide them with protection against competition. Within a national housing system there may be quite separate financing requirements at each stage with each successive actor obtaining the required money in different ways or from different sources. Equally, as we have seen in the previous chapter, the actors involved at each stage may come together in different combinations. The individual who decides to become a developer/builder in order to provide his or her family with relatively cheap home ownership, may require a loan at the outset in order to purchase land, which is topped up as building costs are incurred, and then repaid over a period of 20 or 30 years. A social landlord may finance the development of dwellings with a loan to be repaid, over an extended period of time, from the rental payments. Or, a speculative builder may use share capital in order to finance production which is replenished when the houses are sold to individual purchasers who, in turn, receive finance from a bank. There is, in short, a myriad of different arrangements as between and within countries, and over time.

As with the previous chapter, the aim is to map out both possible and actual arrangements, before moving on to consider explanations. Also like the previous chapter, the relative dearth of literature prevents more than a limited exposition. Here, the main emphasis is on the arrangements whereby home ownership is financed, and the convergence in those arrangements particularly as a consequence of developments in EU countries.

Finance for development

Where large organizations – be they private or public, for profit or not for profit – are involved in the development and construction stages, there are a number of possible sources of finance. Sometimes the organization will fund their activities from their own resources, by which is meant the capital built up within the organization over time. Some organizations may be in a position to raise money through the stock market, others may seek loans from financial institutions such as banks and building societies. Yet others may have access to loan capital provided by national or local government. A detailed breakdown of the relative importance of different sources of capital in all industrial countries even at one point in time is not available. Nevertheless, a number of brief examples illustrate the variation in arrangements.

In the Netherlands during the decades before 1990 about one third of new house building was financed by government loans. Priemus (1990, p. 167) adds that a 'second source of financing is provided by the institutional investors, who not only build for themselves but also finance house building in the nonprofit rented sector'. In France the developers of both owner-occupied and private rental dwellings are eligible for loans at below market rates of interest, which are available through the Credit Foncier de France, 'a State-controlled institution that raises funds in the private market' (McCrone and Stephens, 1995, p. 27). Developers of social housing are similarly eligible for subsidized loans. The same authors report that in Germany finance for developers of private rental dwellings usually takes the form of fixed-rate loans. In the case of commercial companies funding will come from 'a variety of ordinary market sources, including both equity finance and long-term fixed-rate loans' (p. 60). Michael Ball (1983) reports that the large speculative house builders in Britain financed their activities in the 1970s through a combination of share flotation and fixed-interest loans from the financial markets. Local authorities in Britain, in contrast, financed construction at this time from their general loans pools, each of which consisted of a mix of medium- and short-term loans from the private sector, while the current activities of housing associations are financed through a mix of government subsidy and private finance from banks, building societies and other financial institutions.

Finance systems for home ownership

Once dwellings have been built and are available for use by an occupier, there may be other financial requirements. This is particularly significant since the basic problem facing many would-be owner occupiers is that average house prices are high relative to their incomes with the result that 'the timing and size of house purchase [is] dependent upon the availability of mortgage debt' (Miles, 1992, p. 1094). A world in which people had to save, out of earned income, the purchase price of a house in advance of owning and occupying might have markedly different houses and housing systems to those that actually prevail throughout the industrialized countries. The problem of paying for housing is often exacerbated in the case where household structures are strongly weighted towards the nuclear family, since the point at which young people leave the parental home to set up an independent household often coincides with both low incomes and, if the household includes children, high outgoings. In short, over the lifecycle of the individual, income and wealth are sometimes low in the first few decades increasing to a peak in late middle age. What will probably be the individual's most expensive purchase, therefore, can often be least affordable in the first half or so of their lifespan. In fact, in all industrialized countries financial institutions and mechanisms have been developed that have enabled people to borrow all or some of the purchase price of home ownership and to repay over an extended period of years. Generally they have been able to use the dwelling itself as collateral so that they have not needed to find either a guarantor or build up some alternative asset. These arrangements have underlain the expansion of this form of housing tenure to its current status as the most popular over the industrialized world as a whole.

The essence of any effective housing finance system is that money has to be accumulated from those willing to save, and lent on to house buyers for repayment over an extended period of time. In general, the savings originate in the household sector so that house purchase is made possible through one group in the population making money available for another group. Boleat (1985) describes four ways in which this can be achieved.

(1) *The direct route*

This occurs where the house buyer obtains a loan directly from a person who has funds which they are willing to lend. Frequently there may be a family tie between lender and borrower. Although this is typically a feature of house purchase in countries that are not yet economically advanced, it is also practised in those that are. It is unlikely to acquire a numerically significant role, however, since it rests upon individuals with matching financial circumstances making both contact and agreement and, in general, the greater the economic development of a country the greater the degree to which investing and borrowing is done through financial intermediaries.

(2) *The contractual system*

This refers to arrangements whereby the would-be home buyer contracts with a financial intermediary to make regular savings over a period of time. They may receive a low rate of interest on their savings but after a predetermined period they may be eligible to a loan perhaps of a size up to the difference between the full purchase price and the amount of their savings.

(3) *Deposit taking system*

In this system financial institutions attract deposits from those wishing to save, lending the money on to those wishing to borrow. The institutions may take the form of commercial banks which conduct the whole gamut of banking services, savings banks which may deal mainly with the personal sector, and specialist housing banks which lend only to house buyers. In general the loans are given at variable rates of interest.

(4) *Mortgage bank system*

Financial institutions may sell bonds on the capital markets at the prevailing rate. Typically the bonds are purchased by other financial institutions such as pension funds and insurance companies, although some individuals may also be active in the bond market. The money is used to lend on to house buyers.

The distinction (ignoring the direct route) between those that gain their funds directly from the retail or personal savings market (the contractual and the deposit taking systems) and from the wholesale money markets (the mortgage bank system) is an important one. The savings banks operate on the principle that they can borrow from the liquid retail market, paying interest in return for often short-term deposits and lending, on a long-term basis, to purchasers. As a form of protection against fluctuations in interest rates, which could result in depositors withdrawing their savings when market rates rise offering them higher returns elsewhere, savings banks often charge borrowers variable rates of interest. Institutions of the mortgage bank type may attract money from private sector investors including financial institutions owned by share holders, and often charge fixed rates of interest.

A further feature of this typology is that it makes no reference to whether the institution, specifically with the contractual, deposit and mortgage bank systems, are private or public ones. In addition, private institutions may be differentiated into profit-maximizing companies and organizations with a mutuality basis. A distinguishing feature of the public sector institutions is that some or all of their capital and current costs could be met through taxation.

In most countries, up until the 1970s, or even longer, the main institutions that offered loans to the housing sector operated within protected spheres, established by national governments. Thus, in the USA, against a background of deposit rate ceilings, institutions operating in the housing market were permitted a small interest differential. In Britain, the building societies benefited from special tax treatment, which enabled them to attract savings at below the market cost of funds, giving them an advantage over the commercial banks. Such arrangements did not necessarily act against the interests of those wishing to invest in housing. In Britain, the Building Societies Association was able to guide its members on interest rates for savings and lending. The lending rates 'tended to be so low that an excess demand for funds and consequently mortgage rationing characterized the decades prior to 1980' (Roistacher, 1987, p. 100). Those who got over the hurdle of the particular methods of non-price rationing used, benefited from interest rates which in many years were actually negative in real terms. So, any perceived advantages of home ownership were amplified by the advantageous financial arrangements which encouraged people to maximize the size of their mortgage.

Not all countries, however, have developed systems in which there are divisions between mortgage financing and other banking activities. Thus, in Finland, the level of bank specialization was limited with all banking sectors having a significant role in the housing loan market. They were, however, highly regulated. The Bank of Finland imposed constraints on foreign exchange and the issuing of bonds on foreign markets and also imposed interest rate regulations, setting the rate that could accrue to depositors, and, for each type of bank, the average interest rates on loans. With a relatively undeveloped capital market giving households few opportunities to invest, and with a buoyant demand for home ownership, saving to buy a house was a particularly attractive proposition.

The different systems have long histories, of a century or more, with models being transferred from one country to others: what might be viewed as a convergence through policy emulation. Thus, the origins of the savings type of institution are to be found in the British building societies. In the context of the housing difficulties of rapidly expanding urban areas, itself a consequence of increasing industrialization, groups of individuals came together so that, through their shared efforts, they might meet their housing needs. They committed themselves to regular savings which, when pooled, provided, one by one, sufficient funds to purchase a house for each. Once they were all housed the savings club or society was wound up, hence their collective name of terminating building societies. After a while they evolved into permanent societies where the direct link between the body of savers and the body of borrowers was broken; a pool of money was continually topped up by savers, and continually drawn upon by borrowers, paying a rate of interest which compensated the former and provided the society with a small margin to cover operating costs.

The concept of the original terminating societies was transferred by British immigrants to the USA, where they came to be known as thrifts, and also as Savings and Loan Associations (S&Ls). Like their model, in about the mid nineteenth century they took on permanent status. In other respects, the S&Ls differed largely as a result of the specific regulatory framework established following the 1930s Depression when many of them had experienced financial difficulties. As Boleat notes: '[n]o less than 2,800 institutions went out of business, mostly through voluntary liquidation or mergers with others' (1985, p. 67). The new regulations prevented thrifts from operating in more than one state. They were insulated from capital markets and were required to offer housing loans. Interest rate ceilings were imposed on deposit accounts with the intention of reducing competition and encouraging 'more prudent lending policies' (Ball *et al.*, 1988, p. 135). But thrifts were given leave to offer a quarter percentage above other banks as well as being required to operate under an insurance arrangement. These arrangements resulted in 'the fixed rate loan, refinanced by relatively cheap funds resulting from interest rate ceilings on retail deposits' (Ball *et al.*, 1998, p. 135).

The history of the mortgage banks is also a long one, having their origins in eighteenth-century Prussia when the device of offering bonds secured against landed property was developed. The concept was transferred to France in the mid nineteenth century where banks came to provide a means whereby savers and house buyers could come together through the mechanism of offering long-term bonds, or debt papers, secured against the properties being purchased. A characteristic of both the deposit and the bond system was that individual dwellings and the land on which they were built acted as collateral.

Following from these examples of the diffusion of models across national boundaries it might be concluded that there is an Anglo-Saxon model, characteristic of countries with liberal welfare regimes, and a European model. However, whereas different systems may be characteristically represented by the institutions of particular countries, generally each country contains an amalgam of different systems. Lomax (1991) provides figures which show the market shares at the end of the 1980s. In Britain these were: banks 30 per cent; specialist mortgage lenders 66 per cent; insurance companies 2 per cent; and public sector 2 per cent. The equivalent market shares in Germany were 23, 57, 8 and 12; and in Japan 46, 8, 5 and 41.

There is also, as Boleat indicates, a diversity of public and private sector elements. Dominating in the Japanese system, is a public sector body, the Housing Loan Corporation. Set up in 1950 with the main objective of providing long-term, low interest capital for the construction and purchase of housing, it obtains funds through the postal savings system. Individuals invest their savings through Japan's post offices where they are placed at the disposal of the Trust Fund Bureau. The Bureau, in turn, lends them on to a number of government agencies including the Housing Loan Corporation. The government sets the rate of interest at which the Corporation both borrows and lends on these funds so that they establish both the margin enjoyed by the Corporation and the rate facing housing investors. In 1981 about half of the Corporation's lending was to people who intended to build houses for their own use. These loans are restricted to houses of a maximum size of 120 square metres, and to a maximum loan. Repayment is generally over 25 years, often at a fixed rate of interest which is below the market rate. A further one-third of lending is to individuals wishing to buy existing owner-occupied dwellings. The remainder is shared between projects which include rental housing, owner-occupied reha-bilitation and urban renewal projects.

Another example is that of Spain where the mortgage market is dominated by the private sector. According to Boleat (1985), in the early 1980s the confederated savings banks had some 60 per cent of the market with the commercial banks taking a further 20 per cent. The former are non-profit-making organizations which raise their funds mainly through deposits. The remaining 20 per cent is taken by a government-owned institution, the Mortgage Bank of Spain, some of whose funds are raised by bonds quoted on the stock exchange. Again in contrast, in Austria the system is dominated by the public sector with around 70 per cent of new housing units being constructed with the help of public funds. There are four Bausparkassen, each of which has strong affiliations with other banks, operating contract saving systems with the standard contract requiring house purchasers to save 40 per cent of the sum which can be supplemented by a loan for the remaining 60 per cent at an interest rate of 6 per cent. Italy provides another contrast since its 'housing finance market is significantly less devel-oped than that of most other Western European countries' (Lomax, 1991, p. 66). The government takes a central role in the system in part through its ownership of banking institutions. But, in practice, as much as three-quarters of house purchases are financed by borrowers out of their own funds.

Deregulation and convergence

Whereas national systems and their variations were built up over many years, recently there has been considerable convergence. Over the last two decades the pattern typical of western countries of relatively self-contained national banking systems in which their central banks regu-lated the activities of their financial institutions has increasingly been replaced as a result of internationalization and deregulation. Much of the impetus for change has emanated from the strategic decisions of the financial institutions themselves, but governments have played a role, too, in their policy changes. Thus, from the 1960s onwards with more and more national companies expanding into overseas markets and opening up branches overseas, many banks saw it in their interests to follow their corporate customers so that they would be able to compete with local banks in their ability to offer local knowledge. In addition, increasing amounts of dollars, boosted particularly by the oil price rises in the 1970s, were being held in overseas banks, especially in London. Not being subject to the same minimum reserve require- ments laid down by central banks, the financial institutions operating in the so-called Euro-markets were able to generate higher margins. While these developments encouraged increasing internationalization, national regulatory systems came under strain in the 1970s and 80s when volatile and high interest rates presented difficulties for those financial institutions that were subject to interest rate ceilings in their borrowing and lending activities. This created problems, in part as a consequence of depositors shifting their money elsewhere. Finding ways around the regulations then became for the banks an important objective. The resistance of central banks was variable, but in many cases, 'as fast as one loophole was sewn up, canny market operators would find a new one' (*The Economist*, 1984, p. 15) and, in many countries, the same political and ideological shifts that had brought the desirability of welfare provision into question and saw unregulated markets in general as desirable, meant that the financial institutions were often pushing at an open door.

Notwithstanding the pressures from financial institutions themselves, national governments have also played a role, though, as Lomax notes, with some having been more pro-active than others:

> the pace of change has varied markedly between countries. Broadly speaking, a distinction can be drawn between developments in the United States and the United Kingdom and those in other countries which continue to be characterised by higher entry barriers. (1991, p. 60)

In Britain in the early 1980s, there were a number of special devel- opments that contributed to the reshaping of the framework within which the building societies operated. Roistacher (1987) notes that these included the decision by the government aggressively to compete in the savings market through its National Savings programme. In addition, there had been some deregulation of the commercial banks, which because of some decline of their own busi- ness were keen to expand into the mortgage market. The building soci- eties were hit further by some weakening of their tax advantages as a result of changes in investor behaviour. The new competitive pressures made it impossible for the Building Societies Association to maintain its cartel role as individual societies sought new savings schemes and more flexibility over lending rates. Although remnants of the Association's control lingered, by 1986 it formally recognized that the days of the cartel were over. There were also country-specific developments in the USA where inflation played an important role in bringing the previously protected position of thrifts to an end. Arrangements based on long-term, fixed-interest loans were strained when short-term rates rose sharply in the 1970s. One of the first changes came in 1979 with the introduction of regulations which allowed thrifts to offer variable-rate loans. In the 1980s further regulations allowed them to offer money market deposit accounts and to diversify their assets into commercial and consumer loans.

The general picture elsewhere is of similar developments, 'albeit at a less rapid pace' (Lomax, 1991, p. 61). Thus, in Finland, the old system, in which banks had operated within a largely risk-free environment, was not substantially altered until the late 1980s. From the mid 1970s onwards there had been a series of reforms which relaxed the regulatory framework. Excess demand for loans at the regulated rates of interest offered an incentive to the banks to find ways of evading the regulations. Although the Bank of Finland sought to counter such moves it found itself increasingly unable to do so. On the whole, however, as Swoboda indicates, 'the attitudes of the authorities on regulation has been rather passive' (1986, p. 15), with the outcome by the 1990s being that interest rates on housing loans were no longer centrally fixed, but could be set at market clearing rates.

The general picture, as Lomax indicates, then, is that reforms have proceeded less far outside the US and the UK. In the longer run, however, the competitive pressures for change 'may be leading to a degree of convergence between housing finance systems, both between Anglo-Saxon countries and in continental Europe and Japan' (Lomax, 1991, p. 64).

The EU and the single market

A further shift towards convergence in some industrialized countries is being driven by the interest of the EU in the creation of a single market. The formal position is that housing policy will remain in the competence of national governments. Nevertheless, the EU has considerable significance for housing, for example through directives relating to construction practices and standards, building materials, and professional qualifications, and through various associated policy areas (see Drake, 1991). But, perhaps the biggest impact is occurring as a result of the discipline imposed by moves towards economic and monetary union which may lead member countries to adopt similar housing policies. This has been the substance of one view in Britain (see Congdon, 1988). In a reduced form, the argument is that over the long run the inflation rate is related to monetary growth, which, in turn, is related to the creation of credit. The growth of credit in Britain over the 1980s, however, has been very much greater than in Germany whose currency and economy in many ways has formed the benchmark in Europe. Since at least half of the credit in both countries is related directly to the housing market, and credit for non-housing expenditure is frequently secured against house values, explanations for the growth of credit might be sought in the relative attractiveness of investing in home ownership in Britain and Germany. In Britain, the record of house price gains in the two decades before Congdon's paper was one that outstripped many other forms of investment, particularly when the benefit of mortgage interest relief was included. Borrowing to invest in home ownership was thus a financially profitable activity, so much so that it probably resulted in the diversion of investment away from other sectors (see Farmer and Barrell, 1981, for an earlier version of this view). In contrast, the 'situation in Germany has been radically different' (Congdon, 1988, p. 104) with increases in house prices generally not exceeding even the interest rate on housing loans. Congdon summarises the situation:

> we see here a plausible general explanation for the differences in their intensity of credit demand between the United Kingdom and West Germany. Over the last 20 years borrowing to buy houses in the United Kingdom has given an excellent financial return. But borrowing to buy houses in West Germany has been costly for the great majority of homeowners. (It should also be noted that the activities of investors/speculators who have bought houses on borrowed money, with the intention of renting them out, have sometimes been disastrous). Memories, particularly when they are based upon a whole generation of experience, influence attitudes. Attitudes then influence behaviour. There should be no surprise that, at the same interest rate, the pace of credit and money growth is far higher in the United Kingdom than in West Germany. (1988, p. 14)

The point here is that those governments that seek monetary union may be forced to equalize their credit positions, but the requirements of a single market dictate convergence also in the types of institution and the products provided. The primary objective is to create more competition. In practical terms this can be taken to mean that many of the barriers to the entry of firms and products to national markets should be removed, so that the first stage of EU strategy has been to deconstruct existing impediments to competition. The second, and constructive, stage is to create common rules that facilitate a single common market in banking services. The Second Banking Directive is intended to achieve this aim by a principle that financial institutions will be supervised by the governments of their own countries, according to a set of harmonized standards, and once licensed by its own government an institution will be allowed to set up branches in other EU countries. By enabling firms to set up anywhere in the EU the present heterogeneity of prices and products would be reduced. In addition, the competition would, it is argued, ensure greater efficiency and lower prices. The result would be that households in all EU countries would share access to similar types of mortgage:

> The main consequence of the reduction in the barriers to entry to the housing finance industry has been an increase in competition in most countries, accompanied by some blurring of the historical distinctions between commercial banks and specialist mortgage institutions. Mortgage loans are increasingly provided in all countries by multi-purpose financial institutions. Overall, therefore, there has been some convergence of national housing finance systems and this process can be expected to continue. (Lomax, 1991, pp. 21–2)

Considerable progress has been made so that the distinctiveness of national markets is less so than it was even a decade ago. The firms that traditionally dominated the mortgage market have experienced greater domestic competition, and in some countries markets have been opened up to competition from abroad. For example, German mortgage banks have, on a restricted scale, been allowed to operate outside Germany, while Danish institutions have moved into Germany, and British building societies have entered the Spanish mortgage market. Nevertheless, there remain significant barriers to the entry of foreign companies into the mortgage market in each of the European countries. Thus Grilli (1989) points to the importance of national differences in institutional structure when he argues that 'firms structured to operate in one institutional climate may find it too costly to fulfil the requirements they would face in a foreign country' (p. 305). In other respects, also, present arrangements remain diverse. In the United Kingdom building societies frequently grant loans, which are to be repaid over 25 years, sometimes covering 100 per cent of the value of the house. In Spain the maximum sometimes is 80 per cent and the repayment period usually 10 to 15 years; in France the maximum is 80 per cent with 15 years repayment; and in Italy the normal maximum is 50 per cent and the repayment 10 to 25 years (see Lomax, 1991). In Britain, fixed-interest-rate loans remain relatively uncommon, and, where offered, the rate is fixed for a pre-set number of years. In Germany, France, Spain and Italy fixed-interest-rate loans are common. In addition interest rates have varied considerably. Thus, writing in 1990, Laugel and Sovignet noted that in West Germany 'rates had varied from 6.8% to 8.5% in the last few years, while Spain witnessed rates twice as high' (p. 27). The nature of loans for house purchase have thus varied considerably between different European countries.

Conclusions

The comparative literature on the development of national systems of housing finance is, at the time of writing, at a fairly rudimentary stage. It is least rudimentary, though still far from being fully developed, with respect to home ownership. The institutional structure is very varied and even within any one country there are a number of different ways, for example as between public and private sector, in which the home buyer can access finance. It is possible to draw a distinction between an Anglo-Saxon model based on savings banks and a European model based on mortgage banks, but the distinction is very blurred, with home owners in all societies being served by a wide range of institutional types.

Recent decades have witnessed a breaking down of differences both within and between countries. Processes of deregulation and internationalization, which result from a medley of government policies and changes in the nature and role of finance capital, as well as the specific drive towards integration in EU countries have all played a part in this. The latter, of course, provides a specific example of convergence being achieved through the actions of a supra-national body negotiating an agenda on member states.

8

Housing Subsidies

'A subsidy can be thought of as a state-financed reduction in the cost of a specific commodity or asset, relative to the market price it could command' (Gibb and Munro, 1991, p. 3). The reduction can take a number of forms. Housing can be provided directly by the state or an agent operating on its behalf with the user cost being reduced through the utilization of the state's resources. So, for example, the land can be provided free or at a reduced cost, or the finance provided at a below-market rate of interest. The state can provide cash payments to developers to offset the costs of production, or reduce tax rates payable on construction materials. Provided that these subsidies are not retained by the developer, the cost facing the ultimate user is reduced. These supply-side subsidies are sometimes referred to as bricks and mortar (appropriate perhaps only in those countries where they constitute the dominant building materials) or object subsidies.

Notwithstanding the definition above, governments can also intervene on the demand side where they can subsidize occupiers in a number of ways. First, they can provide money payments, which may or may not be specifically tied to housing payments. In the latter form the subsidy constitutes a general redistribution of income and the view could be taken that it should be considered as a social security rather than a housing subsidy. The payments may also be in the form of a reduction of the market rate of interest which is payable on any loan taken out to purchase housing. Second, vouchers can be used as full or part payment to be redeemed only with respect to housing. Third, it is possible for governments to compensate individuals through the system of income tax. Irrespective of their form, demand-side subsidies are sometimes referred to as people or subject subsidies.

Since subsidies can operate on both the supply and the demand sides of the market, they can either reduce the user cost or increase the ability to pay. Whereas the supply–demand distinction is a useful basis for presenting and discussing subsidies, the definition above to which it has been linked is not itself unproblematic. One difficulty relates to the use of the term 'market price' where what is implied is that the market could exist without any state intervention other than subsidies. In reality, all states intervene in a myriad of ways. Even in a country with minimalist government its housing market will exist within a context where government sets rules of behaviour and exchange, establishes institutions for policing them, imposes taxes and implements redistributive measures. All of these may influence market behaviour and modify the costs of provision and the ability of households to pay. Many of these interventions may not be thought of as housing policies but nevertheless have an impact on the cost–income gap. This might be the case with regional or defence policy, for example, since these can influence the geographic distribution of population and thus of need for housing. It can therefore be difficult to ascertain what the market price might be.

Another difficulty with the definition is that some government actions may result not in a decrease, but in an increase, in costs. Thus, as noted in earlier chapters, governments of all advanced industrialized countries have set down some minimum regulations concerning the location of housing, construction standards and materials. These impose constraints within which the market actors are required to operate. In general they have the consequence of increasing the cost of housing – because land is more expensive or higher quality materials are used – although they may also restructure costs, for example as a result of increasing insulation ratings the capital cost may be increased while the running cost is decreased.

It is also useful to recognize that the definition of subsidies as tied to the state purse is too restrictive since actions by the state, such as imposing rent control, may have no financial implications for the state itself, but nevertheless have an impact upon prices actually paid. In this particular case, the policy changes the market and its price structure such that user costs are reduced, and landlords' own assets which are less valuable than they would be in the absence of the policy. A further consideration is that it is also possible that the state could make payments to either, or both, the suppliers and consumers of housing in ways that do not reduce the market price. For example, developers could be given land by a local authority, which did not place restrictions on the selling price of the completed dwellings, so that the outcome could be that consumers pay no less than they would otherwise have done and developers make excess profits.

While there are many difficulties in applying standard definitions of subsidy, the rest of the present chapter recognizes both that reducing the cost–income gap can result from action impacting on both the supply and demand sides of the market, and that, in most countries these state interventions are tenure specific. Even where the housing system has been subjected to comprehensive policy development, the particular instruments, and the balance between them, may differ across forms of ownership. Indeed, any subsidy differences may follow from quite deliberate strategies intended to influence the relative size of the tenures and the relative balance of advantage facing households making tenure decisions. The chapter is arranged firstly by the main forms of tenure and secondly by whether subsidies are on the supply or the demand side.

Home ownership

Supply-side subsidies

According to the preceding discussion, supply-side subsidies reduce the costs to the user. However, the supply–demand dichotomy is not clear cut in the case of self-promoted home ownership since the costs of developing and building may equate to the costs of using or occupying. The loan taken out to finance the cost of building may not, in this case, be repaid with another loan being taken out in order to purchase the completed dwelling. With other forms of provision of home ownership, such as by a speculative builder, however, the existence of specifically supply-side subsidies is clearer. There are a number of ways in which states can reduce the costs of production. These include free or below-market-price land, low – or tax deductible – interest loans, non-repayable grants, and infrastructure. There may be eligibility rules, which restrict the dwellings provided to households with incomes below specified levels, or the dwellings themselves may have specified characteristics. Thus, in Finland, the ARAVA system provides cheap loans but the developer must meet specified quality and size criteria and sell at below specified levels. Household eligibility is limited by house-hold-size related, income criteria (Doling, 1990b). Many other countries – for example Belgium, France, the Netherlands, Norway, Sweden and West Germany – offer supply-side loans (Román *et al.*, 1994). In contrast, Britain provides means-tested grants for rehabilitation only, while in Denmark the supply-side subsidy facility is rarely utilized by home owners (Román *et al.*, 1994).

Demand-side subsidies

A feature of demand-side subsidies for home owners in industrialized countries is that they operate, in the main, through national tax systems. An analytical problem in identifying both the existence and amount of the subsidies relates to the benchmark against which they can be placed. What in other words ought to be considered the 'normal' tax treatment of home owners? The difficulty here is that in many industrial economies there is a distinction, for tax purposes, between 'consumption' goods – such as entertainment and food – and 'investment' goods – such as shares or a business. The distinction is not always hard and fast, but there is a general tendency to treat these two categories of good differently. If housing were to be thought of as a consumption good, a subsidy could be considered to occur where a government provided those people who took loans in order to finance their purchase with deductions against their tax liability, proportionate to the interest payments. This is simply because the purchase of other consumption goods is not generally supported by loans and tax breaks. If housing were to be thought of as an investment good, however, any tax relief against loan interest payments would be consistent with the tax treatment of investment goods in general. The failure to tax the imputed rental value, that is the flow of notional income that owner occupiers enjoy from their investment, equivalent to an income from a business or shares, would in this case be the relevant subsidy.

   This categorization can be turned around. Countries that allow tax deductions against housing loans, but impose a tax on imputed rent, in practice treat housing as if it were an investment good. According to a review by the OECD in the mid 1980s, such an approach was taken by Finland, Greece, Luxembourg, the Netherlands, Spain, Sweden, Denmark, and Norway (OECD, 1988), a list that includes those countries with social democratic welfare regimes together with Spain and Greece. There are other countries that neither allow deductions against loans nor impose an imputed rent tax so that they could be said to treat housing as a consumption good. The three countries identified – Australia, Canada and New Zealand – have liberal regimes and, in Donnison's typology, social housing policies. The remaining countries in the OECD classification – France, Japan, Portugal, Turkey, UK,

USA and West Germany – have mixed systems in which outgoings are treated as for investment goods and benefits as for consumption goods. Whereas the categorization does not itself provide any evidence of the amount or monetary value of subsidy, in terms of structure alone, this third group of countries treat home owners the most favourably since buyers are assisted with the burden of loan repayments but they are not taxed on the benefits they derive from occupation. Perhaps most interesting, however, is the distinction between the social democratic and the liberal countries with the former apparently viewing housing as a commodity that provides long-term benefit. This could be said to fit with the social democratic view, reported in Chapter Four, that welfare, in this case in the form of housing consumption, is not inimical to economic growth.

One limitation of this categorization of countries is that it provides a static picture. There has been a general, though by no means universal, tendency to shift the emphasis from the investment to the consumption view of home ownership. Insofar as this has taken place it has been consistent with a wider tendency to reduce property or bricks and mortar subsidies, which have provided direct incentives to new investment in housing, and to increase people subsidies, which provide direct help to consuming the stock of housing which already exists. This transfer can be seen in the considerable shifts over time in the tax arrangements for both imputed rent and mortgage relief. Perhaps the most frequent shift has been with the treatment of imputed rent where the catalyst for change has often arisen because this type of taxation 'entails logistical and political problems' (Wood, 1990, p. 46). Taxing imputed rent requires some bureaucratic system, which may itself be difficult and expensive to administer, of assessing notional income. In practice the assessments may be periodic and, given the general tendency for values to rise, at any one time they are likely to be at levels below current market values, and since current expenditures may be allowed against liability, the overall yield for the government may be fairly low. Indeed, because of any exemptions that may be allowed, the imputed net rent may be a negative amount. Moreover, the tax can be a difficult one to justify politically in the sense both that it can be interpreted as unfair to tax people for something that they have worked hard to achieve and that, unlike say shares or businesses the acquisition of which is optional, people have to have housing. In the context of these problems Australia, France, Ireland, the United Kingdom and West Germany have all abandoned imputed rent taxation in the postwar era.

There have also been other ways in which owner-occupied housing has been treated for tax purposes. In many countries any capital gains on the value of an asset, such as shares or works of art, are liable to tax but, in general, this does not apply to a household's principal residence. In some countries capital gains are taxable but liability may be offset in specified circumstances. In the USA, the tax can be deferred provided that the gain realized from the sale of one house is used in the purchase of a more expensive house. In Sweden, capital gains can be set against any improvement expenditures. In Spain, households moving to another owner-occupied house are exempt.

In addition to subsidies operating through the tax system, in some countries home owners, along with renters, may enjoy a subsidy in the form of a housing allowance. Sweden is a case in point. Here, home owners can obtain an allowance based, on the one hand, on their income and family size and, on the other, on their housing costs with account taken of tax relief. Elsewhere, this type of subsidy, to be discussed in detail later in the present chapter, may take the form of a cash payment which will have the result of enhancing the ability of the household to meet its housing costs. It is useful to note their existence since there is an important distinction between subsidies that assist with acquisition costs and those that assist with running or occupancy costs. The former refer to those costs that are incurred in the initial purchase of the dwelling; they are all non-recurring and include legal costs, estate agent fees, and the purchase price, perhaps converted into mortgage interest and principal repayments. The latter include all those costs incurred in renewing the physical fabric and in meeting local taxes and utility charges. In those countries in which the balance of subsidies is tilted towards acquisition costs – as in the UK – the overall effect will be to encourage households at the margin to purchase newer properties and to discourage maintenance and improvement.

Finally, it is also common for governments to impose charges on owners. Some countries have systems whereby a property tax is levied on a recurrent basis. This is generally used to finance local authority expenditure and may be based loosely on the market value of the property. Non-recurrent taxes, such as a sales tax, are also frequently levied. Actually, such charges may or may not be specific to owner occupiers. Clearly, however, they do impact on the cost–income gap.

Social housing

Supply-side subsidies

Social housing has been commonly subsidized through the supply side as part of state strategies, particularly in the early postwar period, to increase the rate of new construction. The following details of national systems, taken from Oxley (1993), indicate that within any one country a variety of subsidies and institutions has often been established. In some countries, subsidies commonly take the form of financial help: low-interest loans, tax deductions and non-repayable grants. In other countries, however, the assistance has been through the other factors of production: cheap land or professional expertise, for example.

Portugal has a small social rented sector (some 4 per cent of the stock) which is provided and managed by a public body (IGAPHE). This receives finance from the National Institute of Housing in the form of a subsidy of 50 per cent of the costs of operation and of production loans at 7 per cent interest over 25 years. Rents, however, are calculated according to people's means. Individuals wishing to become home owners may receive help from two sources: from municipalities, which provide and partially prepare land and offer architectural advice; and from housing cooperatives, which provide state-subsidized loans.

In Italy there are four different ways in which social housing is provided and subsidized. The Autonomous Institutions for Social Housing (IACPS), which are public bodies operating at the provincial level, may, along with communes, receive state grants to enable them to build or rehabilitate social housing. Private individuals wishing to provide social housing for rent may draw upon funds accumulated from employee and employer, salary-related contributions which may amount to 75 per cent of the construction costs. The remaining 25 per cent is available as a government grant. Construction companies and housing cooperatives building new social housing or wishing to buy up existing stock for social renting may receive state loans. Private individuals buying existing homes, which they intend to occupy themselves, may also be in receipt of subsidized loans.

In Belgium, social housing is built and managed by public service building companies. Four state credit institutions issue them with loans at low rates of interest providing that the homes are to be let to households of specified types and income levels. They may also receive lump-sum grants. The French system also relies on subsidy. The social housing organizations (HLMs), as well as private individuals, may receive low-interest loans repayable over 35 years for the purposes of both new construction and, in the case of the HLMs, rehabilitation. As in Italy, there is also a fund, which is based on work-based contributions and may be used to supplement other loans, the '1% patronal' scheme, taking contributions from all employers with a workforce in excess of 10 people, equivalent, in its original form, to 1 per cent of the gross wage bill.

Rent setting arrangements

One of the consequences of providing supply-side subsidies is that social landlords are able to offer tenancies at rents below both what would have been market levels and the real costs of production. In general governments have not offered subsidies to landlords without some corresponding restriction on the rents they are allowed to charge. In this way the subsidy has, at least in part, been passed on to households such that the amount and quality of the housing they consume exceeds their ability to pay for it. In practice there are a number of different ways in which rent levels can be determined. There may also be differences between the rent setting principles for each of three stages in the lifecycle of an individual dwelling: for first time lettings, periodic revisions of existing tenancies and where there has been a change of tenancy.

Government at the national or local level may determine rent ceilings, which may in some way be related to market rents in the uncontrolled sectors or to a level that provides landlords with sufficient rent just to be able to meet their costs or even to make a small return on their capital. If the ceiling or break-even rents increase over time with general price inflation, a situation may develop where new lettings have very much higher rents than older lettings even though their quality, location and size may not be superior. This could have the consequence of reducing the desirability to households of new dwellings so that additional construction is deterred. A solution in cases where landlords have a portfolio of properties of varying ages is rent pooling. This involves combining the provision costs of all the dwellings and charging rents that reflect the desirability of individual dwellings but, when summed across all the dwellings, do not provide the landlord with an 'excessive' profit. In some countries there are very different rent setting procedures. Thus, in Belgium and Canada, rent levels are related to the number of dependants in the household and its income so that the rents for neighbouring and identical apartments can be different.

Demand-side subsidies

In general these take the form of housing allowances which are subsidies paid to households. The amount of the subsidy may be decided in relation to household income and the housing costs that they face. The general model is for the allowance to increase with housing costs and decrease with income. The allowance may be varied according to household composition or some group characteristic such as head of household age. The historical context of the introduction of housing allowances was frequently the inconsistencies that arose as governments relaxed rent control, with problems arising in particular where rents were related to historic costs of production since rents for newer properties would be very much higher than rents for older ones. Housing allowances could thus be seen to compensate individuals for the adverse consequences of the cross subsidies which this imposed.

In practice there are wide variations in the detail of housing allowance systems. One area of variation concerns the comprehensiveness of the definition of housing costs against which the allowance is assessed. The rent itself may include, in addition to the costs incurred by the landlord in repaying the loan taken to fund the construction of the physical fabric, amounts to cover the cost of furniture, fittings, heating and other utility charges, property taxes, management costs including an allowance for writing off rent arrears, and the costs of communal services such as street lighting. The concept of 'cold' and 'hot' rents, where the latter includes heating costs, neatly encapsulates the elasticity of the definition of housing costs and the variability of the real significance of housing allowances in different national settings. In addition, a government which retained the same housing allowance system could, by altering the eligible costs, radically change its impact. Other variations across countries include those, such as Britain, where 100 per cent of the rent may be met and the majority of countries where some proportion must be paid from the tenant's own resources. There may also be different rules operating for different categories of person, say older people or students.

Private renting

Supply-side subsidies

The most common practice in industrialized countries is to tax the rental income received by private landlords. Insofar as this is consistent with taxation of profits or dividends from other investments it will have no effect on the level of rent that landlords would seek in order to give them a reasonable return on their investment. Likewise, a tax on any capital gains made by a private landlord is levied in most advanced countries. There are exceptions: in France, for example, landlords who let only one dwelling are exempted, while in West Germany the practice has been to exempt them once the dwelling had been owned for two years. There are also variations in the way gains are computed with the clearest distinction being between real and nominal gains.

In addition to these exemptions, in many cases landlords are able to set specified costs against their tax liability. The first of these is depreciation costs. Without further injections of capital, dwellings become relatively less valuable and, in any case, will have a limited lifespan. Generally, national governments have recognized this through the tax rules imposed on landlords. The OECD has summarized some of the arrangements:

> In France and the Netherlands, gross rental income is subject to a 15 per cent flat rate deduction for depreciation throughout the life of the property. This is a more generous rate than is applied to industrial and commercial assets. In the United States, the treatment of depreciation is a key source of investment financing. The rules in this area, which were already highly concessionary, were eased still further with the adoption of the Accelerated Cost Recovery System (ACRS) in 1981. The period of depreciation of housing investment is normally 20 years... In Germany, housing completed after 27 July 1981 is subject to a generous degressive depreciation rate of 5 per cent for the first 8 years, 2.5 per cent for the next 6 years, and 1.5 per cent for the ensuing 36 years. The United Kingdom is unusual in treating housing as an asset with an infinite life for tax purposes and allowing no deductions for depreciation. (1988, p. 70)

Operating costs are also frequently allowed against tax. In many countries landlords are allowed to deduct the costs of mortgage interest payments, repairs and maintenance, management expenses and insurance. Insofar as such deductions are allowed with respect to other business income, they may not be deemed to constitute subsidies. There is variation in national practice in situations where the deductions exceed rental income. In some countries – Canada and Germany, for example –

the excess may be put against other income; in others it may not. Finally, an investment premium may be permitted. In some countries, for example France and the USA, specific tax deductions are allowed with the intention of encouraging investment.

Rent control

Whereas in many countries the tax treatment of private landlords may appear relatively favourable with respect to businesses generally, during some if not most of the last eighty years they have faced restrictions on the rents they could charge. Often in times of shortage, such as in the aftermath of the two world wars, governments have imposed regulations with the intention of preventing the achievement of market prices which reflected the then current levels of scarcity. At the point in time when rent controls are imposed they constitute a subsidy for tenants who face a lower user cost. While the subsidy is provided as a result of state intervention its cost is incurred by landlords so that the gap between real and user cost is met by landlords. In the long run, when rented dwellings may have been taken into new ownership or new rented properties are brought onto the market, the capital price at which they are exchanged should incorporate the existence of rent control.

There are different ways of imposing controls. These will be examined in more detail in Chapter Eleven, but important is the extent to which controls recognize the mobility of capital and, in turn, that failure to allow investors a reasonable return will have consequences for the long-run viability of the sector.

Demand-side subsidies

As with social housing, in most countries tenants of private landlords may be eligible to housing allowances. Belgium and France are exceptions (Román *et al.*, 1994). Broadly, the same sorts of variation as apply to social housing subsidies also apply to private rental housing.

The volume and distribution of subsidies

A description of the principles which make up the structure of national housing subsidy systems provides an essential, but incomplete, picture. Also important are considerations of who receives the subsidies, that is

Table 8.1 Distribution of housing subsidies

	Direct plus indirect housing subsidies in per cent of GNP		Proportion of direct plus indirect housing subsidies (%)	
	1980	**1988**	**1980**	**1988**
Sweden				
Housing Allowances	1.14	0.73	30	21
Property Subsidies	0.95	1.28	25	37
Tax Subsidies	1.72	1.48	45	42
Denmark				
Housing Allowances	0.38	0.39		
Property Subsidies	0.45	0.43		
Tax Subsidies				
Great Britain				
Housing Allowances		1.14		42
Property Subsidies		0.36		13
Tax Subsidies	0.98	1.23		45
West Germany				
Housing Allowances	0.12	0.17		23
Property Subsidies		0.18		24
Tax Subsidies		0.40		53
Netherlands				
Housing Allowances	0.29	0.40	12	11
Property Subsidies	1.02	1.91	40	54
Tax Subsidies	1.21	1.23	48	35
Belgium				
Housing Allowances		0.01		
Property Subsidies		0.23		
Tax Subsidies				
France				
Housing Allowances	0.13	0.32	10	24
Property Subsidies	0.57	0.45	43	34
Tax Subsidies	0.64	0.55	48	42
Finland				
Housing Allowances	0.41	0.33	28	22
Property Subsidies	0.57	0.48	40	32
Tax Subsidies	0.46	0.66	32	43
Norway				
Housing Allowances	0.16	0.14		
Property Subsidies	0.32	0.28		
Tax Subsidies				

Source: Román *et al.*, (1994) p. 134.

which groups – defined by location, income, age or other character-istic – receive subsidies and which do not. The values of the subsidies are also part of the picture. The total amount indicates the overall finan-cial contribution by the state to the housing sector, providing a measure of the importance of housing relative to other collective goods. The relative shares of the subsidy – by tenure or household type – provide yet another perspective. Unfortunately, much of this information is not available for many industrialized countries so that a systematic comparison of the full subsidy picture in each country is not possible. Papa (1992) and Román *et al.* (1994) have assembled some data but these are limited to a half a dozen or so countries located in western and northern Europe. Overall, then, these provide only very partial pictures of the volume and nature of housing subsidies. The current state of systematically collated knowledge is limited; explanations for the national differences, even more so.

The evidence available shows that the total volume of subsidies varies considerably from one country to another. In the Netherlands and Sweden all subsidies together in 1988 amounted to around three and a half per cent of GNP. The percentage in West Germany is less than a quarter of that level. Although Table 8.1 does not provide the full infor-mation for Belgium and Norway, they too seem to have subsidies which are low by volume. It is also clear that there have been variations over time with the 1980s being characterized in some countries by an overall decrease (Sweden) and in some an increase (the Netherlands).

Existing evidence also indicates the extent to which subsidies are enjoyed universally or are restricted. In Sweden almost all new residen-tial construction attracts property subsidies, and although in some countries such as the Netherlands, France and Norway the proportion is more like two-thirds, elsewhere, such as England and West Germany, it is considerably lower (see Table 8.2). In contrast, in England a far higher proportion of households is in receipt of housing allowances than in any of the other countries for which information is recorded. Although the statistical coverage is extremely limited it does at least indicate that the existence of seemingly similar subsidy arrangements may have very different coverage in different countries.

Table 8.2 Percentage in receipt of subsidies in 1988

Country	Property Subsidies	Housing Allowances
Belgium	53.2	–
Denmark	28.9	14.7
England	14.2	41.1**
Finland	–	5.0*
France	63.0	7.2*
Netherlands	62.7	9.1
Norway	58.6	10.0*
Sweden	99.5	21.1
West Germany	18.6	6.8

* refers to 1987
** Housing allowance figure for Great Britain

Source: Román *et al.*, (1994), pp. 126, 128.

Retrenchment

Peter Kemp (1990) is one of a number of researchers who has pointed out that over the last two decades or so there has been a general tendency, across the economically advanced countries, to shift from producer to consumer subsidies. In explanation, he refers to a number of inter-related processes. First, whereas in the immediate aftermath of the Second World War many governments established producer subsidies as a way of generating the rapid building necessary to make good the shortages, by the 1970s the worst of the shortages had in most places been eliminated. The perception of the policy problem shifted away from new construction towards ensuring that the gap between rents and incomes did not widen. The problem, then, was seen not as one of housing as such, but of the ability to pay so that the solutions were 'more likely to be income supplements tied to housing than subsidies for those who produced housing' (Kemp, 1990, p. 21).

Second, the shift in perceptions of the problem occurred during a period when many national governments saw that they were facing budget deficits so that the ending of the long period of postwar economic growth was associated with forces for the retrenchment of welfare states. When cutting public expenditure in general came to be viewed as a policy goal, housing was often particularly vulnerable, in part because any cuts would not have a wide and immediate impact, since the existing stock would continue to meet the housing needs of the bulk of the population. But, it was also because a shift to consumer subsidies could be packaged as providing protection for those on low incomes. In some countries there was a third re-orientation of the policy making context in that markets were seen increasingly as the best way of responding to consumer wants. On this view, the relaxation of rent controls and the reduction of supply-side subsidies, combined with income-related subsidies, more closely aligned housing with the free market ideal.

The comments above could be taken as evidence that there has over the last two decades or so been a convergence of subsidy policy following from the wider economic changes impacting on industrialized countries. Whereas the observation that the balance of national housing subsidy systems have tipped toward housing allowances has gained prominence in the 1980s and 90s, in many countries the first tipping of the balance occurred somewhat earlier. According to Michael Oxley (1987) they were introduced in France in 1948 while in the Netherlands a rent subsidy was first introduced in 1901, with a major recasting occurring in 1970. Denmark has had a system since 1967, West Germany since 1965 and Britain a national scheme since 1972.

In addition to the timing differences, Kemp, in any case, makes it clear that it is by no means universal. He notes:

> For example, neither Italy nor Switzerland provide housing allowances. Belgium does not have a general system of rent allowances. In Austria there is no general system of housing allowances but a rent supplement is payable in cases where rent increases are excessive and likely to cause hardship. (1990, pp. 22–3)

At the same time, even where housing allowances have become more important they may have been restricted. Thus in many countries, housing allowances are confined to renters. In others, certain groups in the population, for example pensioners and students, are separated out for different treatment. However, the widely reported observation that typically industrialized countries were pursuing a strategy of shifting from supply-side to consumer-side subsidies, taken as evidence of privatization, is empirically testable. It is possible to investigate whether the financial support in the form of housing allowances has grown while subsidies to housing production have shrunk. In this way, the approach could be 'to use housing allowances as a universal indicator of the extent to which housing policy still recognises social responsibility' (Tanninen, 1995, p. 1). While not presenting the data upon which his analyses are based, Tanninen concludes that the pattern of national developments is considerably more complicated than generally thought:

> housing allowance has increased during the 1980s in countries like Holland, France, Denmark and Germany. All the more surprisingly, it has decreased in countries like Sweden, Finland and Great Britain. In other OECD-countries no remarkable changes can be observed. (1995, p. 11)

Actually, the evidence presented elsewhere (Román *et al.*, 1994) at the same time as confirming the variation across countries in the trends in the relative size of housing allowance subsidies, also indicates that the group of countries in which housing allowances increased and the group in which they decreased do not exactly match Tanninen's conclusions.

In addition to these housing allowance developments over the last decades, there have in some countries been developments in the ways in which governments treat home owners; developments which seem to indicate the importance of political considerations. In short, crises in home ownership markets have sometimes been responded to by concessions introduced by national governments, resulting in large redistributions towards home owners. Canada provides an example where such responses occurred early:

> Political pressure on government from would-be home buyers and from the residential construction industry forced the creation of a string of expensive short-term subsidy programs through the 1970s and during the early 1980s... The government invented six new forms of primarily short-term subsidies in the 1970s and four in the early 1980s. (Hulchanski, 1990, p. 306)

In the Canadian case the crises followed from high house price inflation which reduced both the ability of middle-income groups to enter home ownership and, thus, the potential sales by house builders. The new subsidies included exemption from capital gains, a savings scheme for renters who needed a down payment in order to purchase, grants and loans for rehabilitation by existing owners, interest-rate subsidies, and cash grants to would-be buyers. Whereas these measures were popular, they were also expensive and, moreover, provided most assistance to those on middle and higher incomes. They provide evidence, therefore, for the view that social policy does not necessarily follow from the welfare needs of those with the lowest incomes. Most significant of all, however, is that the market developments were perceived as impacting on the electoral position of the party in power so that the programmes were 'an inevitable part of the political process' (Hulchanski, 1990, p. 306).

Evidence of what appears to have been politically motivated developments with respect to home ownership is to be found in some other countries. Thus, in the Netherlands during the period 1977 to 1981 the government set out a programme to curb public expenditure on housing which also entailed encouraging the sale of privately rented housing and the expansion of the home ownership sector. Within just a few years, however, rising unemployment and rising interest rates made greater reliance on home ownership unsustainable, and the government responded by increasing subsidies for rental housing production (Priemus, 1987). In Britain, in 1991, the government introduced a series of measures with the objective of breathing life into a market in which prices had slumped dramatically at the end of the 1980s with consequences in terms of record levels of mortgage arrears, repossessions and negative equity. These included the temporary suspension of stamp duty which is payable as a one-off tax when a house is purchased. One year later they provided funds to enable housing associations to purchase vacant, owner-occupied dwellings, creating a form of de-privatization, but also increasing the level of demand. The fact that in 1991 and 1992 the government was receiving considerable criticism, since its policies appeared to be responsible for the slump in the market, and that 1992 was a general election year, may have been connected with the policy innovations.

Conclusions

Many actions by governments have direct or indirect impacts upon the ability of households to pay for housing. Some of these impacts may make housing less affordable in that they increase the gap between incomes and costs. In many cases, however, the reverse will be true, and the term subsidy can be used to refer to a narrowing of the gap as a result of government action. In most countries subsidies operate both through the supply side by lowering user costs and through the demand side by increasing the ability to pay. Also, in most countries subsidies are tenure specific. Beyond those statements it is difficult to construct generalizations. In part this is because, as evident elsewhere in the book, the comparative literature has not been greatly developed. Quite a lot is known, and appears in the literature, about subsidies in many of the individual industrialized countries, but there have been few attempts to examine across individual countries upon which a comparative analysis could be built. Even where comparisons are explicit, the common patterns are not necessarily clear, as Papa concludes in a useful study of the subsidy arrangements in seven European countries:

> On first sight, the comparative analysis reveals numerous similarities in the way the financial instruments are formulated. ... Each country has some form of individual subsidy as well as forms of property subsidy. ... But when the comparison goes into greater detail, major differences emerge... the systems cannot be compared unconditionally. The coverage of the system, amount of expenditure, and form of subsidy are a few highly diverse aspects. (1992, p. 177)

In part, it is also because the evidence, particularly in relation to the developments in different countries over the last two decades, suggests both convergence and divergence and policy driven both by economic changes as well as by political considerations.

9

Home Ownership

In many industrialized countries tenure is one of the most significant dimensions of housing and housing policy. It is through tenure that issues of achievement and failure are frequently discussed. In the literature, that produced both by individual researchers writing at the level of their own country and by international organizations writing and comparing across countries, reference to and analysis of tenure is common place. So, in one country tenure developments over time are studied, whereas for a number of countries their patterns of tenure are compared, perhaps as the basis of some categorization. Texts on housing policy are invariably organized, at least in part, around tenure chapters. In short, tenure figures everywhere, and the literature to be drawn on is consequently more plentiful than for many other aspects of housing policy. Although it is everywhere, tenure does not provide a complete picture. Tenure describes the way in which real property is held and consumed. In Figure 3.1, tenure relates to stage 3 only, so that much that happens in production and re-production (maintenance and renovation) can happen independently of tenure (though this does not mean that it does not have consequences for tenure). But, in itself, the way in which housing is produced – by small or large company, speculatively or non-speculatively and so on – may not bear any direct relation with its subsequent use.

In this, and the following two chapters, aspects of tenure are considered. The present chapter begins with an issue, which was introduced in Chapter Two, about the variable meanings of concepts, in this case the concept of tenure. It goes on to consider explanations for the developments in the postwar period in home ownership sectors.

The meaning of home ownership

The main analytical challenge arises not so much because tenure provides a partial picture so much as the picture is shifting and non-uniform. As Peter Marcuse puts it: 'lines between ownership and rental, private and public, are often fuzzy' (1994, p. 21). This fuzziness is partly because of the multidimensional nature of tenure. If we refer to home ownership, we refer to a concept of great complexity with meanings on many different levels. As a legal entity, home ownership provides the owner with certain rights and responsibilities. Perhaps these include the right to live in the dwelling, to decorate it to the taste of the owner, to keep domestic pets, to sub-let and so on; but perhaps not the right to alter the physical structure, or to change its usage (maybe to a shop). So, home ownership (throughout this book used synonymously with owner occupation), or indeed any other tenure form, may be thought of as a bundle of legal rights. But, at the social level home ownership might mean entirely different things: status, independence, pride, individualism and achievement; while, at the economic level, the meanings might be investment, financial burden, collateral, and security.

Even having simply listed some of the rights and characteristics sometimes associated with the concept of home ownership, it may be clear that the concept is temporally and spatially contingent. Within any one country changes in the home ownership market over the last decade, for example, may have had the effect of adapting what ownership means. The developments, discussed later in the present chapter, which have resulted in depressed housing markets, falling prices, widespread repayment problems and so on, may have changed notions, associated with home ownership, of investment and status into those of loss and failure. So, what home ownership means in Denmark or France in the 1990s may not necessarily mean the same as it did in the 1980s. Comparisons between one time period and another may simply not be concerned with the same concept so that we may think that we are referring to the same phenomenon, when in reality its meaning – what we associate with it as characteristics – has altered in ways that are more or less significant.

But, there are also large differences between countries. In the English-speaking countries – the USA, Canada, Australia and the UK – as well as some others – Belgium and Finland, for example – home ownership is generally seen as a prize or a dream, something to be aspired to, and something achieved by the more (financially) successful groups in society. In terms of status, legal rights and investment, home ownership has been seen as offering significant advantages over renting. Indeed, those living in social housing are frequently stigmatized. Aspects of this multifaceted and positive picture may be recognized in other countries. There are, however, examples of home ownership in some countries which have very different characteristics.

In Iceland, home ownership exceeds 80 per cent of the entire stock. Much of it, particularly outside the larger settlements where the proportion may be even higher, is produced using pre-industrial modes of production in the sense that couples setting up dwelling arrangements independently of parents may acquire land and obtain the labour of fellow members of their community who give of their time and expertise as part of wider social arrangements. There is here a form of community build. Home ownership is produced in this way, not because it is an investment or a prize, but because it is the way it has been for centuries. In addition, about 6 per cent of the home ownership stock could be described as amounting to a form of social, home ownership. Access is means tested and state loans repayable at 1 per cent are available, so that it is specifically reserved for low-income groups. It thus fulfils a function within the housing system which in many other countries is met by forms of rental housing (Sveinsson, 1992). Even within one country, therefore, the meaning of home ownership can vary. Finland, also, has a large home ownership sector, but much of this also takes forms that would not be immediately recognizable in, for example, the USA or Australia. A large part of the sector takes the organizational form of housing companies where the owner occupiers of individual apartments in a single building share some of the facilities – perhaps the sauna, rest room and laundry – as well as some of the responsibilities – such as maintenance and the cleaning rota (Ruonavaara, 1987). In addition, much of the home ownership stock has been provided with the assistance of state (ARAVA) loans, which are provided on preferential financial terms, but are means and needs tested (in relation to household income and composition) and not available on dwellings above specified prices. These loans might also be deemed to have some social housing characteristics. In the USA, mobile homes have taken a major segment of the housing market. Factory produced, they differ from conventional dwellings in a number of significant respects. They are not subject to the same building regulations governing materials and facilities. They do not attract conventional mortgage finance. The homes have a short life and, far from being investments with an expectation of increasing values, they have value trajectories more like consumer durables. So, owning a mobile home has very different connotations to owning traditional real estate (Ball *et al.*, 1988). In France the Ribot Act of 1908, which set the 'precedent for state subsidies for housing' (Emms, 1990, p. 65) applied to home owners only. After the Second World War this lead was followed by more and more generous subsidies for home owners. As Power (1993) has pointed out: '[w]ithin the social housing movement, there were powerful advocates of owner occupation' (p. 65). As well as loans and grants, low-income home owners could receive housing allowances. Much of the housing built for owner occupation – as much as a quarter of the postwar total – was initially occupied by working-class rather than white-collar households.

Structures of housing provision

Once home ownership in different countries is examined in detail it becomes clear, therefore, that the label is used to describe many different forms of housing. In the words of Ball *et al.*:

> it can be seen that there are not universal forms of provision whose efficacy can be analysed through international comparison of their operation. Cross-country comparison of tenure, one of the bread-and-butter subjects of comparative research, must be aware that distinct structures of provision are being examined even though they exist within apparently common tenure forms. (1988, p. 30)

Their view is that tenure should be approached by way of the concept of structures of housing provision which specify the nature of, and interconnections between, the social agents involved in the provision of housing. These social agents include developers, builders, land owners, consumers and financiers (all of whom can be located at appropriate places in Figure 3.1) linked together by social, economic and political ties. Tenure can thus be described through an audit of the social relations of provision. On this view, there is a wide spread of patterns of social relations across industrialized countries, so that tenure itself is not a uniform phenomenon. Moreover, the structures of housing provision can be seen to have developed considerably over time. Within any one country the shifts can be considerable and arise out of wide social, economic and political forces: 'the changes are not consequences of government policy but of shifts in the nature or role of agencies within a process of provision and the subsequent reaction of others to those changes' (Ball *et al.*, 1988, p. 30). In turn, the consequences of a myriad of forces, continually acting and re-acting and reformulating relationships are those of continual change, so that 'structures of housing provision never stay constant' (p. 30). Tenure concepts, including those of home ownership, are therefore both spatially and temporally contingent.

This can also be taken to mean that the perceived advantages and disadvantages of tenure forms are also contingent. Thus, with respect to home ownership there could be structures of provision where 'central planning by state agencies, a nationalised building industry, and state ownership of land [meant that] the provision of housing would not necessarily be unstable, nor would home owners benefit from capital gains' (Hayward, 1986, p. 213). One result could be that home owners actually had fewer advantages than did social housing tenants. It should not necessarily be assumed, as much housing analysis currently does, that those in some tenures, generally home ownership, are in a preferential and privileged position.

The conclusion that tenure is contingent has important implications for comparative analysis because it throws open the whole question of the value of tenure as a classificatory aid. The issue has been posed by Ruonavaara:

> If the content of tenures as bundles of rights and duties is wholly determined by historically specific institutional and social arrangements there is little point in trying to classify them into a single typology. A category such as 'owner occupation' would denote to such a bewildering variety of nationally specific tenure forms having little in common that it would confuse more than clarify. (1992, p. 4)

So, the label 'home ownership' provides an example of the way, as discussed in Chapter Two, that language can confuse by providing a single understanding for a variable phenomenon. In the literature there are three main responses to this. The first approach, by far the most common, is to ignore the contingent nature of tenure and to undertake research as if there was no issue to address. There can be a number of reasons for taking this position. Researchers may be unaware of the issue, that is that they are not aware that the concept is problematic; they may disagree with the view that it is problematic; or, they may have adopted a pragmatic response that alternative concepts and labels are difficult to construct. The second response consists of finding ways to analyse housing in which structures of provision are explicitly explored with the result that the complexity and contingency of tenure

is recognized. The third involves attempts to identify common characteristics of tenure forms which can be taken to constitute inherent
features. The second and third responses are discussed below.

Tenure characteristics as contingent

The introductory chapter of one book on comparative housing lays out
the case for viewing tenure as contingent:

> Most forms of housing provision prevalent in advanced capitalist countries have
> changed in significant ways over the past 40 years... Changes in the nature of
> housing provision, therefore must be part of the explanation of shifts in housing
> policies and subsidies. (Ball *et al.*, 1988, p. 36)

The remaining chapters of their book are set out in ways that are
largely consistent with this. Thus the chapter on home ownership traces
the characteristics and developments in each of the six countries under
review, drawing systematically on comparable data, but emphasizing
the inter-country differences and similarities.

Another study, more limited in scope, starts from the observation
that there exists a correlation between high rates of unemployment and
high levels of mortgage default experienced by home owners in
Britain, USA and Germany (Doling, 1990c). But, in Finland this link
did not exist. High rates of unemployment appeared to have little
impact on the ability of people to meet their housing loans. The
analysis was based on a schema which facilitated examination of key
differences in the system of home ownership in Finland compared with
the other countries. This showed that many home owners in Finland
had built their own homes and even where they had bank loans the
repayment period was short; the Finnish home owner had been relatively unexposed to unemployment; the welfare system provided a
strong safety net; and the banks were prepared to reschedule loan
repayments. Altogether this painted a picture of home ownership that
differed greatly from that in the other countries examined. A recognition of the contingent nature of the characteristics and advantages of
home ownership thus aided explanation.

A more systematic examination of home ownership has been carried
out by Barlow and Duncan (1988) who note that not only does the
meaning of tenure change over time and space, but that there has been
a confusion among housing researchers between tenure as a statistical
label which describes a bundle of housing rights and tenure as corre-

sponding with 'significant break-points in concrete real world categories like housing class, social status, or financing mechanisms' (p. 219). There has, in their words, been an 'elision between taxonomic and substantive collectives' (p. 221) which may have relevance in some 'political cultures where they were originally used – Britain, North America and Australasia – but they have much less meaning in other countries' (p. 222). In other countries other substantive shorthands – flat/non-flat and urban/rural may have more significance. Their solution to what they see as the inappropriateness and ethnocentricity of tenure 'is to drop the search for some single universal housing shorthand' (p. 226). The researcher is urged to consider first what, exactly, is the substantive question and then to devise or use appropriate taxonomic concepts. Tenure may be one of those, on its own or in combination with others, but it should not retain its present, privileged status. Their own explorations of this proposal in the context of an interest in the ways in which states finance housing provision demonstrates how more complex categorizations can provide a richer and more diverse picture than that provided by tenure alone.

Tenure characteristics as inherent

Several authors, while recognizing the specificity of the characteristics of home ownership, have attempted to identify which of its characteristics might be non-contingent, that is inherent in the tenure. Thus Whitehead (1979) argues that although many of the putative advantages of home ownership are actually correlates of income, with tenure constituting an intervening variable, there were some characteristics that could not be disassociated from tenure. Likewise, Saunders argues that home ownership 'offers inherent rights of use, control and disposal' (1990, p. 99). He adds that they are not unlimited, and 'some of them may also be enjoyed to some extent by tenants' (p. 99). Nevertheless, they are inherent because although it would be possible for them to be removed by legislation, to do so would be destroy the tenure, to be 'tantamount to abolishing private property ownership itself' (p. 99) so that it is not the case that all the 'current advantages could be removed while still leaving the tenure intact, for many of its key advantages are synonymous with its legal status as private property' (p. 100). It is, for Saunders, the merits of these intrinsic rights as well as any other contingent advantages of ownership that give ownership its attraction to many households.

Ruonavaara (1992) furthers the argument by proposing that a distinction should be recognized between types and forms of tenure, the first general and the second specific. His types are based on a restricted view of tenures as modes of possession. From this he recognizes two ideal types: owner occupation and renting. These constitute the two 'institutions through which rights of possession are accommodated with rights of ownership' (p. 9) and, expressed as ideal types, incorporate the mode of possession but separate this from all other aspects linked to tenure such as forms of promotion and finance. These historical and spatially specific characteristics are described by forms of housing tenure and include the specific institutional arrangements such as housing companies, housing associations, public housing and so on. Examining tenure at these two levels enables the use of the ideal types as categories through which cross-national comparisons can be conducted as well as a 'means of organising the inquiry into real forms of tenure observable in historic societies' (p. 13).

Statistical trends

Following the Ruonavaara position we can turn to an examination of some of the broad trends and differences that have occurred in home ownership sectors. One dimension of this examination is that of growth. Along with demographic growth and increasing economic prosperity in all industrialized countries in the postwar era, there have been increases in their housing stocks. It has not just been a case of increasing numbers of dwellings per 1000 population, but household units have generally become smaller in size as birth rates have dropped, extended family networks weakened, and more adults live on their own. But any increase in the absolute size of national housing stocks has been more than matched by the increase in their home ownership sectors. Table 9.1 indicates that in all the countries recorded – with the exception of Japan and Canada – there was, over the period up to 1990, an increase in the relative size of the sector. It is true that in some countries, during some decades, there were actually decreases in the relative size of home ownership. Nevertheless, over the long run, home ownership has become statistically more dominant in most advanced countries. The extent of this dominance is recorded in the statistics for the 11 countries in Table 9.1 which have home ownership rates recorded for both 1960 and 1990. In 1960 the average size of the sector was about 48 per cent. By 1990 this had grown to 58 per cent, so that, on average, the owner-occupied sectors in these 11 countries had, over the 30 years, increased their share by about a fifth, and the average household in these industrialized countries had come to be a home owner.

Within these averages there are some important variations. First, Table 9.1 indicates that the rate of increase varied considerably from country to country. It was by far the highest in the UK, where the increase from 1945 to 1990 was almost 40 percentage points; but, it was also high in Australia, Austria, Belgium, Ireland, and Italy. In a number of countries, in particular West Germany and Switzerland, the owner-occupied sectors have increased hardly at all. By contrast, we know from the case study in Chapter One that, whereas in Japan there was a large-scale shift towards home ownership after 1945, Table 9.1 suggests that the size of the home ownership sector had peaked by 1960 only to decline subsequently. Second, in some countries the increase in owner occupation has petered out with the appearance – in Australia, the USA, Denmark, Switzerland and Sweden, for example – of having reached a plateau. However, the plateaux are at different heights so that they do not represent a universal law about a saturation level for owner occupation.

Table 9.1 The postwar growth of home ownership

	Percentage share of total stock by year				
	1945/50	*1960*	*1970*	*1980*	*1990*
Australia	53	63	67	71	70*
Austria	36	38	41	48	55
Belgium	39	50	55	59	63
Canada	66	66	60	62	64
Denmark	–	43	49	52	51
France	–	41	45	51	54
Finland	–	57	59	61	67
Greece	–	–	–	70	77
Ireland	–	–	71	76	81
Italy	40	45	50	59	67
Japan	–	71	59	62	61
Netherlands	28	29	35	42	44
Norway	–	–	53	59	59
Portugal	–	–	–	57	58
Spain	–	–	64	73	76
Sweden	38	36	35	41	42
Switzerland	–	–	28	30	30
UK	29	42	49	56	68
USA	57	64	65	68	64
West Germany	–	–	36	40	38

* 1985

Source: Hägred (1994) Table 6; Oxley (1993) for Belgium in 1990.

This leads in to the third variation apparent from Table 9.1: the current levels of home ownership vary considerably across industrialized countries. Ireland has an owner-occupation rate of around 80 per cent, with Greece and Spain just a few percentage points behind. There are a cluster of countries – Australia, Italy, Britain and Finland – with between 65 and 75 per cent. Next are Japan, Canada, and United States all with 60 per cent or more, while at the lower end of the distribution West Germany and Switzerland have two-fifths or less. The distribution of the relative size of owner-occupied sectors thus stretches right across a range from 30 per cent to 80 per cent. Even within small groups of countries with similar cultures, histories and economic development, such as the Nordic countries or those of the Iberian peninsula, there are wide differences.

Explaining variation in size

Given the existence throughout the postwar period of wide cross-country variation in the level of home ownership, as well as the apparent importance of home ownership in the lives of people in industrialized countries, a challenge for the comparative analyst is both to seek for explanations for the variation and to use the variation to search for theoretical understanding of the origins of national housing systems.

This search can begin by identifying which theoretical models are not consistent with the variation in home ownership sectors. First, it is possible to discount any marked correlation between level of home ownership and the models suggested by either David Donnison or Gosta Esping-Andersen. Donnison's 'social' housing countries included Ireland, Britain and the USA, which all have large sectors, but also Switzerland which does not. Likewise the spread of home ownership levels within Esping-Andersen's corporatist cluster (West Germany, Austria, Belgium, Italy and France) and within the social democratic cluster (Sweden, Norway, Holland and Denmark) are extremely wide. It is not possible at this broad statistical level, then, to relate home ownership to these more general taxonomies describing welfare states. It is also clear from even a rapid assessment that the size of a country's home ownership sector is not related to the level of national prosperity. It is not the case that high GDP per capita has been translated into high home ownership levels. Indeed, home ownership is often high among rural, and frequently non-industrialized, populations such as those in Ireland, Greece and Spain. It is not difficult therefore also to recognize that levels of home ownership do not appear significant in a convergence theory setting (Schmidt, 1989).

Tenure as contingent

Where, then, should the search for explanation go? One avenue which could be pursued would begin from recalling the earlier discussion about the inherent and contingent dimensions of home ownership. It is quite possible that in trying to explain variation in the level of the ideal type encapsulated in a particular mode of possession the analysis is too coarse. It is also possible that progress could be made by trying to establish significant dimensions of the other aspects of tenure – what Ruonavaara describes as the 'real forms of housing tenure observable in historic societies' (1992, p. 13). This avenue would thus recognize that home ownership may have significantly different meanings in different countries, which are not encapsulated by the statistics about relative size, but which might be correlated with measures of convergence and so on.

Ideology and political tenure strategies

A second avenue is to develop along the lines of Kemeny and his work on political tenure strategies, explored initially in Chapter Five. The presentation of these strategies has to this point been descriptive of some general processes which are deemed to lead to two family groups: those countries favouring home ownership and those favouring cost renting. In short, some countries have established legislation and institutions that have encouraged households to seek housing solutions in home ownership; some countries in cost renting. This statement begs the question, however, of the origins of each country's particular strategy: why do some countries pursue home ownership and others cost renting? For Kemeny the explanation is to be found in the wider orientation of the mode of consumption in each country. Simply, in some countries privatized modes of consumption dominate and, consistently, their housing systems will also reflect this orientation so that they will have developed home ownership sectors. In other countries, with a more collectivized dominant mode of consumption, cost renting will have been pursued. Tenure may thus reflect the more general orientation of a country along the privatization–collectivization continuum. Moreover, there is, for Kemeny, an extent to which housing and other areas of consumption become mutually reinforcing.

There is thus a strong connection between housing policy and other social policy, which occurs, in part, because housing constitutes such a large part of the 'household budget that tenure differences will have profound implications for resistance to or acceptance of public collective intervention' (Kemeny, 1992, p. 121). Any resistance may be exacerbated because the greatest burden of house purchase cost typically falls at a point in the household lifecycle that coincides with the expenses of child rearing and salaries which have not reached their maximum. The intense financial pressure which faces many households at this point perhaps acts as a downward pressure to vote for political parties that promote high social costs. So, high mortgage payments in home-owning societies influence political opposition to high tax rates and collective arrangements in other areas of welfare. Moreover, once households have passed through the high mortgage repayment stage the growth in the value of the home may have created a nest egg which the household may see as meeting its future needs, for example with respect to a pension. Kemeny saw from his comparison of Australia, Britain and Sweden that home ownership often coincided with low density, detached and semi-detached houses and cost renting with high-density apartment blocks. In the former, low density, circumstances the costs of providing collective services, such as public transport, are frequently higher.

These arguments have been stimulating in raising issues about the relationships between housing and other areas of social policy, placing them together in a symbiotic relationship, the existence of which apparently explains national tenure origins and divergence. But, they have also attracted considerable criticism. Ruonavaara (1987) argues that the privatism–collectivism distinction is rather crude, and 'somewhat original: he [Kemeny] tends to pay special attention to how consumers *pay* for housing' (emphasis in original, p. 163). The assumption seems to be that in private forms of provision the owner pays all the costs and accrues all the benefits, whereas in collective forms the costs and benefits are shared. In reality, 'the distinction between the two forms of housing consumption is a polarisation out of a continuum, and actual tenure patterns to be found in different societies can be placed somewhere between the opposites of purely privatised and purely collectivised systems of housing consumption' (p. 165). He takes specific issue based on the case of Finland where tenure cannot be as closely correlated with housing form as Kemeny found elsewhere, so that the putative processes militating against collective provision cannot operate.

Ball *et al.* (1988) add to this critique with their arguments that in practice Kemeny sees tenure 'as universally the same' (p. 33) and that referring to countries as having 'privatism' or 'collectivism' embedded in their social structures explains little. Kemeny himself has been critical of his own work and in a series of publications over the subsequent decade has further explored and developed his argument (see Kemeny, 1992). One aspect of this is 'to move away from the simplistic identification of owner occupation with privatism' (Kemeny, 1992, p. 119); to recognize, in other words, that notions of privatism and collectivism are highly complex and cannot simply be correlated with forms of tenure.

But at least some of the thrust of the Kemeny thesis has been given some support by Schmidt's statistical analysis (Schmidt, 1989). This provides evidence that home ownership cannot be explained by reference to variables describing degrees of socialist party influence in national governments. So, it does not appear possible to read off tenure strategy from political party orientation. However, his analysis does show a strong correlation ($r = 0.88$) between national home ownership rates and what Schmidt refers to as 'welfare ideological orientation', namely public welfare expenditure as a proportion of both gross national product and of total, public expenditure. Simply, the greater the extent to which countries are willing to allocate their resources to welfare consumption in such forms as family allowances, pensions, sickness benefit, and unemployment support the more they are also willing to emphasize collective forms of rental housing, with the corollary that the weaker the general welfare orientation the greater the emphasis on home ownership. The particular categorization is based of course on a continuum reflecting total commitment rather than type of commitment or recipient and a more detailed analysis relating tenure to welfare regime type might be informative. But, given this level of coarseness, Schmidt emphasizes that 'it is not very likely that the scope of public welfare determines the structure of the housing market, or vice versa' (p. 95) and thus he does not confuse correlation with causality. In other words it is not clear whether high levels of owner occupation, once established, lead, as Kemeny argues, to downward pressure on taxation and collective expenditures. Equally, both owner occupation and welfare expenditure might be heavily influenced by a third factor. The latter view – pursued by Schmidt – supports a general feature of the Kemeny thesis namely that the 'observations suggest that the structure of the housing market is affected by the same factors as public welfare in general' (p. 95) which Schmidt expresses also in the view that both 'are expressions for more fundamental social values concerning the appropriate balance between public/collective and private/individual spheres' (p. 95).

Pursuing this, Schmidt suggests that, whereas the balance of political parties, expressed as the distribution of seats in national parliaments, may change, countries may have deeper and more enduring ideological structures. These may encapsulate widespread beliefs about life goals and take linguistic form in catch phrases about home ownership: 'The Great Australian Dream', 'The American Way of Life', 'The Belgian born with a brick in his tummy', and 'The Englishman's Castle'. The point is that they have been enduring, transcending short-run developments at the political level, but continually informing the discourse of housing politics. A British, as well as comparative, perspective on this has been provided by Peter Saunders in comments about culture:

> The popularity of the twentieth century tenurial revolution in Britain is testimony to the strength of 800 years of a cultural tradition which is distinctive from that of mainland Europe. This is not to suggest that continental European cultures do not carry strong individualistic values, nor that their peoples have not desired their own homes. Before the First World War, for example, German factory workers apparently 'yearned' for small private houses of their own... however, only around 40 per cent of the West German population has even today fulfilled this yearning, and this does suggest that the desire for individual private property may run deeper in English culture than it does in the German. (1990, p. 40)

Notwithstanding some confusion evident in the juxtaposition of 'Britain' and 'English' as well as some over generalization about the tenure homogeneity of the countries of mainland Europe, the argument supports the Kemeny–Schmidt position about a relationship between tenure and underlying ideology.

Further support for some connection with ideology comes from Pooley (1992) who, summarizing case studies of 11 European countries, concludes that the housing interventions at the end of the last century were commonly motivated by desires to ensure political stability within which capitalist production could prosper. Commonly this was expressed through twin objectives:

> promotion of the single family house which was thought to engender stable family life, and the extension of home ownership which was meant to produce responsible citizens within a stable capitalist society. The two concepts were

linked in the minds of most reformers and politicians, and could be seen to have the dual function of encouraging self-help within the working classes, yet at the same time exercising a degree of social control over a potentially disruptive population. (1992, p. 333)

In Pooley's estimation these objectives constituted a tendency in most countries to encourage home ownership. It was particularly strong in Belgium where, for the politically dominant Catholics, family and property were deemed the foundation stones of society. Access to living space was essential for the promotion of traditional family values, while 'the integration of the worker into bourgeois society through the ownership of property was necessary if that society was to survive' (p. 334). State intervention designed to support these aims through the private market was strongly supported taking the form of channelling 'finance into appropriate building projects through national savings and housing banks' (p. 334). Whereas politicians had similar policy aspirations in many other countries, 'in almost all [of them] economic and political factors restricted the extent to which individual home ownership could be achieved' (p. 334).

Inflation

An entirely different avenue to these ideas is suggested, with little further elaboration, in an article in *The Economist* (1992–3). This relates levels of home ownership to inflation. It asserts:

> Historically, there has been a fairly close link between rates of home ownership and inflation: high-inflation countries tend to have the highest rates of owner-occupation... as property has been a popular hedge against rising prices. (p. 97)

The implication, therefore, is that high inflation environments have encouraged households to seek the financial security of investment in real property. It might be added that, where purchase is undertaken with the aid of a loan, high rates of inflation act quickly to reduce the burden of repayments, making buying relatively more attractive than paying rent. But, as with Schmidt's correlational analysis, it might equally be argued that the causation operates the other way: the demand for owner occupation as well as increases in house prices have had inflationary tendencies. This may particularly be the case when and where there is rapid growth of prices in the owner-occupied sector. An observation made with respect to Britain may have wider applicability:

there is a recognition that housing policy and subsidy arrangements encourage house price inflation by stoking inflationary wage demands and by encouraging higher levels of consumer expenditure. (Maclennan *et al.*, 1993, p. 12)

Retrenchment

Following a general tendency throughout the postwar period for home ownership sectors to expand in most advanced countries, the wider economic and political developments experienced over the last two decades have had, in some countries, significant consequences for policies towards home ownership.

In those advanced countries, which experienced a combination of economic sluggishness, change and high levels of unemployment, along with perceived difficulties in raising money to meet public spending, and a political shift towards more right-wing governments, early responses often took the form of placing greater emphasis on the private sector. In the case of housing, this sometimes meant home ownership. Britain is the archetypal case. The legislation in 1980, which introduced a statutory right to public housing tenants to purchase their homes, constituted a shift from collective to individualized welfare. By the end of the decade well over a million dwellings had been transferred into the home ownership sector. Such sales, though in smaller numbers, also occurred in Belgium and Ireland (Hägred, 1994) and the USA (Silver, 1990).

A different response by some governments to the economic and political situation with which they were faced in the late 1980s and early 1990s, was to reduce tax subsidies to owner occupiers. In the case of the USA, this was a side effect of reforms aimed at the system of personal taxation. As the highest marginal rate of taxation has, progressively, been reduced from 70 per cent in 1980 to 28 per cent in 1992, the monetary value of tax deductibility, with respect to mortgages and any other concession, has also been reduced. The level of the highest tax rate has also been reduced in Britain. But, some countries have introduced reforms which have been focused specifically on the house buyer. Thus, in Britain and Sweden, tax deductibility on housing loans has been limited to the lower marginal rates of income tax. In Finland and Denmark the reforms have additionally placed limits on the proportion of the mortgage that is eligible for relief. Such reforms could be seen as consistent with desires to reduce both the fiscal tensions of high social spending as well as government intervention in markets. Their effect, while holding everything else constant, however, is to increase the user cost of home ownership. In turn this can be expected to act as a downward pressure on demand and house prices.

It may be that such reforms have contributed to slumps in housing markets in many countries over the last decade. Thus, in some countries home ownership markets have been displaying symptoms that indicate that their former buoyancy and steady expansion may be limited. Not only can this be seen in the widespread phenomenon of falling or static prices, but also in the increasing incidence of purchasers experiencing difficulties in meeting loan repayments. Problems of high levels of arrears have been a feature of the US market for at least two decades, though by the early 1980s they reached what was then a peak (Dreier, 1982). In the early 1980s they had also begun to increase rapidly in Britain (Doling *et al.*, 1988) and in West Germany (Potter and Drevermann, 1988). By the early 1990s this had also happened in the Scandinavian countries – Sweden, Finland, Denmark and Norway (Kosonen, 1995).

In many of the countries in which house ownership markets have been depressed over the last decade, this has been recognized as a consequence of earlier house price booms, themselves brought about by the liberalization of financial markets (Kosonen, 1995). But, there is also recognition of the role of changes in labour markets. Not only may the problem be that rates of unemployment are high in many industrial economies, particularly outside south and east Asia, but labour markets have in many cases changed in other ways. One of the responses of some firms and some governments to the economic difficulties faced in many countries has been to strive to achieve greater flexibility in workforces. A consequence has been that increasing numbers of the workforce are employed on a relatively insecure basis. Working part-time, on a fixed-term contract basis or just at risk of dismissal may make it difficult to sustain mortgage payments (Doling and Ruonavaara, 1996). There may, in other words, be a contradiction between greater reliance on a form of housing provision where households are expected to make long-term commitments to the repayment of loans, and labour markets which increasingly have failed to produce jobs that provide long-term job (and income) security. So, attempts by capital and by national governments to protect capital accumulation may have resulted in the development of housing markets which in turn limits capital accumulation:

> Falling house prices and uncertainty about the future have had a depressing effect on geographical mobility of labour. High levels of indebtedness have deflated

consumer demand for manufactured products while increasing the reluctance to borrow. All of these factors reduce the opportunities for capital accumulation. (Doling and Ruonavaara, 1996, p. 43)

Insofar as national governments in their policy making have contributed to the developments in both housing and labour markets they have contributed to such a contradiction. Such situations are not necessarily unusual. Offe (1984) has referred to such crises as 'the tendency inherent within a specific mode of production to destroy those very preconditions on which its survival depends' (p. 132). One of the interesting features of this crisis of home ownership is not only how far such a contradiction is characteristic across advanced countries, but how government policy will respond to it. Some evidence of politically motivated developments was presented in the previous chapter. In contrast, if the central importance of the processes of globalization with its associated impacts on labour markets are stressed, the developments in home ownership markets could be viewed as evidence of a convergence brought about by economic development.

Conclusions

The subject matter of this chapter has illustrated one of the difficulties facing the comparativist, namely that concepts such as tenure may take on different meanings in different countries. Indeed, they can differ within a single country at one point in time, as well as over time. While recognizing the difficulties that flow from these differences, a practical problem is that the available statistical information is based on a taxonomy of tenure which does not take into account the variations in meaning.

The available statistical information shows that, taking the last half century as a whole, the dominant trend has been for home ownership sectors in industrialized countries to increase in size. In some countries the trends have seemingly plateaued out, but overall the growth has reached the point where the majority of households in the industrialized world are home owners. However, there are also large differences between countries with some having home ownership rates around 80 per cent, and other as low as 30 per cent, so that there are some countries to which the label 'home owning' society clearly applies, and others to which it does not. On the question of what has driven this spread of home ownership rates there are different views, but arguably the best developed is that by Kemeny in which he builds an explanation based on countries developing sets of policies and institutions that influence the balance of advantage and disadvantage associated with each tenure. In some countries the balance is weighted very firmly with home ownership. But even accepting the significance of government intervention in making home ownership more attractive and available in some countries, this begs a further question of why have governments of different countries intervened differently. Can the differences be attributed simply to ideology as some have suggested?

A further development in home ownership sectors, and one which is currently presenting a challenge to policy makers, is the depressed state of housing markets in many countries, as indicated by trends in prices, mortgage debt and repossessions. There is some evidence that processes largely outside the control of individual governments – the globalization of financial markets and manufacturing industry – bear a responsibility for these developments, but the policies of some governments seem also, directly and indirectly, to have been instrumental.

10

Social Housing

This chapter begins, as did the previous one, with a discussion of meanings, in this case the meanings attached to the label 'social housing'. Notwithstanding the definitional difficulties it goes on to use the existing literature to address a number of issues. First, why is it that countries which have politico-economic systems to which principles of profit and willingness to pay are central have developed systems of housing that run counter to those principles? This is of course the 'why welfare states' debate, rehearsed in Chapter Four, in microcosm. It is not the intention here to repeat that debate but to concentrate specifically on explanations related to social housing. Second, the chapter explores explanations for the variations in the size and the nature, including the institutional form, of social housing sectors, both across countries and over time. Finally, as in previous chapters, consideration is given to the evidence that, as part of more general tendencies towards retrenchment, governments have been reducing their commitment to social housing.

The meaning of social housing

Although the term 'social housing' is widely used in the international literature, it is not at all clear what, precisely, it means. Michael Ball and his colleagues suggest that '[i]t is easier to provide an approximate rather than a universally applicable general definition of social rented housing' (Ball *et al.*, 1988, p. 42). Most observers, however, probably agree with them that there are three key features that distinguish it from other forms of housing. First, rent levels are not set primarily according to considerations of profit, such that in their activities as landlords the owners of property are concerned to achieve only limited or no profit. Second, dwellings are allocated according to principles of need, with ability to pay not being paramount. Third, the amount and the quality of social housing is strongly influenced by the level of social demand. In other words, the extent to which governments are willing to pay for housing is important in determining the size and nature of social sectors. Together these dimensions add up to principles that differ from those of the market. There may be private sector organizations involved in their provision but the distinguishing feature is that social housing is not a pure commodity. In the decommodified form, it shares with other areas of the welfare state notions that labour market position is not the sole, or even the main, determinant of access.

The proposition that the adjective 'social' implies a decommodified form needs qualification, however, particularly with respect to the nature of subsidy. Subsidy may be important for closing the cost–income gap, but the nature of the subsidy will have a bearing on the consequences. Subsidies, such as rent control, that reduce user costs facilitate access to housing according to principles other than those of the ability to pay. Such subsidies are tied to the house so that it is the house that can be deemed to be 'social'. In themselves, such subsidies only partially decommodify since unless the controlled rent is close to zero it may not be affordable by someone who is unemployed. On the other hand, subsidies that increase the ability to pay may have different characteristics. First, they are person rather than house based. Second, subsidies paid through the tax system do not decommodify at all since they are linked directly to income. Third, those paid in the form of housing allowance do decommodify. Indeed, they may more fully decommodify than subsidies reducing user cost, but since they are not necessarily house linked we have the position that the label social may be contingent on the nature of the occupier rather than the house. Individual houses may move from social to non-social as occupiers, or at least their income and subsidy position, change.

Notwithstanding this qualification, if there is otherwise frequent agreement about the three characteristics that define social housing, so is there frequently an assumption (and this chapter also in practice pursues the same line) that social housing is necessarily rental housing. In fact, as indicated in the previous chapter, an exploration of the social relations of housing provision may indicate that forms of home ownership have many, if not all, of the characteristics outlined above. Government subsidies may reduce the gap between housing costs and household incomes and they may be inversely related to income; allocation may be limited to low-income groups; and provision limited by public expenditure considerations. Even if such a close match is not found everywhere, in most industrialized countries home ownership is supported by subsidy systems, such as mortgage interest relief, which may enable households to pay more for housing than they would otherwise be able to do. In any case, as Hindess (1987) has argued, generally, housing markets are social in the sense that most are moulded and structured by governments who exert direct and indirect pressures on supply and demand. Markets in general cannot be disassociated from their social context and housing markets can be seen as frequently being driven by policies that reflect social goals. Notwithstanding the recognition that the adjective 'social' need not be limited to one tenure, in practice the conventional approach is indeed to limit it to a certain type of rental housing.

Even so, there is nothing in the definition that specifies the landlord type or sector; that is, the particular institutional form. The definitional morass here can be illustrated by the example of postwar West Germany where housing in all sectors has been so heavily influenced by the state through subsidies and regulations that it is difficult to distinguish the social from the non-social. In the aftermath of the Second World War, the government sought to utilize the private landlord by creating a regime whereby tax incentives were tied to rent regulation. Private landlords could write off capital costs against tax and rents were related to the costs of provision so that, while this meant that they obtained a secure capital asset, they were largely prevented from profiteering. Owner occupation was encouraged by a mixture of grants, low-interest loans and guarantees. Having saved 40 per cent of the cost of a home through a savings bank, households could get the remaining 60 per cent at a low interest. Owners who chose to build homes with a rental flat attached could also get the same special tax incentives as landlords. Whereas these arrangements reduced user prices and thereby made allocation less dependent on individual, household income, other arrangements fitted the social housing label even more closely. As an alternative to the regime described above, private landlords were eligible to direct subsidies which 'met the differences between the controlled or registered rent and the real cost of producing and running the dwelling' (Power, 1993, p. 111). In return the landlord had to allocate the dwelling to a tenant nominated by the local authority, and the rent was tied to the provision costs for the duration of the subsidy. Broadly similar arrangements applied to the limited dividend companies and cooperatives. Many of them could be considered part of the voluntary sector and had their origins in churches, trade unions and other voluntary organizations. They received subsidies and operated under statutes which required:

that they would operate only for the *public good*... that they would charge cost *rents* rather than economic or market rents; that dwellings would be no larger than 120 square meters so as to be able to accommodate the majority of households on moderate incomes. (original emphases, Power, 1993, p. 114)

At the same time many of the organizations operating under these arrangements were not strictly 'non-profit'; rather they invested with an expectation of receiving a 4 per cent return on capital.

In combination, the ambiguities in the meaning of social housing exacerbate the general problem of obtaining truly comparable international data about the size of the sector in different countries. It is, as Emms (1990) notes of the German housing system, 'abundantly plain that the blurred demarcation lines between tenures make it nearly impossible to provide aggregate data for the social rented sector as such' (p. 128). However, as elsewhere in this book (as frequently also in other books) available statistical evidence is reported and largely taken as equivalent across countries.

Why social housing?

The reasons why industrialized countries have social housing sectors, and the nature of those sectors, have been considered by a number of authors. The various perspectives they bring to bear reflect the more general analyses of the origins of the welfare state. The books by Emms (1990) and Power (1993) could be seen as adopting theoretical positions which broadly reflect a convergence approach. Each considers the development of social housing in a sample of countries: the UK, France, West Germany, Netherlands and the Soviet Union in the first; and, the UK, France, Ireland and West Germany in the second. They present factual and detailed accounts which provide investigators with valuable introductions to the content and nature of policy developments. Power discusses the development of social housing against the context of McGuire's four-stage model of policy development (see Chapter Five) which proposes that, as they developed, the economically advanced countries at first initiated limited social housing interventions but, after the Second World War, pursued mass development. This continued until the 1970s when the emphasis turned from quantity to quality. Emms's book provides the reader with illustrations of interpretations of social housing interventions viewed as technical solutions to need. The 'reasons' for the West German solution, for example, are claimed to be 'twofold, and not far to seek': war damage and immigration (Emms, 1990, p. 115).

A different perspective, one which derives from the nature of the good under review, has been adopted by some economists. In their analyses of welfare states they have frequently argued that the nature of some goods and services is such that market provision results in a level of output below that collectively demanded (for example Culyer, 1980). Public and semi-public goods – national defence, libraries, education, health care, housing and so on – have positive externalities, that is benefits, which accrue to people whether or not they themselves purchase the particular good or service. In these circumstances, it is argued, unless governments impose some form of compulsory provision, through taxation and state provision, for example, many individuals will be tempted to pursue a free rider strategy so that the total amount provided will be below the socially desired level. Specific examples of how this might occur have been presented by Gibb and Munro:

> if an individual allows a house to deteriorate greatly, passers-by might be in danger of it falling on them or, if conditions in one part of the housing stock are so insanitary that diseases are spread, the risk of disease is an externality imposed on people living near or passing by… The individual imposing such externalities faces no costs in imposing disbenefits on neighbours. Equally a very beautiful garden fronting an immaculate house is an external benefit which passers-by and neighbours enjoy, but for which the provider of the benefit receives no recompense. (1991, pp. 38–9)

In fact, the theory of externalities provides a view about just one way in which markets may fail to produce efficient outcomes. There may also be imperfect competition in supply, for example resulting from monopoly suppliers of construction materials. Or, the slowness of housing markets to respond to changes in demand may mean that landlords are, in effect, local monopolists who are able to exploit any excess demand (Hills, 1991). Yet another example of market failure is provided by those categories of good where, although they can be supplied by for-profit organizations, it is difficult for those paying to know whether the good has been supplied to the expected level of quality, or indeed at all. Such cases may occur where the person consuming is different to the person paying, as with the provision of nursing homes for the elderly. They also occur where, as with health care, the good may be complex and the consumer has insufficient knowledge of quality. Hansmann (1980) has argued that the need for trust with respect to such goods and services necessitates provision by non-profit organizations.

The neo-classical perspective thus views housing policy development, including the decision to provide social housing, as a technical
exercise pursued by governments with the intention of correcting
market failures. Even so, not all neo-classical economists are in agreement with these arguments, with some (such as Minford, Peel and
Ashton, 1987) taking the position that state intervention generally
creates more problems than it solves, in particular causing problems of
excess demand.

A quite different perspective on the development of social housing is
provided by studies working in the Marxist tradition in which the
dynamic of capitalist societies takes centre stage. One of the most
comprehensive and well-crafted examples has been published by
Michael Harloe who comes straight to the heart of the social housing
issue: '[t]he interesting question... does not concern why housing has
been such a marginal component of the welfare state but rather why it
has sometimes been provided through the agency of the state in a
partially decommodified form' (Harloe, 1995, p. 4). In short, the issue
is not 'why not more', but 'why at all'? Harloe comes to this position
after first rejecting the Torgerson view that housing is vulnerable to
welfare state retrenchment as well as being a doubtful candidate for
social investment in the first place because, unlike other welfare goods
and services, access once granted is permanent (Torgerson, 1987). But
any such arrangement around access, not being part of some universal
characteristic of real property, is clearly contingent, as the case studies
of the USA and Japan in Chapter One indicate. In fact, there are other
differences between housing and the major welfare services such as
education and health care, which may be more relevant. Of the three
reasons Harloe puts forward, the first is the most basic: the private
ownership of property constitutes a foundation stone of capitalism. As
Harloe (1995) puts it: '[h]ousing is property and in capitalist societies
the defence of all forms of private property rights is deeply entrenched'
(p. 536). On this view any attempt to promote forms of housing that
would undermine the principle of private ownership would likely to be
more vigorously rejected than decommodifications in other areas.
Moreover, because housing provision offers an avenue for both manufacturing and financial capital to accumulate surplus value, 'there
might be similarities between the obstacles to housing socialization
and, for example, those facing plans to socialize the ownership of
industry or agriculture' (p. 236). How convincing is the argument that
similar threats to capital accumulation do not operate with areas of
welfare provision other than housing, or if they do, this has been

historically recent? A counter argument is that schools, hospitals, urban parks and roads are also extensive users of land which have been isolated from the general market in land. In other words, private ownership of land and opportunities for capital accumulation have elsewhere been compromised.

Second, Harloe argues that in the case of housing there had always existed private forms of provision and this was not the case for health care, education and pensions. Further, in the latter cases government interventions did not pose the sort of threat to vested interests that they did with housing. Set against this argument, social housing is not in itself inconsistent with private capital accumulation. At this point reference back to earlier chapters is useful. A distinguishing feature of social housing could be said to be that either user cost is reduced below market level or incomes are raised to enable low-income groups to pay market-level rents. But, neither strategy precludes capital accumulation from at least some points in the provision process depicted in Figure 3.1. Thus private landowners may extract development betterment, private builders may make profits by winning, and successfully fulfilling, house building contracts gained from local authorities, and private financiers may generate profit by making loans available. Indeed, only in the limited case of housing provision in the former USSR and its eastern European satellites might social housing perhaps be equated with zero opportunity for capital accumulation. It can be added that transport routes existed in their commodified form – toll roads, for example – long before, as well as during, the nineteenth century, and in many industrialized countries the exacting of road tolls remains common.

Third, Harloe argues that because housing is a durable commodity that can act as collateral, the high capital cost can be converted into a stream of payments (in the form of rent or mortgage payment). This characteristic helped to bring about provision of housing in a commodified form within the means of a large proportion of the population of western societies, particularly if government subsidies were available. In contrast, Harloe argues, the lumpy costs of other areas of welfare – education, health care, unemployment benefit and so on – are not so easily formed into affordable financial packages. Harloe suggests that because of the unpredictability of some events – unemployment and sickness, for example – and the fact that education is required in advance of entry into the labour market, it is not easy 'to see an immediate opportunity for profitable private sector provision of education, unemployment and disability benefits for the broad mass of the population' (p. 537). But, here too, the case for difference is perhaps over-stated. The questions might be raised of to what extent have pure, private sector solutions to housing provision produced acceptable housing for people at the lower end of the income distribution scale, and to what extent has the inventiveness of financial capital been stretched? More generally, Harloe admits that the distinctions between housing and other areas of welfare are 'incompletely drawn' (p. 537). There are, arguably, differences between housing and other areas of welfare but these are relative and contingent rather than absolute and universal. This, too, has been the thrust of the counter arguments presented here. Yet, it remains the case that while throughout industri-alized countries there is no example of a total absence of housing which can be labelled 'social', equally, there is no example where intervention has been as comprehensive as it often has been for health care or education, for example. So, if housing is different, the nature and foun-dation of this difference has yet to be fully specified.

Public or voluntary provision

It was noted earlier that social housing could be provided through different institutions. In many countries the voluntary, that is private, non-profit, or, third sector was responsible for the provision of social housing in the early years of industrialization. Though in many coun-tries this sector has continued to play a, if not the, major role, in some other countries the state has taken over the lead. For example, in Britain and Ireland the major responsibility came to be vested with local authorities. Of the former, Emms states:

> The trend in the allocation of social housing responsibilities is part of a general pattern in Great Britain in the first half of this century of relying on the state directly rather than on state-supported agencies to provide welfare organization. In housing as in other respects it therefore sets the British social rented sector totally apart from its western European counterparts, where socially rented housing is almost entirely owned and managed by organisations constituted on the lines of British housing associations. (Emms 1990, pp. 17–18)

It is not clear what the significance of the two types of institutional arrangement might be. Heidenheimer *et al.*, (1975) suggest with respect to the voluntary sector, that, either because governments provide subsi-dies or their officials take management responsibilities, there is considerable government influence on their actions. Michael Ball *et al.*, on the other hand, argue that such influence may be resisted:

> An important aspect of the differing institutional structures of social rented housing provision concerns the relative autonomy of social landlords in respect of political control. In the four mainland European countries examined here there has often been considerable resistance to attempts by central and/or local government to control how these landlords allocate or manage other aspects of their housing. (Ball *et al.*, 1988, pp. 44, 47)

Whether or not there are political consequences deriving from the institutional arrangements by which social housing is delivered, the reasons why those arrangements differ across countries have not been widely explored in the literature. In the standard economic analysis of state intervention in housing, in which the conditions under which the market may not be an appropriate mechanism for welfare provision are identified, a distinction between different forms of collective provision – the state or the voluntary sector – largely goes unexamined. This challenge has been taken up, however, in a book by Douglas (1983) in which he considers government failures. His argument is that although there are circumstances in which welfare provision should not be left to the market, there are equally circumstances in which the state may also not be the best alternative. In constructing this argument he draws heavily upon the earlier work of the economist Burton Weisbrod (1977), a reduced form of whose model is presented here.

The model starts from an assumption that each citizen will have a different demand function for public goods. Some will be prepared to pay a lot, others not so much. In these circumstances how do governments decide how much to spend on public goods and therefore how much to levy in taxes to enable their provision? Weisbrod assumes that governments will provide to the point where as many citizens would be willing to contribute more in taxes as would be willing to contribute less: that is the position of the median citizen-voter. This may not, of course, be the 'actual way in which government sets the level of public expenditure' (Douglas, 1983, p. 111), but the crucial element in the argument is that 'there will always be some citizen-voters who are undersatisfied with the level of production of the public good, and some citizen-voters who are overtaxed by that level' (p. 111). In Weisbrod's view this may lead to the position where 'consumers are likely to be left in non optimal positions in both private and government markets, being over or undersatisfied in government markets and making socially inefficient choices in private markets' (Weisbrod, 1977, p. 59). One role for the voluntary sector will thus be of meeting the interests of the undersatisfied by supplementing state provision, of which in the extreme case there may be none. In some cases the supplementation may be by the private, for-profit sector, but where the public good element is dominant the private, non-profit sector may be active.

Weisbrod provides an historical dimension to this in his consideration of the sequence of responses. He argues that it is likely that:

> the government sector will not be the first to respond to consumer demands for collective goods. The reason is that demands by all consumers do not generally develop simultaneously, and so the political decision rule will at first determine a zero level of government provision, leading the undersatisfied demanders to nongovernmental markets. (1977, p. 60)

His proposition is, then, that, taking an historical perspective, in any country the demand for public goods may at first be low and the non-profit sector meets that demand, but that as the country's wealth increases and the demand for public goods spreads through the population, state provision is likely to replace it.

Weisbrod's analysis has been subjected to a number of criticisms, for example that in many countries the voluntary sector supplies largely private, not public goods (see Ware, 1989). Nevertheless, the question can usefully be asked: does the Weisbrod model fit, at this level of generality, the historical development of the state and voluntary housing sectors in western European countries? The case could be made that in some respects at least it does, though perhaps with significant reservations. In many countries the voluntary housing sector has a long history: from at least the Middle Ages, religious orders were involved in providing accommodation for the poor and the sick; but philanthropic initiatives around housing developed considerably in the nineteenth century when previous arrangements for meeting the welfare, including housing needs, of the urban populations were replaced by the market. The precise timing varied from country to country and followed the course of industrialization and urbanization as a result of which increasing numbers of the poorer sections of society were concentrated in areas of unsatisfactory housing. The housing produced by the voluntary sector, in response to the private slums, has been described as 'built criticism of the private market' (Prak and Priemus, 1992, p. 164). The driving forces behind the many initiatives were frequently located in the medical and religious professions. There was also the development of cooperatives (they flourished particularly in Scandinavia) which were sometimes the direct product of working people. But, overall the contribution of the voluntary sector was small.

Although the initiators of the voluntary sector lay outside and independent of government, usually, as Pooley (1992) has indicated, they 'interacted with and reflected government policy' (p. 4). Moreover, following the Weisbrod model, they also offered one particular (among several) strength in that they 'often responded more quickly and directly than most government policy to economic and social factors' (p. 4). In that sense the voluntary sector provided examples of solutions to housing problems which, later, governments sometimes came to emulate.

If the period before the First World War saw in many countries the development of the voluntary sector, the period after saw growing intervention by the state. In many ways the stated objective remained the same – to remedy some of the consequences of the private market – but in some countries, notably Britain, state intervention meant strategies of state provision on a scale that overshadowed the voluntary sector. In other countries, such as Sweden and the Netherlands, there was also state encouragement of municipal housing provision, although that was accompanied by state encouragement of the voluntary sector. In some countries, therefore, the voluntary sector also became a major part of national strategy at an early date.

A far larger expansion of state intervention in housing occurred after the Second World War where throughout most parts of western Europe there was a combination of large housing shortages, the need for economic reconstruction, social expectations and tensions, and private capital and housing markets which were inadequately functioning. As in the inter-war period, different countries adopted different strategies. In Britain, policy concentrated almost exclusively on provision by local authorities, leaving the voluntary sector – and for a while the private market sector also – in a residual position. In Spain and in Italy, the private market sectors continued to play the dominant role. In West Germany, the state placed the major onus on non-profit organizations, which mainly took the form of limited liability companies, and housing cooperatives. They are managed by a variety of organizations ranging from the churches to labour unions. As in West Germany, the non-profit sectors in Denmark and the Netherlands were selected as a major plank of national housing policy, and were both closely regulated by government, as well as subsidized.

National variations

It will be clear from the previous section that, whereas in European countries there may have been a tendency – by no means universal – during the present century to replace the activities of the voluntary sector with those of the state sector, the extent of replacement has been variable. Indeed in some countries, the voluntary sector has been actively promoted by their governments, with relatively minor roles for their public sectors. This brings us back to the issue about the balance between the state and the voluntary sectors for which Weisbrod offers an explanation when he argues that:

> if two political units (such as countries) differ in the degree of heterogeneity of their populations, the more homogeneous unit will, ceteris paribus, have a lower level of voluntary-sector provision of collective-type goods or their private-good substitutes. In short, that country will tend to have relatively smaller voluntary and private sectors, and a relatively large public sector. (1977, p. 67)

So, the argument is that where a country is socially and economically homogeneous the more likely are its citizens to want the same public service to the same extent. In these circumstances there will be a tendency for a dominance of public provision. In countries character-ized by heterogeneity, however, the voluntary sector is more likely to look after the welfare of the different interest groups. The latter has been the case in the Netherlands where the:

> extreme cultural heterogeneity, in the form of intensely held religious cleavages (between Catholics, Calvinists, and liberal Protestants) that characterised Dutch society at the turn of the century led to a highly privatized system in which the nonprofit sector produces most of the country's quasi public goods – albeit financed almost exclusively by government. (James, 1989, p. 53)

Cross-national differences in the balance between state and voluntary sector provision can, on this view, thus be attributed to the hetero-geneity of the population. So, in deciding how public goods are to be provided, a 'social choice is often made between the nonprofit sector and local governments as the chief producer of education, health and social services' (James, 1989, p. 5) with this social choice reflecting the power of interest groups. The generalizability of this proposition has not yet been adequately examined.

Nature and size

At this point the discussion moves on to considerations of the variations in the size and nature of social housing solutions. An important source is the book by Michael Harloe (1995) which although largely limited to six countries – Britain, Denmark, France, Germany, the Netherlands and the United States – is, in other respects, arguably the most comprehensive and detailed study of social housing yet carried out. The latest milestone in a decade or more of comparative writing, it provides a detailed analysis of policy developments. Reminiscent of Donnison, he identifies two models of social housing provision which he calls the 'residual' and the 'mass' models. The residual model describes social housing which has been built up through small-scale programmes, targeted on poorer groups in society. Historically these were frequently associated with slum clearance programmes, and more recently with specific, disadvantaged groups who are not catered for by mainstream, private market solutions. Targeted in these ways, residual social housing has generally been a stigmatized form of provision which, at the same time as improving the quality of the physical fabric recipient households enjoyed, more or less reinforced their marginalized position within society. The Harloe argument is that residual social housing provision was initiated in Europe in the period before the First World War, but as it has become more and more apparent that private sector provision was not capable of meeting the legitimate needs of the urban poor, this form of social housing has become institutionalized. Whereas there have been periods of more comprehensive interventions, until now residual social housing has been part of the 'normal' response of European governments. In Harloe's words:

> the residual form of provision has been incorporated within welfare capitalist regimes on a more or less permanent basis. In other words, this is the normal form of social rented housing provision in 'normal' times. (1995, p. 7)

On this view the 'abnormal' response is represented by the mass model where large-scale programmes are targeted much less narrowly on the poor. The level of stigma is considerably less and subsidies have tended to be directed at the property (supply side) rather than the person (demand side). With the exception of the United States in the countries examined, there have been periods in which governments have gone beyond the residual model to pursue the mass model. These periods have coincided with system wide crises and/or restructuring. The first such period occurred in the immediate aftermath of the First

World War as a means of restoring the status quo. The second period stretched from the end of the Second World War to the mid 1970s and coincided with the reconstruction and restructuring of national economies, and in the case of some countries with the final stage in the transition to urbanized and industrialized economies. Mass social housing was also an expression of the postwar, welfare state consensus.

For Harloe, then, developments in social housing need to be located in wider processes of change, to periods in which national systems as a whole have undergone fundamental reconstruction and restructuring. Identifiable periods or epochs of capitalism – labelled as 'structures of accumulation' – can be seen in a number of countries to have generated social housing responses. Harloe describes the consecutive structures as follows:

> The first was liberal capitalism, the initial form created by the Industrial Revolution which reached its peak in the late nineteenth century. Its dissolution was hastened by the First World War and, despite a concerted attempt to revive the system after 1918, the events of 1929–32 marked its death-knell. The second welfare capitalist (or, as some prefer, Fordist) structure of accumulation began to emerge in the inter war period... came to dominate in the years after 1945 but, from the 1960s, became increasingly unstable and conflict-ridden. The final phase of this regime occurred in the years after the mid-1970s recession. The consequences of its breakdown, in terms of economic instability, industrial and labour market restructuring, political realignments and new patterns of social stratification and social divisions, are still being worked through. (1995, p. 8)

Harloe's argument is not that these identifiable periods effected social housing responses as necessary and functional to the processes of reconstruction, but that there have been some broad similarities in the responses that nations took (as well as some notable exceptions). Generalizing, the characteristic response was the development of residual social housing provision in the first period, the move towards mass provision in the second, and the reversion to the residual model in the third.

Wherever and whenever the mass model dominated, however, the poor were not a significant recipient group. Rather, as with the development of institutional models of welfare in some countries, the respectable, employed working classes and the lower middle classes constituted a major part of the beneficiary group. The same point has been made by Emms (1990) who concluded that from the outset social housing was intended for the deserving poor – skilled manual workers and clerks – and rarely for the 'really indigent' (p. 3). Rather than seeking to house the very poorest, then, social housing landlords 'have always been concerned to select tenants who were likely to be unproblematic both economically and socially' (p. 3). Pooley summarizes the literature in like fashion:

> The conclusion drawn by most case studies – that short-term state involvement in housing did little to help those in most housing need – is based on a careful evaluation of the quantitative and qualitative contribution that state strategies made to the housing stock, and an assessment of the characteristics of families helped by such schemes. (1992, p. 329)

Further, Harloe draws a significant distinction between social housing, even in its institutional form, and other areas of social policy which were the product of middle-class settlements. For the latter the benefits generally extend beyond the poor into the middle-class strata so that all but the very richest directly benefited. In that sense the services are 'universal'. In the case of social housing, however, the poor have generally been excluded and been forced to seek solutions in the private market which have been inferior to the social sector. So, the mass social housing model has not generally involved an extension of the welfare state blanket to warm both the poor and the middle-class groups, and in that sense been a solidaristic service, but one that has maintained, if not reinforced, existing stratification based on labour market position. This also suggests that reservations, about explanations of the origins of social housing being located in the housing needs and aspirations of the very poorest strata of industrialized societies, are appropriate.

However, in some respects this picture may also be changing. A combination of a number of processes including the achievement in many countries of a rough balance of households and dwellings, the continued growth of owner occupation to incorporate many middle- and lower-income groups, and the rise of mass unemployment, which has had profound effects on social and economic structures within the population, has sometimes altered the nature of the social housing tenant. Both Emms (1990) and Power (1993) provide details of these developments in a number of European countries and the resulting challenges to social housing landlords who have been faced with a conversion of their stock not simply to a residualized form but to a highly stigmatized and disadvantaged form.

Running alongside these broadly similar trajectories in the social housing sectors in the countries examined are variations in size. These can be identified statistically in the final column of Table 10.1. Differences in the level of social housing commitment can be attributed to a number of national characteristics. The extent to which the private market, whether supported or not by state subsidies, has been able to satisfy the housing needs of all sectors of the population has been an important influence on the pressure for government intervention in the form of social housing. In Harloe's analysis this is the only characteristic that could be described as being internal to the housing system, arising from the existence of housing need. Other factors have their locus elsewhere: the extent to which decent housing was perceived to be an important element in resolving crises in the wider system; the strength of political support and particularly the degree of middle-class support; and legal and institutional variations which have facilitated or impeded policy developments. Also important are ideological differences, including liberal ideas about the relation of the individual to the state and the role of markets. In the United States these notions were significant in maintaining a housing system in which social housing had a very small part. In France and Germany family-centred ideologies, and in the Netherlands 'cross-ideological corporatism' were moulding influences (Harloe, 1995, p. 526). In contrast to (perceptions about) other areas of welfare, however, social democratic ideologies were rarely significant. Social housing did not develop so as to break the relationship between labour market position and housing quality, nor did it become 'a right of social citizenship for all' (Harloe, 1995, p. 527). There is a direct parallel here, then, with explanations, also built on ideological predilections, about the relative importance of home ownership sectors. In addition, it may be noted that social housing sectors are small in most of those countries falling into either Donnison's embryonic group (Barlow–Duncan's rudimentary group) or his social group (liberal).

Retrenchment

The reference in many of the previous chapters to the period of the last two decades during which the governments in many industrialized countries have been re-thinking their commitment to meeting the housing needs of their citizens is also relevant here. Indeed, there might be an *a priori* case for concluding that if retrenchment is apparent anywhere it would be in social housing sectors. This is reflected in the literature, although much of it has looked across whole housing systems being as concerned with owner occupation and private renting as with social housing (for example, Lundquist, 1992a; Tosics, 1987).

Of the literature on retrenchment of social sectors, some has been country specific (for example, Silver, 1990) with a great deal being Britain specific, discussing its dramatic council house sales policy (for example, Forrest and Murie, 1988). The substance of two studies which are both cross-country comparative and confined (though only partly in one case) to social housing are presented here.

Lundquist (1986) takes three countries – Britain, Germany and the USA – in which during the 1980s there had been the implementation of policies that resulted in tenure conversions. Although he does present evidence about the extent and nature of conversions, this is not his primary aim. One of his arguments is that these conversions cannot simply be thought of as privatization, as retrenchment or as a weakening of commitment towards housing needs, but may more appropriately be thought of as special cases of government promotion of home ownership. The main focus, however, is on a comparison and evaluation of the effects of conversion, searching for answers to the questions about who gains and who loses. It thus provides an example of the use of comparative analysis in order to learn policy lessons, in which, in this case, the distributional consequences of conversion are found to be regressive.

A different measure of the extent to which states have withdrawn, or not, from their involvement with meeting the housing needs of their populations is the change in the percentage of new housing construction (see Doling, 1994). It might be concluded that a relatively greater reliance on the private sector as the source of new housing represented a view by national governments that housing needs could adequately be dealt with through the market. Empirical evidence suggests considerable inter-national differences (see Table 10.1). Over the period 1975 to 1990 there were considerable reductions (below 100 per cent in the second column) in the share of new production taken by social housing in the UK and Ireland, with reductions also in Germany. In the other countries, for which data are available, the share of new production did not greatly decrease and in some – Sweden and Denmark in particular – significantly increased. There are similar variations apparent in the third column.

The non-conformity of the change in this aspect of housing production is significant in terms of conclusions about welfare state retrenchment and about the extent of convergence or divergence in any developments. One aspect of the pattern of national developments is that broadly it conforms with Esping-Andersen's welfare state regime types: reductions in social housing production in liberal regimes and increases in the social democratic ones. One explanation for this pattern is provided through consideration of national approaches to combating the impact of economic forces. In some countries, there has been a continued, and central, commitment to maintaining full employment. In part this has been attempted by strategies of high welfare, including housing expenditure. In these countries the role of the government, as a central part of the postwar welfare state project, in managing the economy in ways to protect employment, has been retained.

Table 10.1 Social housing's share of production and stock

	Production			Stock
	1960 *(% of total)*	*% change 1975–1990*	*% change 1980–1990*	*1990 (% of total)*
Australia	–	–	–	7
Austria	40.3	77.4	104.1	20
Belgium	–	64.5	142.9	7
Canada	–	–	–	5
Denmark	32.3	179.2	187.1	18
Finland	44.7	100.9	96.2	15
France	–	–	66.5	17
Germany	33.2	4.4	6.9	15
Greece	–	–	–	0
Ireland	33.6	17.1	25.5	11
Italy	–	–	68.4	3
Japan	–	–	–	8
Netherlands	49.9	123.9	116.3	44
New Zealand	–	–	–	6
Norway	30.0	76.1	98.4	4
Portugal	–	–	–	4
Spain	–	–	–	1
Sweden	60.6	178.9	153.9	22
Switzerland	12.5	138.8	116.9	4
UK	43.9	28.1	32.1	25

Source: Doling (1994) Table 1; Hedman (1994) Table 5.

In some other countries, the focus of concern has shifted away from full employment to considerations of international competitiveness. In Britain and the USA, and to a lesser extent France and Germany, competitiveness imperatives came to mean reducing what were seen as burdens on the private sector. Among these burdens were high levels of welfare spending since these were predicated on high levels of taxation. In reduced form, if economic prosperity was to be rekindled, some governments believed that it was necessary to reduce the size of their welfare states. They pursued strategies that had this effect, reducing expenditure on social housing and other areas of welfare. However, their policies had other consequences in the form of developments in unemployment, which applied their own and further pressures on government spending. The net result has been an increased fiscal tension arising not simply despite, but in part because of, reductions in expenditure on social housing provision.

Conclusions

Although the precise meaning of the label 'social housing' is contestable, an examination of the development of housing interventions in all industrialized countries shows the development of sectors in which the rules of allocation erode the iron law of housing. Citizens, or at least some of them, are enabled to gain housing of a standard and cost that exceeds their ability to pay. Much of this housing is provided on a no, or a limited, profit basis often through local authorities or voluntary organizations. Even so, the extent to which social housing solutions have developed has generally been less than the development of social health care, social education and so on. Housing has not been accorded such a central place in welfare states as some other goods or services, and the reasons for this constitute an interesting debate. Moreover, in the earlier decades of its provision access to it was generally not restricted to the very poorest members of industrial societies.

There are clearly wide differences in the nature and size of the sectors which result from these incursions into the housing system. In some countries the sectors are large, in others small. In some the local authority role has been dominant, in others minor. Equally, there have been large variations over time. As in other respects government policies have not been static. Harloe draws attention in particular to the mass and residual models, where the former has characterized some countries for limited periods when unusual circumstances have come together, with the residual model being the one to which, sooner or later, they have tended to revert. Many authors have seen a particular shift in this direction in recent decades as part of the more general retrenchment of welfare states. The evidence, however, is not clear cut.

11

Private Renting

A reading of the previous two chapters indicates that tenure definition is not unproblematic. This applies equally to the private rented sector where one common definition is that it consists of housing that is not considered to fall into either the home ownership or the social sectors. This is defined as the residual. An alternative approach involves making reference to some of the common characteristics of the sector. First, perhaps, that the dwelling is owned by a person or body other than the occupier so that ownership is separated from use. Second, decisions about who gets to use the dwellings are taken through the marketplace as the outcome of negotiations between suppliers and consumers, and with the former having regard to profits and the latter to ability to pay and value for money. But such an approach to definition has difficulties, which by now will be familiar to the reader, stemming in part from the varying extent and consequence of state intervention. Thus, the market relations may be more or less constrained by interventions such as rent control and security of tenure provisions, while subsidy arrangements may, as seen earlier, give social housing characteristics to some parts of private sectors.

The present chapter begins with a consideration of the historical links in many countries between private renting and the processes of urbanization and industrialization, and of the early policy initiatives commonly taken by governments. Perhaps more than in previous chapters, therefore, there is a strong emphasis placed upon the historical development of housing policy. Although in the course of doing this some variations between countries are noted, the main emphasis is on the policy changes over time and their relation to key historical milestones. This also has connection with what was termed in Chapter One, the European paradigm and so provides a link back to one of the starting points. The second part of the chapter concentrates more on different national approaches to placing restrictions on rents with particular regard both to the relationships between the private and social sectors and to the long-run fortunes, in terms of its size, of the private sector.

The historical background

The course of industrial development as well as its timing – in the nineteenth century and later, perhaps primarily the second half of the twentieth – has varied considerably across countries. Nevertheless, in many countries any initial numerical significance of private rented housing developed further as part of the process of industrial and urban development. As Mulder notes:

> the privately rented sector may be considered as a typical byproduct of the industrial revolution. In former ages most inhabitants of the urban areas of Western Europe used to own their own dwellings. In the early days of the industrial revolution however the privately rented sector started to grow. (1988, p. 11)

Thus, in their pre-industrial eras, the focus of economic life in European as well as other countries with which we are concerned was frequently in the countryside and small towns. Under agrarian capitalism a large proportion of the population built their own homes – self-promoted, home ownership – or had them provided by employers. With industrialization and urbanization these social relations were replaced by market relations. As Ginsburg (1979) argues with respect to Britain, the 'free market' in labour power was extended to free markets in other commodities. In these terms housing became a market commodity subject to forces of supply and demand. At the same time there was in most countries a shift towards private renting. The standard, though not universal, model was of people with small amounts of capital becoming landlords (perhaps also acting as developers) and seeking tenants from whose rent they received a return on their investment.

The rise of this model can be largely explained in general terms by reference to the supply and demand conditions which frequently prevailed in rapidly industrializing towns. On the demand side, wages were often low and irregular, making long-term financial commitments to a housing loan impossible for many sectors of the new, urban population. They also translated into an ability to pay only a limited level of rent which afforded low rates of return for landlords. Rental housing with its relatively easy access, generally without the prepayment requirements of ownership, and easy egress did mean, however, that households could relatively rapidly adjust housing consumption to income. On the supply side there was often a strong psychological incentive for small investors in that, in comparison with investing in other people's enterprises, they could literally keep their eye directly on their investment. In any case, alternative avenues for investment for the small investor were in many countries limited so that some money flowed into the housing sector for want of somewhere else to put it. Whereas in most countries private landlordism thus developed rapidly, it was also common for employers themselves to take on this role, finding it necessary to do so in order to attract labour to their factories in the first place. It was for them, therefore, part of their growth strategies.

Harloe (1985) makes it clear that state intervention in this market was not unknown at an early date, and in some countries even well in advance of the big phases of urbanization. In many countries, however, the first legislation, which fundamentally changed the relationship between market actors, and between them and the state, could be seen as responses to the conditions and relationships in the private rental market. In general, these interventions took three forms: regulations concerning standards, price control and tenant rights.

Standards

One of the features of housing for the urban proletariat delivered through the marketplace was that the dwellings themselves were often built using poor materials in poor designs. In northern climes, they were often difficult to keep warm. Their densities were extremely high, they sometimes lacked adequate sewerage and fresh water supply systems, and households were frequently forced, because of low incomes, to live in crowded circumstances. Sharing common facilities such as kitchens and lavatories was not unusual. At least some of the impetus for early legislation was to be found in the health consequences of this type of provision. Thus, in Denmark, the criticisms of working-class housing at the end of the century 'continued to come from doctors… [b]ut whereas previously they had emphasized the danger of epidemics, after 1880 they increasingly rested their case on the general health of the working population' (Hyldtoft, 1992, p. 48). In Belgium, as van den Eeckhout indicates, working-class housing in urban and industrial areas was perceived as a problem even earlier:

The cholera epidemic of 1832–3 alarmed the urban elite; inquiries into working-class dwellings in Brussels (1838) and into the working and living conditions of the labouring classes throughout Belgium (1843–6) drew attention to the condition of urban housing; and doctors, statisticians and philanthropists produced other reports which blamed bad housing for high urban mortality. (1992, p. 198)

Frequently, and in response to such concerns, national governments introduced legislation which laid down minimum standards. Such legislation covered aspects of housing provision such as maximum densities, minimum space standards, construction materials and specifications, and infrastructural requirements. The overall effect was to improve the quality of dwellings constructed after legislation was introduced, but this was achieved only at the expense of an increase in the real resources used in the construction of each dwelling. This had the effect, then, of widening the gap between costs and incomes.

Rent control

In the absence of any further intervention by national governments, the likely consequence of a widening of the cost–income gap is that entrepreneurs may take the view that opportunities to find consumers willing to pay a rent that provided an acceptable return would be limited and consequently reduce their speculative investments in housing. In these circumstances, any shortage of housing, in relation to the number of households, may be exacerbated. In turn, the response of landlords to a situation of excess demand was sometimes to try to increase rents. The tensions that resulted from such actions came to a head in a number of European countries, as well as the USA, at the time of the First World War when there were additional reasons for shortage. Thus in the Netherlands, despite not being directly involved in the war, '[h]ousing production fell from approximately 23,000 units in 1913… to approximately 6,000 in 1917' (Prak and Priemus, 1992, p. 177). Likewise in Denmark, similarly not directly involved, housing production 'almost halted due to uncertainty, rising costs and a slump in the bond market, while urban in-migration accelerated' (Hyldtoft, 1992, p. 60). So, in many countries the consequences of the actions of governments in attempting to increase standards, which themselves contributed to shortage and increasing prices, were exacerbated by the special circumstances of war.

The characteristic response, as Harloe (1985, p. 28) writes 'was to introduce rent controls, starting in France in 1914… in Britain in 1915, in Denmark in 1916 and in Germany and the Netherlands in 1917'. In each of these countries, and others, governments passed legislation with the intention of preventing landlords from charging rents that reflected the market value of their dwellings with vacant possession. The result is that '[r]ent control, and in particular rent freeze, is probably the oldest deliberately wielded instrument of housing costs policy in America and Western Europe' (Priemus, 1982, p. 29).

Rent control resulted in a reduction in the user cost of housing. This had the consequence of narrowing the gap between user cost and user income, while at the same time leaving the real costs facing the provider at a high level. In effect the introduction of rent control meant that if there had been additional costs of provision resulting from an increase in standards these would be met by landlords. Governments may have intervened in rental markets but they did so in ways that did not impose direct costs on the public purse, rather turning landlords, willingly or not, into benefactors.

Security of tenure

The same tensions that had led governments to introduce rent control, also persuaded many of the desirability of providing some, if not all, tenants with greater levels of security. As Priemus observes:

> A rent freeze never came singly. Rent control was always accompanied by legal measures in order to protect the tenants better. (1982, p. 30)

In the pre-control period, the contract between landlord and tenant could, subject to the contractually defined period of notice, generally be rescinded at any time by either party. Landlords were sometimes tempted to evict tenants knowing that there were others eager to rent at higher rents. In the post-control period, the absence of security of tenure provisions would have facilitated landlords finding a way around the rent restrictions by getting in new tenants, so those governments that introduced rent control also introduced security of tenure provisions designed to prevent landlords from taking unilateral action to end a contract. The security was not absolute but the measures had the effect of shifting the balance of property rights from landlord to tenant. This restriction in the ability of landlords to obtain vacant possession also had the effect of reducing the liquidity of their investment. They were in other words locked into the sector, a result of which may have been to make the sector even less attractive than before as an avenue for investment. Since lower liquidity would normally be compensated for by higher returns, this restriction had the affect of increasing the cost of provision, and thus the gap between real and user costs.

The inter-war years

In the period after the end of the First World War in many countries there were further policy developments which broadly reflected views that a less restricted operation of private housing markets was to be sought. In the USA rent control was phased out. In Europe the developments were more complex. Thus in Denmark, the period from 1917 to 1927 was one of intense intervention in housing with large amounts of subsidy going to local authorities, housing associations and private builders. However, at the end of that period not only did the government cease to provide such support, but in 1925 rent control was withdrawn outside the capital (Hyldtoft, 1992). In Belgium, rent control had been introduced in 1919, but after currency devaluation in 1926, increases in rent were permitted with the level of increase and its timing varying with house type.

The Depression in the 1930s had a differential impact on western countries but in general it created circumstances where an unsubsidized and uncontrolled housing market was problematic. Thus in Denmark in 1936, new rent controls were introduced. In some countries subsidies to landlords became more important. Notwithstanding these policy developments, throughout the urban areas of Europe and North America the typical inhabitant was, by the outbreak of the Second World War, renting their housing from a private landlord. At the same time, as Michael Harloe points out, the general picture was that this form of housing was not left to the unfettered market:

> the unaided private landlord had proved no more capable of supplying housing at socially acceptable standards to low income workers in the twentieth century than he or she had in the previous century. In practice rent control was the main means by which many governments tried to ensure that rents stayed within the means of the working class, even though this involved an enforced subsidy by landlords to tenants. (1985, p. 40)

The postwar period

Similar housing tensions to those that characterized the period of the First World War and its immediate aftermath also widely prevailed during and after the Second World War. National policy responses with respect to the private rental sector were also often similar, leading Priemus to the view that:

> Rent freeze is of the nature of an emergency brake, applied by the government only in very tight corners. Such circumstances resulted from the two world wars: many dwellings were destroyed, the construction industry was practically idle for years and gigantic shortages thus developed in a short time. (1982, p. 29)

The subsequent policy developments have been numerous and in some industrialized countries far reaching. A review carried out by Wiktorin of Sweden, Denmark, Great Britain, West Germany, Netherlands, Belgium, France, Switzerland and Canada (reported in Román *et al.*, 1994) indicates some of the resulting similarities and differences in national systems of rent setting. Averaged over all the countries reviewed, the picture is that first-time rents of new rented property are the least controlled, rent increases where there is a sitting tenant are the most controlled, and increases where there is a change of tenancy are subject to control that is neither as free as the first nor as restrictive as the second. Overall, these arrangements provide most protection in cases where there is an existing tenant with two of the overall effects being to dampen down pressures for rapid increases in rents and to discourage mobility. Because landlords are restricted in their ability to benefit from any upsurge in market prices brought about, say, by general increases in property values, tenants have some certainty about their housing costs.

National variations

Having examined some general tendencies, as well as country differences, in the historical development of policies towards private renting, the focus turns to contemporary and recent variations in both the size of private rental sectors in each country and the nature of their regulatory systems.

Within the general pattern indicated by Wiktorin there is considerable cross-country variation, not only in the degree of control but also in the way in which any control mechanism is constructed. Nevertheless, in all the countries reviewed, first-time rents are, with minor exceptions, those freely negotiated between landlord and tenant. Thus in Sweden, rents are normally set in relation to those prevailing in the municipal sector whereas in Denmark a rent ceiling operates. Of the countries reviewed, Sweden is the most restrictive with respect to rent increases, these being the outcome of collective negotiations involving the interested parties. Great Britain, with respect to tenancies commencing after 1988, is the least restrictive, such rents being freely negotiated. In all the other countries there is some form of rent control. Thus in West Germany, where any proposed increase in rents is not agreed by the tenant, the onus is upon the landlord to take the issue to court. In the Netherlands, rent increases should not exceed a nationally determined trend, while in France a rent ceiling is operative. Where a new tenant takes occupation of a dwelling there is, in some countries, relaxation of rent controls with no example in the countries reviewed of greater restrictions being imposed than those applying to the previous tenants.

It is also relevant to note that there is a broad correlation between the existence of government restrictions on rent negotiations and security of tenure, such that where the former is weak so is the latter. Román *et al.* (1994) provide a number of examples:

> In the Netherlands, where the most expensive apartments have freely set rents, standards of assessment are lacking in cases where a tenant feels that the rent increase undermines security of tenure. In Great Britain it is said that security of tenure has deteriorated in connection with the transfer to the free setting of rents. Switzerland, which has the free setting of rents as a basic principle, has now found itself in a difficult situation when regulating which rent increases and which grounds for the notice of termination should be regarded as valid. (p. 120)

A few, slightly more detailed, examples may usefully illustrate the variety of arrangements with respect to rent control. In the USA, rent control systems operate in only a few states and only in New York City has such regulation been in place continually since World War Two. Even where rent control does operate, it generally does not have a strong influence on rents. Generally, new tenancies provide landlords with an opportunity to set rents at unregulated levels. Moreover, while controls 'hold rentals down somewhat', they do not do so to the extent 'that poorer tenants can afford' them because, even in areas with relatively strong controls, 'rent-income ratios rise' (Marcuse, 1990, p. 362). The Australian private landlord is also relatively uncontrolled in the opportunities to negotiate free market rents. In most of the postwar period there has been a fairly buoyant demand for rental accommodation deriving from young, newly formed households, but these households face a sector in which 'controls are minimal, and in the case of rent controls, virtually nonexistent... [while]... security of tenure for tenants remains limited' (Burke *et al.*, 1990, p. 729). The position in Italy is different again. In the 1960s and 70s there had been rent freezes. But the new legislation in 1978 established a system whereby rent levels, the rate of increase and the duration of any contract, were determined by law. In practice this has meant that rents have not followed the movement of the market, but landlords and tenants often reach informal agreements which allowed the legal position to be circumvented (Tosi, 1990). It is important, following the Italian example, to recognize that there may be a difference between formal national housing policies, as statements of what should happen, and implementation which may be with more or less vigour and with more or less effectiveness.

Yet, whatever the policy details and the national environment, there has been, as Harloe (1985) has traced, a general tendency for the fortunes of the sector in most countries, as measured by size in absolute and relative terms, to decline. The explanation for this decline has formed the focus of a great deal of debate in the literature. Most forceful have been the views developed by neo-classical economists, that the decline can be primarily attributed to the existence of rent control. Thus, Albon and Stafford (1987) report on the basis of 'research into the effects of rental market controls in various parts of the world at various times [that] the same picture emerges', and that this picture is one which is 'devastating – similar to the impact of bombing' (p. v). The impact in terms of reducing the supply of rental housing is 'unambiguous' and one which is 'agreed by virtually all economists' (p. viii), and arises because they deny landlords an economic return on their investment, leading them to 'sell as soon as an opportunity presents itself' (p. 24).

But, while economists in all industrialized countries have come down fairly unanimously in attributing decline to the existence of rent control, this view is not universal as the following extract about Australia testifies:

In the postwar period, the private rental sector has declined from 43 percent to 19 percent of the total housing stock. The steady decline in the 1950s and 1960s was related to the growing affluence of households, enabling many to achieve their preference for ownership. Combined with the effects of substantial direct and indirect government subsidies to the other two tenure sectors, the proportion of the stock either owner occupied or publicly rented grew at the expense of the private rental sector... In Australia the relative decline of private rental as a tenure form does not reflect the effects of restrictions on this sector such as residential tenancy legislation or rent controls. By world standards, such controls are minimal and, in the case of rent controls, virtually nonexistent. (Burke *et al.*, 1990, p. 729)

On this view, then, the decline of private renting in industrialized countries can be attributed as much to increases in overall prosperity and national policies resulting in inducements to households to become owners or tenants of social landlords, as it can to policies that have restricted rents.

Table 11.1   Rental sectors (1990)

Country	Size of private rental sector (%)	Type of policy model	Combined size of all rental sectors (%)
Australia	19	Dualist	26
Austria	25	Unitary	45
Belgium	31		
Canada	31	Dualist	36
Denmark	26	Unitary	44
Finland	9		
France	23		
Germany	43		
Greece	23		
Ireland	8		
Italy	23		
Japan	24		
Netherlands	12	Unitary	56
New Zealand	23	Dualist	29
Norway	18		
Portugal	32		
Spain	17		
Sweden	19	Unitary	41
Switzerland	66	Unitary	70
UK	7	Dualist	32
USA	33	Dualist	38

Source: Hedman (1994) Table 5; Kemeny (1995).

Whatever the interpretation put on the consequences for the size of the sector, however, rent control remains a significant, and widely discussed, dimension of policy. At the same time, as Table 11.1 indicates, taken over all the countries for which information is collated, the private rented sector by 1990 still accounted for approximately a quarter of their combined stock. Notwithstanding the extent of the decline, therefore, the sector is far from insignificant. The variation in the national situations is, however, large with Switzerland at one end of the spectrum having two-thirds of its stock in this sector, and the UK at the other with a mere 7 per cent.

One approach to looking at these variations in sector size is to seek to identify some patterns in the national arrangements. The most unrestricted systems exist in those countries that have liberal welfare states – the USA, Australia, Switzerland, Belgium, and, since 1988, Great Britain. The most restricted exist in social democratic countries, particularly Sweden and to a lesser extent Denmark. But, this classification does not correlate strongly with the size of the private rented sectors as recorded in Table 11.1. There is, however, another important distinction, one which provides a stronger basis for correlation between policy approach and sector size, that being between those countries in which governments have responded to the private and public rental sectors in an uncoordinated and those which have responded in a coordinated fashion. Jim Kemeny has, in a number of publications, identified a distinction between those countries in which there have developed deep, institutional cleavages such that housing standards, types, prices and means of access differ considerably from the private to the cost renting sectors, and those countries in which the two sectors have been treated in a coordinated way.

At the heart of this distinction is a process, referred to by Kemeny (1995) as 'maturation', which describes the decline over time in the real value of the outstanding debt on an individual or a set of dwellings. In other words there can be a growing differential between the debt on an old dwelling and the debt that would be incurred on a newly constructed dwelling. This may occur for a number of reasons: for example because some of the loan on an old dwelling may have been paid off over time, or, because of the seemingly inexorable rise in the cost of residential development. In a private rental system in the absence of rent regulation, the benefits of this differential may be enjoyed by the landlord, representing the investment return or profit allowed by the market. The landlord is able to privatize the gain from maturation, and thus to benefit rather than the tenant. In public or social systems of renting, however, maturation may be dealt with differently. If rents are allowed to reflect the cost of provision, tenants of old dwellings will pay rents that are lower than market rents. This may create anomalies such as where the rent on a high quality old property may be lower than the rent on a newer, lower quality dwelling. Social housing organizations may deal with this in different ways, such as rent pooling where the benefits of maturation can be used as the basis of cross subsidy with rents reflecting market differentials but being significantly lower. The point is, however, that a social housing system in which rents reflect, individually or collectively through rent pooling, the cost of provision has the clear potential to undercut the rents set by the market. Herein lies both a challenge and an opportunity to which, Kemeny (1995) argues, national governments have responded in two broad ways.

The dualist model has been established in those countries in which governments have sought to discourage cost or social renting. The latter has been nationalized and segregated from private renting so that it is not placed in direct or open competition. This puts governments in a stronger position to deflect pressure 'to either increase the supply of cost rental housing in order to satisfy the growing demand, or to dampen demand both by making cost renting less attractive and by reducing its availability' (Kemeny, 1995, p. 51). This has also enabled them to protect and to promote the role of home ownership, even though this may not have been the original intention:

> the prime motivation for setting up a state-run cost rental sector in the first place was to provide a safety net to the private rental market. But by the time a historic juncture occurs it is only a secondary purpose to shelter the private rental market from cost rental competition. Dualist rental systems primarily prevent the emergence of a rental market that might tempt large numbers of households to continue renting rather than to buy into owner occupation. (Kemeny, 1995, p. 53)

Those countries that have developed a unitary model, by contrast, have encouraged cost renting. In this, advantage is taken of the process of maturation by allowing cost renting to compete with profit renting (and indeed with home ownership). The integration of the markets allows maturation to exert a downward pressure on market prices, because '[o]nce cost rental organisations gain a significant share of the rental market they act as market leaders, determining the maximum level of private rents by their market preponderance' (Kemeny, 1995, p. 56). Thus a distinction between the two systems is that in the former governments are seeking to protect the primacy of the private, for-profit sector by subjugating the cost-rental alternative: in the latter they are seeking to use the cost-rental sector to ensure that the housing system as a whole meets specified social ends.

It is the Anglo-Saxon countries – Canada, New Zealand, USA, Australia, and Britain – that have pursued the dualist option. In these countries cost renting has been provided and managed by the state as a supplement to the national housing stock where the private sector has not been able to provide. However, at some point in the postwar era there occurred such tensions over the demand for social renting that governments were compelled to act. In Britain this happened much later than in the other countries, but there has been a similar outcome in terms of government efforts to reduce and marginalize the cost-rental sector. One result is that these countries have smaller proportions of their total stock in the rental sectors (see final column Table 11.1). The unitary option countries, which include Austria, Denmark, Sweden, Switzerland, Germany, the Netherlands, generally have state cost-rental sectors which are small relative to the non-state cost-rental sectors. In other words social housing has been provided through private institutions. The unitary model countries have all maintained a large, at least 40 per cent, rental presence in their national housing stocks. The distinction between these two approaches also casts some light on the issue explored in the previous chapter, namely the relative contribution to social housing of the state and the voluntary sectors. Broadly, the provision of social housing directly by the state has dominated in those countries where the state has also sought to protect the primacy of the private, profit-driven, rented sector.

It is also worth noting that the membership of Kemeny's two groups matches closely with other classifications discussed at earlier points in this book. The Anglo-Saxon group consists of those English-speaking countries with liberal social welfare regimes distinguished by Esping-Andersen. The countries with unitary systems, while encompassing those of Esping-Andersen's social democratic as well as corporatist regimes, according to Kemeny (1995) all demonstrate high levels of corporatism. Before the Second World War, they have, in their housing sectors, as well as elsewhere, been strongly influenced by German culture and have constructed markets which have sought to strike a balance between economic and social objectives.

Conclusions

The literature that looks at the private rental sector across countries is relatively limited in size. Researchers have not paid nearly as much attention to it as they have to other tenure forms, even though across industrialized countries as a whole it constitutes around a quarter of the stock. Nevertheless the work of Harloe, in particular, provides considerable information about the development and variations in the sector showing the development of three policy areas – standards, rent control and security – and the general conformity with the European paradigm. Kemeny's identification of two opposing models of the relationship between the private and social rented sectors is especially useful in drawing together approaches to policy across all tenure forms. Together these two authors throw light on the relationship between policy approaches and the size of rental sectors. It is also worth noting that Kemeny's two models also provide some leverage on the issue, discussed in Chapter Nine, about the relative contributions of the state and non-state sectors to social housing.

12

Which Policies Work Best?

At the outset of this book – in the Introduction and Chapter Two – the case for undertaking the comparative analysis of housing policy was argued on two grounds: as an aid to theoretical understanding and for learning policy lessons. Up to this point, however, the emphasis has been on the former with a particular focus on theories of convergence and divergence. In the present chapter the emphasis is shifted to policy lessons. Implicit in this re-orientation, especially under a heading that uses a notion of 'best' applied to policy, is the possibility of convergence, not as a direct consequence of the logic of industrialism but of the considered judgements of policy makers. One process leading to such convergence would occur where housing policy is driven by rational policy makers who seek out knowledge from their own and other countries in order to put the best policies onto statute books. If the world were one in which housing problems and objectives were common across industrialized countries, cross-country lesson learning and policy making on the basis of those lessons might be expected to lead to a narrowing of differences. There might be another process through which the same convergence outcome was achieved, a process driven not by individual countries seeking better policies but by the growing importance of supranational bodies – the EU, the World Bank, the UN and so on – seeking to guide policy making in individual countries. Convergence through policy choice could thus be either bottom up or top down.

In this chapter studies which have sought to identify successful and unsuccessful policies will be considered. Although it is useful to note Peter Ambrose's assertion that '[c]omparative housing analysis has so far devoted little attention to assessing the performance of national housing systems' (1992, p. 163), there is nevertheless a growing body of literature that has attempted to evaluate the relative effectiveness of policies in different countries. The starting points are frequently questions such as: which national governments have produced the best policy regimes; which might benefit from learning from elsewhere; which policy approaches work best, which the worst; and, starting with a blank sheet of paper, what should a government do in order to produce the best housing system? The first part of the chapter considers some of the methodological issues, in part dealt with in Chapter Two and elsewhere, involved in answering such questions. The second part presents some of the answers.

Evaluating government rhetoric

One approach to evaluating housing policy is to consider statements made by national governments about commitments adopted by them. Often these will be found in written constitutions, which may of course be the product of much earlier governments, in the preambles to statutes or in government papers. They will include commitments made to citizens as a whole or to specific groups, and may be contingent on some qualification or condition to be met by potential recipients. Such statements could be compared in order to ascertain their relative strength and orientation, for example which offered the highest standards of housing and which were most comprehensive in their inclusion of all groups in their populations.

Actually, there is no shortage of such statements of intent, but, perhaps unfortunately for evaluative and comparative purposes, there is often little difference between the expressions of different national governments. As Christine Whitehead has indicated:

> The preamble to almost every Housing Act passed in advanced industrial economies in post war legislation includes something of the form that the government aims to provide 'a decent home for every family at a price within their means'. (1994, p. 1)

In some respects, the commitments are even stronger and more uniform since a 'right to adequate housing is embodied in numerous international human rights texts' (Avramov, 1995, p. 12). Thus in Article 21 of its Universal Declaration of Human Rights, established in 1948, the United Nations promoted the concept of an adequate standard of living, of which adequate housing was a cornerstone, for all. In Avramov's view this declaration, along with other statements, reflects the fact that the right to adequate housing is recognized '[u]nequivo-cally... by all member States as one of the basic human rights founded in international law' (p. 23). At the level of the individual nation, some have enshrined such a right into their constitutions while others have included it in legislation.

In fact, these and other statements of intent are not, on their own, very useful for policy evaluation. Because many of them are very similar – and in the case of the UN Declaration, by definition, it applies across member states – the grounds for comparison are limited. There is another problem in that many such declarations and statements are little more than rhetoric. In practice, they are often statements of intent which are necessary but not sufficient measures. They may, and are, interpreted differently in different countries. Of the commitment to decent housing in the United States, for example, it is generally agreed that 'it is a matter of rhetoric and aspiration rather than of the commitment of resources' (Whitehead, 1994, p. 1). Elsewhere there may be stronger or weaker practical commitments to improving housing conditions. Thus, Avramov (1995) has identified a number of steps, each substantial, which lie between statement and realization:

> The constitutive components of the social process of realization of rights include:
> – statement of intent;
> – establishment of rights;
> – provision of means;
> – monitoring of implementation;
> – affirmation and reaffirmation of principles in order to exert moral and political pressure to maintain acquired rights. (1995, p. 9)

So, a number of obstacles can be identified: the law may not be applied; there may be resources of an inadequate level earmarked for its implementation; some groups in the population might be deliberately excluded from any legal right; and the multiplication of procedures may make responsibilities diffuse. Some of these are, of course, obstacles that can be recognized somewhere in most areas of public policy (see for example, Pressman and Wildavsky, 1973; Bardach, 1977). Others, such as the deliberate exclusion of specified groups, may reflect the unwillingness of the policy makers to make the right to housing a universal one. However, the conclusion that can be drawn is that the acid test of policy is less what governments say they will do or will guarantee, and more what they achieve. It may be, in other words, outputs rather than inputs that are of the more relevance to evaluation.

Evaluating outcomes

So, evaluating housing policy requires going beyond the face value of what governments say they are doing, or even what they would like to do. How can this be done? One approach starts from the policies and attempts to identify their consequences. In other words, the task is to gauge the impact of a piece of legislation or the whole set of policies. This can be couched in terms of exploring which groups in the population gain and which lose: who benefits most from interest subsidies to house buyers – existing owners, land owners, buyers, or builders, for example? In fact, in most cases analysts have found it difficult to provide accurate answers to these sorts of question. It may, for example, be possible to describe the first order, or formal incidence of tax reliefs or housing allowances, but as O'Sullivan (1984) has observed in relation to the UK, which groups gain and lose, overall, in most cases will often be a matter of conjecture.

A second approach to evaluation starts by breaking the exercise down into two steps. The first step is the identification of appropriate criteria against which to evaluate policy performance. The criteria might include the objectives stated by the policy maker or measures derived from principles such as the Burns–Grebler disequilibria discussed in Chapter One. They might include measures of the number of dwellings per 1000 inhabitants; the average floor space of dwellings; the rate of owner occupation; and the rate of housing production. The selection of specific criteria reflects views about what governments are, or should be, aiming to achieve by introducing policy in the housing area. The second step is to assess which countries, or which policies, can be associated with the highest and lowest levels of the appropriate criteria; which policy regime has resulted in the highest rate of production, for example.

There are a number of possible limitations to this approach. One is that it might be seen to rely on an assumption that policy making is part of a problem solving world, in which governments are essentially benign and set out to solve the problems facing members of the societies they represent, and those problems are housing related ones. In this world, the extent to which policies contribute to the eradication of stated housing problems is the relevant measure against which they should be evaluated. But, it should be clear from earlier chapters (particularly Chapter Four) that not all researchers accept that this is a helpful or accurate interpretation of policy making. From a Marxist perspective, for example, policy may be interpreted as fulfilling the interests of the capitalist class in maintaining the conditions under which capital accumulation can be maintained. Housing policy may thus have very little to do with solving housing problems, and very much to do with social stability. Some, non-Marxist, observers have seen public investment in housing production being utilized primarily as a means of regulating national economies. On both these views, a criterion against which to evaluate the success of housing policy, more appropriate than those listed above, might be national prosperity. The argument would be that success in social policy terms, in general, ought to be measured by success in building a prosperous economy so that GDP per capita would perhaps be the relevant criterion.

A further limitation is that the approach could in any case be deemed essentially positivistic leading to the identification of a putative universal law which states that policy 'x' will be best in all circumstances and in all places. Even without this concern, there are several important assumptions. The association between policy and achievement may be confused with causation when in reality the links between the two may be much more complex. For example, both the policy and the achievement may be a consequence of some other, unidentified, variable. Or, any statistical association may ignore the importance of the social and economic framework, and what emerges as the 'best' policy may not work in another framework. In short, this type of study may lead to propositions of policy superiority irrespective of the wider national setting.

There are further methodological difficulties, which apply irrespective of whether the criteria are housing or economy related: for example, it can always be argued that with a different housing policy regime economic growth would have been even greater. There is, in other words, the familiar counterfactuals problem which derives from our inability to be able to specify what would have happened if the world had been different in some respect. One consequence is that looking at data that describe outcome measures and comparing them with national characteristics such as policy type, welfare regime or economic development is, as Nesslein (1988) points out, 'a weak test'.

Notwithstanding these methodological and theoretical difficulties, there is a growing literature that has identified appropriate criteria and grappled with the problems of finding data that are comparable across a range of countries. A number of such studies are presented here.

Homelessness

Statistics on homelessness provide measures that focus on the extent to which the housing system fails, completely, to meet the housing needs of some groups. So, the most successful policy regime could be considered one that results in the lowest number of people excluded from access to housing. The problems of appropriate definitions are particularly acute here since what constitutes a homeless person is highly contestable: whether it includes those who are literally without a roof over their heads or someone who does not have housing of a socially acceptable standard is just one dimension of this. Problems associated with counting are also prevalent since much enumeration of individuals in industrialized societies is based on their place of residence, which by definition may exclude some homeless people. In response to these difficulties, Table 12.1 is derived from a variety of sources that provided indications of the numbers of people in each of the countries who approached voluntary and statutory organizations in response to their lack of housing. In presenting an earlier set of statistics Avramov (1995) concluded that they show a clear picture related to national commitment to counter exclusion:

> From the European Union perspective, it may be said that countries with high standards of general welfare protection, namely Belgium, Denmark, Luxembourg and the Netherlands, have implemented more efficient policies and measures to deal with the prevention of homelessness. France, Ireland, Germany, and the United Kingdom have been less successful in removing structural obstacles to adequate housing. (1995, p. 163)

Table 12.1 Estimated average annual number of people who may have been dependent on services for the homeless in EU member states in the early 1990s

Austria	8,400
Belgium	5,500
Denmark	4,000
Finland	5,500
France	346,000
Germany	876,540
Greece	7,700
Ireland	3,700
Italy	78,000
Luxembourg	200
Netherlands	12,000
Portugal	4,000
Spain	11,000
Sweden	14,000
UK	460,000

Source: Avramov (1996) Table 5.

A further factor, which may considerably inflate the German statistic, has been the hiatus in its housing system resulting from the large surge of people from the former East Germany. However, in general, of particular importance is the extent to which countries have ensured an adequate supply of low-cost social housing, organized in ways that make it accessible to low-income groups, who might be expected to experience housing difficulties.

But, Avramov also recognizes that differences in the statistical picture may reflect not only national differences in the strength of welfare provision but also the 'general socio-cultural background against which individuals in difficulty develop their coping strategies to deal with housing exclusion' (Avramov, 1995, p. 164). Turning to the voluntary and statutory sector may be only one of the possible strategies facing individuals in the event of homelessness, but the numbers doing so may reflect the availability of those services. Where provision is limited, as in southern European countries, people may pursue private solutions as evidenced by the large numbers of people living 'in shacks, tents, caravans, containers, staircases, elevator cages and other "unconventional dwellings"' (Avramov, 1995, p. 164). In other words the provision of services may mean that 'homelessness becomes more visible' (Avramov, 1995, p. 164), with a consequence that to an extent the figures in Table 12.1 reflect the availability of support services rather than homelessness per se.

Dwelling space

Other measures of the success of housing policy could be the number of dwellings and the amount of dwelling space available to the population. All the measures contained in Table 12.2, however, must be treated with some caution. The number of dwellings per 1000 inhabitants is counted in at least three different ways: all dwellings including vacation homes; all dwellings excluding vacation homes; and, only those dwellings inhabited on the day of the survey. Thus, the figure of 463 for France conceals the fact that around 9 per cent are vacation homes so that a more directly comparable figure would be 430. Likewise, the figure for Portugal should be reduced from 360 to 268, for Spain from 413 to 306 and for Switzerland from 493 to 410 (Colleen and Lindgren, 1994). As a measure of policy achievement, dwellings per 1000 inhabitants is also problematic because the level will reflect not only policy but will also depend 'to a large extent on a country's economic development and degree of urbanization, the number of children per family, and the age structure of the population as well as on cultural conditions' (Colleen and Lindgren, 1994, p. 70).

Table 12.2   Dwelling space (around 1990)

	Dwellings per 1000 inhabitants	Average number of persons per room	Average space sq. m. per person	Average floor space sq. m.
Austria	384	1.00	28.0	85
Belgium	390	0.56	–	–
Canada	377	0.48	–	114
Denmark	471	0.59	49.0	107
Finland	458	0.68	30.0	74
France	463	0.61	31.5	85
Greece	470	0.84	25.0	–
Iceland	354	–	–	–
Ireland	295	0.80	25.7	91
Italy	361 ·	0.77	29.0	–
Japan	–	–	–	90
Luxembourg	–	0.52	38.2	–
Netherlands	394	0.54	–	–
Norway	412	0.60	43.0	–
Portugal	360	0.96	–	–
Spain	413	0.76	23.5	–
Sweden	471	0.51	47.0	92
Switzerland	493	0.70	34.0	–
Turkey	–	–	–	107
UK	400	0.55	26.8	–
USA	426	–	–	152
West Germany	439	0.58	34.9	86

Source: Hedman (1994) Tables 3, 3.4 and 6.2.

There are similar interpretational difficulties with the other measures. Practices with respect to recording floor area and rooms vary considerably from country to country, with one of the major sources of variation being whether or not the kitchen is counted. Even so, inter-pretation of policy effectiveness is again complicated by social and economic factors, broadly defined: for example the high floor space for Turkey 'should be seen in the light of an average household size of 5.6 persons' (Hägred, 1994, p. 18).

Notwithstanding these caveats, the general, and marked, pattern which can be seen in the data of Table 12.2 does not bear any strong association with the Donnison or Esping-Andersen groupings of countries, but rather indicates that economic performance dominates housing achievements. The amount of housing enjoyed by the average Swede, Dane or North American is greater than that achieved by the average Spaniard, Irishman or Greek. This might be taken to suggest that housing policy is less important than economic progress in determining the amount of housing consumed in a country, and in that sense fuel is added to the case for convergence.

Production and investment

The influence of housing policies on the production of housing has been the focus of research by Nesslein whose starting point is that:

> A central goal of welfare state housing policy has been to raise substantially the average housing standard. In this respect the primary focus of policy has been to increase significantly new residential construction. (1988, p. 297)

The assertion is clearly questionable, as Nesslein acknowledges, since the intention might be to redistribute the cake rather than increase its size. It is, nevertheless, testable. Nesslein does so using data that indicate gross capital formation in housing as a percentage of GNP over each of the decades from the 1950s to the 60s and 70s. He finds that there is no clear correlation between those countries with the strongest welfare states, or the most interventionist housing policies, and housing investment. In some decades what he views as some of the more market-oriented countries, such as Switzerland and Italy, had the highest levels of investment at the same time as another, the United States, has often had one of the lowest. On this evidence social expenditure on housing is not money well spent, since it does not appear to result in higher levels of production. Overall his analysis and his conclusions are consistent with arguments developed by a number of economists, namely that government intervention in the housing field has been generally counter productive (see, for example, Albon and Stafford, 1987; Minford *et al.*, 1987). In the words of one commentator:

> It is no wonder that some observers have not only questioned the value of government intervention but have concluded that it is precisely this intervention which has been responsible for perpetuating the housing 'problem', in short, that the doctor has been the cause of the illness. (Wood, 1987, p. xi)

Efficiency

Since housing commonly accounts for a significant proportion of both average household expenditure and GDP, the issue of the appropriate types of housing policy has been of concern to the World Bank. Its two main strategic guidelines have been presented as:

- Economic development is the most effective way of improving housing conditions in developing countries.
- To ensure the maximum benefits, governments should promote the efficiency of the housing sector and should avoid policies that cause significant market distortions and produce counterproductive results. (Mayo *et al.*, 1986, p. 198)

The evidence presented earlier in the present chapter suggests that the first of these guidelines may apply equally to developed countries. With respect to the second, the objective of housing policy is seen as the creation of competitive markets. The view taken is that, in general, the major obstructions to competition exist in the markets in inputs to the production of housing. Specifically, the problems are seen as:

(a) their ownership may be so concentrated that owners can fix prices, as in some land markets; (b) large economies of scale may make the production of some inputs a natural monopoly, as with some types of infrastructure; and (c) government regulations may restrict the competitive allocation of inputs, notably finance. (Mayo *et al.*, 1986, p. 189)

The World Bank's advice about how to create the circumstances in which competitive markets can function, is consistent with a number of critiques of housing policy in industrialized countries. Thus there is near universal (at least in the universe of economists) opprobrium of rent controls mainly on the grounds that the restriction on landlords, which prevent them charging prices that reflect the scarcity value of lettings, discourages investment. In general the optimum level of government intervention is seen as a minimal one.

There have been studies, also from an economics perspective, that have examined aspects of the efficiency impacts of housing policies. Thus, Strassmann (1990), on the basis of an empirical analysis of thirteen countries – both industrialized and industrializing – concludes that residential mobility, which may be important since it facilitates the adjustment of housing consumption to changes in household resources and needs, including the needs of industry, is higher in those countries with the least state intervention in housing. There is a tendency, in other words, for housing policy to decrease the will or the ability of households to move. A further example of such studies is based on the general observation that public investment crowds out private activity has been applied to housing. On the basis of his analysis Murray (1983) concluded that for every 100 public dwellings built in the United States in the 1960s and 70s, the construction of private dwellings was reduced by about 85 dwellings so that much of the public investment was wasted. Finally, on the basis of a multi-country statistical study of housing investment, Annez and Wheaton (1984) concluded that the amount of public housing had no apparent effect on the overall size of the stock or on the average consumption of housing. Each of these studies therefore supports the view that efficiency is hindered by government intervention.

The identification of the efficiency of different national structures for the provision of new housing has also been dealt with in a recent study by Barlow and Duncan (1994) with the conclusions they reach being very different to the World Bank orthodoxy. They start from the position that, while there has been considerable debate about the market versus the state, such a debate makes little sense beyond ideological rhetoric. The real choice is not one, to the exclusion of the other, but between different market–state mixes. The authors also reject the widely held view that the market–state mixes of different European countries are converging. Rather, they build on the Esping-Andersen liberal, corporatist and social-democratic models of welfare states. They then take one country as a 'typical' example of each – Britain, France and Sweden respectively – as the case studies through which the efficiency of different market–state mixes can be explored. In each of the case study countries they also concentrate their empirical research on particular high growth regions, justifying this with the argument that in such regions the market should be expected to work best, thus providing an acid test of market efficiency.

The question of the appropriate acid test is resolved for them with the identification of production, and allocative and dynamic efficiency. In turn, these are operationally defined as: the volatility of output and production costs; the diversity of output costs to the consumer; and technical innovation and increased productivity. On the basis of these, the authors conclude that systems of provision with the most direct state regulation – of the three cases here, Sweden – are the most efficient, at least throughout the 1980s. Those with least state regulation – as evidenced by Britain – are the least efficient, with France having an intermediate position.

This conclusion runs contrary to the received wisdom of much of the rest of the industrialized world in the 1980s. The Barlow–Duncan view is that there are two main determining factors. The first is the extent to which regulation facilitates tenure diversity, and in particular the scope that is provided for non-profit provision and self-promotion. These are important because their political and familial motivations can act counter cyclically. As a result they can help to reduce the severity of troughs in the housing provision cycle. The second is essentially a re-statement of the view explored in Chapter Six that state regulation may sometimes encourage developers to seek to make the major part of their return from speculation in the land element as opposed to concentrating on labour productivity and product quality.

Conclusions

It is important to note that this examination of the literature comparing the effectiveness of national policy regimes has been limited in a number of ways. It has not sought to define the circumstances, such as the cultural and economic framework, which might be most conducive to policy transfer, nor has it provided examples of actual policy trans-fers. Rather it has sought only to look at some of the possible criteria researchers might use if they were seeking to draw up league tables of policy models such that those countries with the most successful models are identified. Of course, the use of efficiency and other measures as criteria, the operational definitions used and the interpreta-tions of the empirical studies are all contestable. Indeed, the very foun-dation of the generalizability of their sort of conclusions has been questioned in the view that '[o]ne no longer expects to learn, if in fact one ever expected to learn, grand lessons from comparative research about universally applicable efficient and effective social policies' (Maddox, 1992, pp. 355–6). Whether or not this view is endorsed by the reader, the reality is that individual governments continue to look overseas for policy lessons, and supranational organizations continue to offer advice, and indeed, may demand submission to a preferred model. Convergence may thus come about if not as a result of economic deter-minism then through the search for better policies.

References

Albon R and Stafford D (1987) *Rent Control.* Croom Helm: London.

Ambrose P (1991) The Housing Provision Chain as a Comparative Analytical Framework, *Scandinavian Housing and Planning Research,* **8**(2):91–104.

Ambrose P (1992) The Performance of National Housing Systems: A Three Nation Comparison, *Housing Studies,* **7**(3):163–76.

Annez P and Wheaton W (1984) Economic Development and the Housing Sector: A Cross-National Model, *Economic Development and Cultural Change,* **32**(4):749–66.

Avramov D (1995) *Homelessness in the European Union: Social and Legal Context of Housing Exclusion in the 1990s.* Fourth Research Report of the European Observatory on Homelessness. FEANTSA: Brussels.

Avramov D (1996) *The Invisible Hand of the Housing Market: A Study of Effects and Changes in the Housing Market on Homelessness in the European Union.* Fifth Research Report of the European Observatory on Homelessness. FEANTSA: Brussels.

Ball M (1983) *Housing Policy and Economic Power: The Political Economy of Owner Occupation.* Methuen: London.

Ball M, Harloe M and Martens M (1988) *Housing and Social Change in Europe and the USA.* Routledge: London.

Bardach E (1977) *The Implementation Game.* MIT Press: Massachusetts.

Barlow J (1992) Self-promoted Housing and Capitalist Suppliers: The Case of France, *Housing Studies,* **7**(4):255–67.

Barlow J and Duncan S (1988) The Use and Abuse of Tenure, *Housing Studies,* **3**(4):219–31

Barlow J and Duncan S (1994) *Success and Failure in Housing Provision: European Systems Compared.* Pergamon: Oxford.

Barnett I, Groth A and Ungson C (1985) East-West Housing Policies, in Groth A and Wade L (eds) *Public Policy Across Nations.* JAI Press: Greenwich.

Boddy M (1989) Financial Deregulation and UK Housing Finance: Government-Building Society Relations and the Building Society Act, 1986, *Housing Studies,* **4**(2):92–104.

Boelhouwer P and van der Heijden (1992) *Housing Systems in Europe: Part 1, A Comparative Study of Housing Policy,* Housing and Urban Policy Studies 1. Delft University Press: Delft.

Boleat M (1985) *National Housing Finance Systems*. Croom Helm: London.

Bullock N (1991) Comparing European Past with Third World Present, in Saglamer G and Ozukran S (eds) *Housing for the Urban Poor*. ENHR International Symposium. Istanbul Technical University.

Bulmer M (1982) *The Uses of Social Research*. Allen and Unwin: London.

Burke T, Newton P and Wulff M (1990) Australia, in van Vliet W (ed.) *International Handbook of Housing Policies and Practices*. Greenwood Press: New York.

Burns L and Grebler L (1977) *The Housing of Nations: Analysis and Policy in a Comparative Framework*. Macmillan: London.

Clapham D, Kemp P and Smith S (1990) *Housing and Social Policy*. Macmillan: Basingstoke.

Cardoso A and Short J (1983) Forms of Housing Production: Initial Formulations, *Environment and Planning A*, **15**:917–28.

Colleen L and Lindgren P (1994) Housing Construction, in Hedman E (ed.) *Housing in Sweden in an International Perspective*. Boverket: Karlskrona.

Congdon T (1988) *Note on the Origins of the United Kingdom Dilemma over EMS Membership*. Memorandum to the Treasury Select Committee.

Culyer A (1980) *The Political Economy of Social Policy*. Martin Robertson: Oxford.

DoE (1977) *Housing Policy: A Consultative Document*. Department of the Environment, Cmnd 6851. HMSO: London.

Deakin N (1993) Privatism and Partnership in Urban Policy, in Jones C (ed.) *New Perspectives on the Welfare State in Europe*. Routledge: London.

Dickens P, Duncan S, Goodwin M and Gray F (1985) *Housing, States and Localities*. Methuen: London.

Doling J (1990a) Housing Policy and Convergence Theory: Some Comments on Schmidt, *Scandinavian Housing and Planning Research*, **7**(2):117–20.

Doling J (1990b) Housing Finance in Finland, *Urban Studies*, **27**(6):951–69.

Doling J (1990c) Mortgage Default: Why Finland is not Like Britain, *Environment and Planning A*, **22**:321–31.

Doling J (1994) The Privatisation of Social Housing in European Welfare States, *Environment and Planning C, Government and Policy*, **12**:243–55.

Doling J, Ford J and Stafford B (1988) *The Property Owing Democracy*. Avebury: Aldershot.

Doling J and Ruonavaara H (1996) Home Ownership Undermined. An Analysis of the Finnish Case in the Light of the British Experience, *Netherlands Journal of Housing and the Built Environment*, **11**(1):31–46.

Donnison D (1967) *The Government of Housing*. Penguin: Harmondsworth.

Donnison D and Ungerson C (1982) *Housing Policy*. Penguin: Harmondsworth.

Donnison D and Hoshino S (1988) Formulating the Japanese Housing Problem, *Housing Studies*, **3**(3):190–5.

Douglas J (1983) *Why Charity? The Case for a Third Sector*. Sage Publications: Beverley Hills.

Drake M (1991) *Housing Associations and 1992: The Impact of the Single European Market*. London: The National Federation of Housing Associations.

Dreier P (1982) The Housing Crisis: Dreams and Nightmares, *The Nation*, August, 21–8.

The Economist (1984) International Banking Survey, *The Economist*, 30 March.

The Economist (1992–3) I Own, I Owe, So Off to Work I Go, *The Economist*, 26 December–8 January, 95–7.

van den Eeckhout P (1992) Belgium, in Pooley C (ed.) *Housing Strategies in Europe, 1880–1930*, Leicester University Press: Leicester.

Emms P (1990) *Social Housing: A European Dilemma?* School for Advanced Urban Studies: University of Bristol.

Esping-Andersen G (1990) *The Three Worlds of Welfare Capitalism*. Princeton University Press: Princeton.

Farmer M and Barrell R (1981) Entrepreneurship and Government Policy: The Case of the Housing Market, *Journal of Public Policy*, **1**(3):307–32.

Folin M (1985) Housing Development Processes in Europe: Some Hypotheses from a Comparative Analysis, in Ball M, Bentivegna V, Edwards M and Folin M (eds) *Land Rent, Housing and Urban Planning: A European Perspective*. Croom Helm: London.

Forrest R and Murie A (1988) *Selling the Welfare State*. Routledge: London.

Friedman J and Weinberg D (1985) *The Great Housing Experiment*, Urban Affairs Annual Review 24, Sage: Beverly Hills.

George J (1986) Comparative Social Research: Issues in Comparability, *Acta Sociologica*, **29**(2):167–70.

Gibb K and Munro M (1991) *Housing Finance in the UK*. Macmillan: Basingstoke.

Ginsburg N (1979) *Class, Capital and Social Policy*. Macmillan: London.

Ginsburg N (1992) *Divisions of Welfare: A Critical Introduction to Comparative Social Policy*. Sage: London.

Gough I (1979) *The Political Economy of the Welfare State*. Macmillan: London.

Government Statisticians' Collective (1979) How Official Statistics are Produced: Views from the Inside, in Irvine J, Miles I and Evans J (eds) *Demystifying Social Statistics*. Pluto Press: Cambridge.

Grilli V (1989) Financial Markets and 1992, *Brookings Papers on Economic Activity*, **2**:301–24.

Hägred, U (1994) The Housing Stock – Age, Quality and Forms of Tenure, in Hedman E (ed.) *Housing in Sweden in an International Perspective*. Boverket: Karlskrona.

Hallett G (1993) *The New Housing Shortage: Housing Affordability in Europe and the USA*. Routledge: London.

Hansmann H (1980) The Role of Nonprofit Enterprise, *Yale Law Journal*, **89**:835–91.

Harloe M (1985) *Private Rented Housing in the United States and Europe*. Croom Helm: Beckingham.

Harloe M (1995) *The People's Home: Social Rented Housing in Europe and America*. Blackwell: Oxford.

Harsman B and Quigley J (1991) Housing Markets and Housing Institutions in a Comparative Context, in Harsman B and Quigley J (eds) *Housing Markets and Housing Institutions: An International Comparison*. Kluiver Academic Publishers: London.

Harvey B (1994) Europe's Homeless People and the Role of Housing, in Kristensen H (ed.) *Housing – Social Integration and Exclusion*. Danish Building Research Institute: Horsholm.

Hayakawa K (1990) Japan, in van Vliet W (ed.) *International Handbook of Housing Policies and Practices*. Greenwood Press: New York.

Hayward D (1986) The Great Australian Dream Reconsidered: A Review of Kemeny. *Housing Studies*, **1**:210–19.

Hedman E (1994) *Housing in Sweden in an International Perspective*. Boverket: Karlskrona.

Heidenheimer A, Heclo H and Adams C (1975) *Comparative Public Policy*. St Martin's Press: New York.

Heidenheimer A, Heclo H and Adams C (1990) *Comparative Public Policy*, 3rd edn. St Martin's Press: New York.

Higgins J (1981) *States of Welfare: A Comparative Analysis of Social Policy*. St Martin's Press: New York.

Hills J (1991) *Unravelling Housing Finance*. Clarendon Press: Oxford.

Hills J (1992) *The Future of Welfare: A Guide to the Debate*. Joseph Rowntree Foundation: York.

Hindess B (1987) *Freedom, Equality and the Market: Arguments on Social Policy*. Tavistock: London.

Holmans A (1987) *Housing Policy in Britain*. Croom Helm: London.

Homan R (1991) *The Ethics of Social Research*. Longman: London.

Howenstine E (1993) The New Housing Shortage: The Problem of Housing Affordability in the US, in Hallett G (ed.) *The New Housing Shortage: Housing Affordability in Europe and the USA*. Routledge: London.

Hulchanski J (1990) Canada, in van Vliet W (ed.) *International Handbook of Housing Policies and Practices*. Greenwood Press: New York.

Hyldtoft O (1992) Denmark, in Pooley C (ed.) *Housing Strategies in Europe, 1880–1930*. Leicester University Press: Leicester.

James E (1989) *The Non Profit Sector in International Perspective: Studies in Comparative Culture and Policy*. Oxford University Press: Oxford.

Johnson N (1987) *The Welfare State in Transition: The Theory and Practice of Welfare Pluralism*. Wheatsheaf: Brighton.

Jones C (1993) The Pacific Challenge, in Jones C (ed.) *New Perspectives on the Welfare State in Europe*. Routledge: London.

Kemeny J (1981) *The Myth of Home Ownership: Public Versus Private Choices in Housing Tenure*. Routledge: London.

Kemeny J (1992) *Housing and Social Theory*. Routledge: London.

Kemeny J (1995) *From Public Housing to the Social Market: Rental Policy Strategy in Comparative Perspective*. Routledge: London.

Kemp P (1990) Income-Related Assistance with Housing Costs: A Cross National Comparison, in Maclennan D and Williams R (eds) *Housing Subsidies and the Market: An International Perspective*. Joseph Rowntree Foundation: York.

King D (1987) *The New Right: Politics, Markets and Citizenship*. Macmillan: London.

Klein R (1993) O'Goffe's Tale, in Jones C (ed.) *New Perspectives on the Welfare State in Europe*. Routledge: London.

Kosonen K (1995) *Pohjoismaiden Asuntomarkkinat Vuosina 1980–1993*, Vertaileva Tutkimus. Palkansaajien Tutkimuslaitos. Tutkimuksia 56: Helsinki.

Laugel J-F and Sovignet E (1990) Mortgage Credit: The Impact of 1993, *Housing Finance International*, 26–9.

Le Grand J (1982) *The Strategy of Equality: Redistribution and the Social Services*. Allen and Unwin: London.

Lisle E (1985) Validation in the Social Sciences by International Comparison, *International Social Science Journal*, **37**:19–29.

Lomax J (1991) Housing Finance – An International Perspective, *Bank of England Quarterly Bulletin*, February, 56–66.

Lundquist L (1986) *Housing Policy and Equality: A Comparative Study of Tenure Conversions and their Effects*. Croom Helm: London.

Lundquist L (1988) Corporate Implementation and Legitimacy, *Housing Studies*, **3**(3):172–82.

Lundquist L (1992a) *Dislodging the Welfare State? Housing and Privatization in Four European Countries*. Delft University Press: Delft.

Lundqvist, L (1992b) *Policy, Organisation and Tenure: A Comparative History of Housing in Small Welfare States*. Scandinavian University Press: Gothenburg.

McCrone G and Stephens M (1995) *Housing Policy in Britain and Europe.* UCL Press: London.

McGuire C (1981) *International Housing Policies.* Lexington Books: Lexington.

Maclennan D, Gibb K and More A (1993) Housing Finance, Subsidies and the Economy: Agenda for the Nineties, in Maclennan D and Gibb K (eds) *Housing Finance and Subsidies in Britain.* Avebury: Aldershot.

Maddox G (1992) Long Term Care Policies in a Comparative Perspective, *Ageing and Society,* **12**:355–68.

Malpass P and Murie A (1994) *Housing Policy and Practice.* Macmillan: Basingstoke.

Marcuse P (1990) United States of America, in van Vliet W (ed.) *International Handbook of Housing Policies and Practices.* Greenwood Press: New York.

Marcuse P (1994) Property Rights, Tenure and Ownership: Towards Clarity in Concept, in Danermark B and Elander I (eds) *Social Rented Housing in Europe: Policy, Tenure and Design.* Housing and Urban Policy Studies 9, Delft University Press: Delft.

May T (1993) *Social Research: Issues, Methods and Process.* Open University Press: Buckingham.

Mayo S, Malpezzi S and Gross D (1986) Shelter Strategies for the Urban Poor in Developing Countries, *World Bank Research Observer,* July, 183–203.

Miles D (1992) Housing Markets, Consumption and Financial Liberalisation in the Major Economies, *European Economic Review,* 36, 1093–136.

Minford P, Peel M and Ashton P (1987) *The Housing Morass,* Hobart Paper 25. Institute of Economic Affairs: London.

Mishra R (1981) *Society and Social Policy,* 2nd edn. Macmillan: London.

Mishra R (1990) *The Welfare State in Capitalist Society.* Harvester-Wheatsheaf: London.

Mishra R (1993) Social Policy in the Postmodern World, in Jones C (ed.) *New Perspectives on the Welfare State in Europe.* Routledge: London.

Molotch H and Vicari S (1988) Three Ways to Build. The Development Process in the United States, Japan and Italy, *Urban Affairs Quarterly,* **24**(2):188–214.

Mulder A (1988) Housing Tenures in Europe, in Kroes H, Ymkers F and Mulder A (eds) *Between Owner-Occupation and Rented Sector: Housing in Ten European Countries.* The Netherlands Christian Institute for Social Housing: Delft, 11–22.

Murray M (1983) Subsidized and Unsubsidized Housing Starts: 1961–1973, *Review of Economics and Statistics,* **15**:590–7.

Needleman L (1965) *The Economics of Housing.* Staples Press: London.

Nesslein T (1988) Housing in the Welfare State. Have Government Interventions Raised Housing Investment and Lowered Housing Costs?, *Urban Affairs Quarterly*, **24**(2):295–314.

OECD (1985) *Social Expenditure 1960–1990: Problems of Growth and Control*. OECD: Paris.

OECD (1988) *Urban Housing Finance*. OECD: Paris.

O'Connor J (1973) *The Fiscal Crisis of the State*. St Martin's Press: New York.

O'Sullivan A (1984) Misconceptions in the Current Housing Subsidy Debate, *Policy and Politics*, **12**:119–44.

Offe C (1984) *Contradictions of the Welfare State*. St Martin's Press: New York.

Oxley M (1987) The Aims and Effects of Housing Allowances in Western Europe, in van Vliet W (ed.) *Housing Markets and Policies under Fiscal Austerity*. Greenwood Press: New York.

Oxley M (1991) The Aims and Methods of Comparative Housing Policy Research, *Scandinavian Housing and Planning Research*, **8**(2):67–77.

Oxley M (1993) *Social Housing in the European Community*. European Housing Research Working Paper Series Number 2. De Montfort University: Leicester.

Papa O (1992) *Housing Systems in Europe, Part 2, A Comparative Study of Housing Finance*. Delft University Press: Delft.

Pierson C (1991) *Beyond the Welfare State: The New Political Economy of Welfare*. Polity Press: Cambridge.

Pickvance C (1986) Comparative Urban Analysis and Assumptions About Causality, *International Journal of Urban and Regional Research*, **10**(2):162–84.

Pinker R (1971) *Social Theory and Social Policy*. Heinemann: London.

Pooley C (1992) *Housing Strategies in Europe, 1880–1930*. Leicester University Press: Leicester.

Potter P and Drevermann M (1988) Home Ownership, Foreclosure and Compulsory Auction in the Federal Republic of Germany, *Housing Studies*, **3**(2):94–104.

Power A (1993) *Hovels to High Rise: Social Housing in Europe since 1850*. Routledge: London.

Prak N and Priemus H (1992) The Netherlands, in Pooley C (ed.) *Housing Strategies in Europe, 1880–1930*. Leicester University Press: Leicester.

Pressman J and Wildavsky A (1973) *Implementation*. University of California Press: Berkeley.

Priemus H (1982) Rent Control and Housing Tenure, *Planning and Administration*, **9**(2):29–46.

Priemus H (1987) Economic and Demographic Stagnation, Housing and Housing Policy, *Housing Studies*, **2**(1):17–27.

Priemus H (1990) The Netherlands, in van Vliet W (ed.) *International Handbook of Housing Policies and Practices*. Greenwood Press: New York.

Pugh C (1990) *Housing and Urbanisation*. Sage: New Delhi.

Roistacher E (1987) The Rise of Competitive Mortgage Markets in the United States and Britain, in van Vliet W (ed.) *Housing Markets and Policies under Fiscal Austerity*. Greenwood Press: New York.

Román R-E, Bengtsson P and Johansson J (1994) The Volume of Housing Subsidies, in Hedman E (ed.) *Housing in Sweden in an International Perspective*. Boverket: Karlskrona.

Rose R (1986) Common Goals but Different Roles: The State's Contribution to the Welfare State, in Rose R and Shiratori R (eds) *The Welfare State East and West*. Oxford University Press: Oxford.

Ruonavaara H (1987) The Kemeny Approach and the Case of Finland, *Scandinavian Housing and Planning Research*, **4**(3):63–77.

Ruonavaara H (1992) Forms and Types of Housing Tenure: Towards Solving the Comparison/Translation Problem. Paper given at European Cities: Growth and Decline Conference, The Hague, April.

Saunders P (1990) *A Nation of Home Owners*. Unwin Hyman: London.

Schmidt S (1989) Convergence Theory, Labour Movements and Corporatism: The Case of Housing, *Scandinavian Housing and Planning Research*, **6**(2):83–101.

Schmitter P (1974) Still the Century of Corporatism, *Review of Politics*, **36**:85–131.

Short J, Fleming S and Witt S (1986) *Housebuilding, Planning and Community Action: The Production and Negotiation of the Built Environment*. Routledge & Kegan Paul: London.

Silver H (1990) Privatization, Self-Help, and Public Housing Home Ownership in the United States, in van Vliet W and van Weesep J (eds) *Government and Housing: Developments in Seven Countries*, vol 36, Urban Affairs Annual Reviews. Sage: Newbury Park.

Strassmann W (1990) *Residential Mobility and Housing Markets: An International Comparison*. Paper given to International Housing Research Conference. CILOG: Paris.

Sveinsson J (1992) The 'Scandinavianisation' of Icelandic Housing Policy, in Lundquist L (ed.) *Policy, Organisation and Tenure: A Comparative History of Housing in Small Welfare States*. Scandinavian University Press: Gothenburg.

Swoboda A (1986) *Ongoing Changes in Finnish Financial Markets and their Implications for Central Bank Policy*. Bank of Finland: Helsinki.

Tanninen T (1995) Housing Allowances as a Social Indicator of Changing Housing Policies in the Nordic Countries. Paper given at Nordic Sociological Congress. Helsinki, 9–11 June.

Taylor-Gooby P and Dale J (1981) *Social Theory and Social Welfare*. Edward Arnold: London.

Titmuss R (1963) *Essays on the 'Welfare State'*. Allen & Unwin: London.

Torgerson, U (1987) Housing: the Wobbly Pillar under the Welfare State, in Turner B, Kemeny J and Lundquist L (eds) *Between State and the Market: Housing in the Post-Industrial Era*. Almqvist and Wiksell: Stockholm.

Tosi A (1990) Italy, in van Vliet W (ed.) *International Handbook of Housing Policies and Practices*. Greenwood Press: New York.

Tosics, I (1987) Privatisation in Housing Policy: The Case of Western Countries and Hungary, *International Journal of Urban and Regional Research*, **11**(1):61–77.

Turner B, Kemeny J and Lundquist L (1987) *Between State and the Market: Housing in the Post-Industrial Era*. Almqvist and Wiksell: Stockholm.

Turner J (1972) Housing as a Verb, in Turner J and Fichter R (eds) *Freedom to Build: Dweller Control of the Housing Process*. Macmillan: New York.

van Vliet W (1990) *International Handbook of Housing Policies and Practices*. Greenwood Press: New York.

van Vliet W and van Weesep J (1990) *Government and Housing: Developments in Seven Countries*, vol 36. Urban Affairs Annual Reviews. Sage: Newbury Park.

Ware A (1989) *Between Profit and State: Intermediate Organizations in Britain and the United States*. Polity Press: Cambridge.

van Weesep J and van Kempen R (1993) Low Income and Housing in the Dutch Welfare State, in Hallett G (1993) *The New Housing Shortage: Housing Affordability in Europe and the USA*. Routledge: London.

Weisbrod B (1977) *The Voluntary Non-Profit Sector*. D C Heath: Lexington.

Whitehead C (1979) Why Owner-Occupation? *Centre for Environmental Studies Review*, **6**:33–41.

Whitehead C (1994) *Demand versus Need in Housing Economics*, Paper given at the Invigning Institutet for Bostadsforskning. Uppsala Universitet: Gavle.

Wilensky H (1975) *The Welfare State and Equality*. University of California Press: Berkeley.

Wilensky H and Lebeaux C (1965) *Industrial Society and Social Welfare*. Free Press: New York.

Williamson P J (1989) *Corporatism in Perspective*. Sage: London.

Wolman H (1975) *Housing and Housing Policy in the US and the UK*. Lexington Books: Lexington, Mass.

Wood G (1990) The Tax Treatment of Housing: Economic Issues and Reform Measures, in Maclennan D and Williams R (eds) *Housing*

Subsidies and the Market: An International Perspective. Joseph Rowntree Foundation: York.

Wood J (1987) Preface to Minford P, Peel M and Ashton P, *The Housing Morass*, Hobart Paper 25. Institute of Economic Affairs: London.

Wynn M (1983) *Housing in Europe.* Croom Helm: London.

Index